IRISH ON THE MOVE

Studies in Theatre History and Culture

Heather S. Nathans,
series editor

IRISH
ON THE
MOVE

*Performing Mobility in
American Variety Theatre*

Michelle Granshaw

UNIVERSITY OF IOWA PRESS, IOWA CITY

University of Iowa Press, Iowa City 52242
Copyright © 2019 by Michelle Granshaw
www.uipress.uiowa.edu

Printed in the United States of America
Design by April Leidig

ISBN: 978-1-60938-681-8 (pbk)
ISBN: 978-1-60938-682-5 (ebk)

Printed on acid-free paper

Cataloging-in-Publication data is on file with the Library of Congress.

Portions of the introduction and chapter 1 were previously published in
Popular Entertainment Studies, republished with permission from University of
New Castle, Australia, and in *Theatre History Studies*, republished with permission
from University of Alabama Press. A portion of chapter 3 was previously published
in *Nineteenth Century Theatre and Film*, republished with permission from SAGE
Publications Ltd. Sketch and afterpiece quotes from *Irishman in Cuba*, *Americans in
Turkey*, *High Life and Low Life in New York*, *The Match Girl of New York*, and *Irishman
in Greece* from the Tony Pastor Collection at the Harry Ransom Center
are reprinted with permission from University of Texas at Austin.

2019002934

To my parents,
Patrick and JoAnn Granshaw

CONTENTS

ACKNOWLEDGMENTS

THIS BOOK WOULD NOT EXIST without a bit of serendipity. With a late registration time and my first and second choice classes full, I registered for Marion R. Casey's Irish in New York course while studying at New York University. Along with subsequent classes with Mick Moloney and Robert Scally, the course sparked questions that continue to weave through my research. While reading nineteenth-century newspapers, coming across a random, opaque reference to the hibernicon started the intellectual journey that ultimately led to this project. At the time, I could not imagine the many places these inspirations would take me, and I am grateful for all the support that helped my research and this book along the way.

I researched and wrote most of this book while working at the University of Pittsburgh. The institution generously supported my work through a Third Term Research Stipend and Richard D. and Mary Jane Edwards Endowed Publication Fund Grant. A UCIS Hewlett International Grant, Global Studies Center Domestic Travel Grant, and European Studies Center Small Grant for Faculty Research and Travel funded trips to present my research at the Association for Theatre in Higher Education and American Society for Theatre Research. The faculty, staff, and students in the Department of Theatre Arts, past and present, provided a welcoming community that helped sustain the momentum on this project through their encouragement and conversations. Many thanks to Annmarie Duggan, Kathleen George, Bruce McConachie, Cynthia Croot, and Gianni Downs. I appreciate my research assistants, Claire Syler, Le'Mil Eiland, and Amanda Olmstead, who helped with newspaper research and transcribing notes and sketches. Teaching Pitt's undergraduate and graduate students challenged me to rethink my ideas about historiography and performance, and this project benefited from those conversations. Thank you especially to my advisees Vicki Hoskins, Le'Mil Eiland, Kristin O'Malley, Amanda Olmstead, and Nic Barilar.

I am grateful for the support of institutions and professional organizations that made this research possible. The Hibernian Research Award from the Cushwa Center for the Study of American Catholicism at the University of Notre Dame funded my research at the Archdiocese of New York Archives. The American Theatre and Drama Society Faculty Research Award supported travel to New York and Belfast. At the University of Texas at Austin, the Harry Ransom Center Research Fellowship in the Humanities, 2016 to 2017, sponsored by the Dorot Foundation Postdoctoral Research Fellowship in Jewish Studies, made it possible to visit the Tony Pastor Collection. The David Keller Travel Grant and Thomas Marshall Travel Grant enabled me to present my research in various stages at the American Society for Theatre Research annual conference.

I thank the archivists, librarians, and staffs who assisted me with my research at the New York Public Library (especially Bob Kosovsky and the staff at the Performing Arts Library), New York Historical Society, Library of Congress, Tamiment Library and Robert F. Labor Archives at New York University, Harry Ransom Center at the University of Texas at Austin, British Library, Harvard Theatre Collection, Archdiocese of New York Archives, John Hay Library at Brown University, Princeton University Special Collections, Kent State Special Collections, Southern Illinois University, Carbondale Special Collections, Abraham Lincoln Presidential Library, American Antiquarian Society, International Center for Photography, Mary Evans Picture Library, and State Library at New South Wales.

My work on the hibernicon started at the University of Washington and the mentorship of the UW faculty was invaluable during my time there and beyond. I am grateful for the UW Graduate School Presidential Dissertation Fellowship. Thanks to Herb Blau for his stories and insightful conversations. I have great appreciation for the intellectual support and wise counsel of Thomas Postlewait and Odai Johnson. Sarah Bryant-Bertail's incisive critical commentary helped me become a more thoughtful and imaginative scholar. I had the great fortune of working with Barry Witham. It is not possible to fully thank him in a few lines for all his intellectual and professional support and generosity. The excitement, curiosity, and joy in his work and ability to craft a rigorous and enticing historical narrative continue to inspire me. His thoughtful feedback and respect for his students and their voices vitally shaped my aspirations as a scholar, teacher, and mentor.

This research would not have been possible without the immense generosity of Tim and Judy Dobler. I can never adequately repay them for providing me with a place to stay in Seattle, which made it financially possible to pursue this project. Parts of chapter 3 and 4 were written while sitting on their balcony across from Green Lake and eating a delicious croissant from Urban Bakery. I aspire to pay their generosity forward.

Working with the University of Iowa Press was a delight from the beginning. The anonymous readers' insightful comments were extremely helpful in revising the book. I am grateful to everyone at the press and on the editorial team for their enthusiasm and support of this project. I especially thank Ranjit Arab, Meredith Stabel, and Daniel Ciba. Thank you to Matt DiCintio for compiling the index. It has been a pleasure and an honor to work with Heather Nathans as my editor. Her expertise, rigor, support, and contagious excitement have made this a stronger book and an enjoyable process. I am immensely grateful for her generosity and mentorship.

Parts of the introduction and chapter 1 appeared as "Inventing the Tramp: The Early Tramp Comic on the Variety Stage," *Popular Entertainment Studies* 9, no. 1–2 (2018): 44–63. Sections of chapter 3 appeared in "Performing Cultural Memory: The Traveling Hibernicon and the Transnational Irish Community in the United States and Australia," *Nineteenth Century Theatre and Film* 41, no. 2 (Winter 2014): 76–101. I am very appreciative of the Mid-America Theatre Conference's recognition of my research from chapter 1 through the Robert A. Schanke Theatre Research Award, which led to the publication of my conference paper, "Inventing the Tramp: The Early Tramp Comic on the Variety Stage," in *Theatre History Studies* 38 (2019). I am thankful to my editors, Gillian Arrighi, Sharon Marcus, Katherine Biers, and Sara Freeman. I also thank the journals for permission to reprint parts of the articles and conference paper.

Colleagues and friends at Pitt and in the field offered fruitful conversations, advice, and necessary distractions over the years. I thank AnnMarie Saunders, Mimi Kammer, Chrystyna Dail, Amy Hughes, Naomi Stubbs, Jennifer Josten, Liz Coen, Douglas A. Jones Jr., Samer Al-Saber, Adrienne Macki, and Elizabeth Osborne. Aaron Tobiason read early versions of the chapters and provided crucial feedback that greatly improved the project. My conversations with Lezlie Cross and Gibson Cima helped renew my intellectual excitement and belief in this project at crucial times, and I am grateful for their friendship. It is not possible to say thank you enough to Jyana Browne for all the emails and conversations as I navigated the ups and downs of this project.

Many people beyond academia have supported me throughout this process. My grandmothers, Connie Granshaw and Jean Losito, provided vital encouragement and support. Since NYU, Elizabeth Dobler has patiently listened to my ramblings about performance and Irish America, attended shows, and generously offered coffee, cookies, and wake-up calls from near and far. Thank you, Elizabeth, for all the long calls, a place to stay on research trips, and many years of friendship. As the fellow theatre person in the family, my brother Patrick Granshaw never fails to put a smile on my face or remind me why I love the theatre. Thank you to my sister-in-law and brother, Ali Granshaw and Mark Granshaw, for the encouragement, support, and much needed distractions. While working on this book, watching my nephew James Granshaw grow up into a thoughtful, compassionate, baseball-loving young person has been a distinct joy. My sister, Lisa Granshaw, was always there when I needed her to read a passage, to spend several hours talking through a new idea, or to provide a place to stay on innumerable research trips. Thank you, Lisa, for everything.

My parents, Patrick and JoAnn Granshaw, pushed their children to think beyond what our family had considered feasible before. They made it possible for me to imagine that maybe, just maybe, this career and book might be more than an unattainable dream. Their patience, love, and unfailing support have meant more to me than I can ever say. I am so fortunate to have them in my life.

IRISH ON THE MOVE

INTRODUCTION

I N THE RUN-UP TO the 2018 midterm election, President Donald
Trump and the Republican Party based their election platform on
the supposed threat posed by a group of Central American migrants walking to the Mexico–United States border to apply for
asylum. Even though the migrants were weeks away from reaching the
United States, stories about their journey covered the front pages of
national newspapers. The *New York Times* and Fox News ran multiple
segments every day on their progress and whether they posed a threat
to democracy in the United States. On Twitter, the president characterized the migrants as an "assault on our country by Guatemala, Hon-
duras, and El Salvador, whose leaders are doing little to stop this large
flow of people, INCLUDING MANY CRIMINALS, from entering Mexico to
U.S."[1] Trump threatened to eliminate aid to countries "which seem to
have almost no control over their population."[2]

In this national conversation, "the caravan" became a representative
shorthand that denoted a mobile experience. As Cesar Rios, director of
the Salvadoran Institute for Migration, remarked, "El Salvador experiences a migration dynamic where 200 to 300 people migrate each day.
A caravan is the visibility of this hidden reality."[3] More than a concrete
manifestation of the migrants' journey, through repetition, the caravan
became symbolic of a white nationalist, Republican political ideology.
From their perspective, the caravan represented mobile, nonwhite foreign threats that would inevitably attack citizens and undermine order
once they reached the United States. The caravan helped transform
the migrants' journey into a concrete meaning to be perpetuated and
contested.

In Central America and the United States, government officials, writers, activists, and commentators advocated for alternative interpretations of the migrants' journey. Instead of viewing the migrants' journey only in relation to U.S. identity, Salvadoran officials explained its meaning for their people. In response to Trump's accusations, Salvadoran Minister of Justice and Public Security Mauricio Landaverde stressed that "mobility is a reality and a right."[4] Salvadoran President Salvador Sánchez Cerén echoed his statement, explaining "For us, migrating is a right, and so migrants' rights have to be respected."[5] Others in the United States have framed the migrants' journey within the tradition of the American Dream. Describing a flight from economic hardship and violence, these writers argue that the migrants represent the historical and contemporary foundation of the United States, which was built by immigrants "hop[ing] for a new life."[6] Some cite Emma Lazarus's poem "New Colossus," which appears on the base of the Statue of Liberty, as evidence of the nation's dedication to migrants: "Give me your tired, your poor, your huddled masses yearning to breathe free, the wretched refuse of your teeming shore. Send these, the homeless, tempest-tossed to me, I lift my lamp beside the golden door!"[7] In this view, the migrants' journey embodies the persistence, hard work, and hope that built the nation.

The complicated debate over migrants, their mobility, identity, and role in U.S. society has preoccupied the national conversation since its founding. Although many factors change over time, including, but not limited to, racial, economic, geographical, gender, sexual, religious, and political dynamics, the country continues to struggle over how to make sense of the mobile existence of migrants, the poor, and the working class. Figures and narratives in the cultural imagination, such as the caravan, have helped make these debates concrete. Although they might transform over time, their repetition makes a transient experience—movement—tangible and memorable. They are shaped by who produced them as well as by how they are perceived and responded to by readers and audiences. For example, Trump's supporters spread the narrative he discussed on the White House lawn and shouted on Twitter. When a reporter pointed out the nation's long history of welcoming poor migrants, a Trump supporter responded, "Either you don't know

what you're talking about or you're trying to convince me of something that isn't true."[8] For the figures and narratives to effectively create
meanings from mobility, they need a receptive audience.

This book argues for a methodology that examines how meaning
is created and perpetuated surrounding migrants and movement in
the United States. Although it might be applied to different types of
movement and people, I purposefully examine one of the first large-
scale, despised migrant groups to freely enter the United States: the
Irish. Anglo-Protestant discrimination, public debates over their migration and assimilation, and anxiety over the Irish's mobile threat laid
a framework for how the nation dealt with future large-scale migrations perceived as threatening. It also illustrates how migrants and Irish
Americans utilized physical and imagined mobility to resist a dominant
culture determined to erase their humanity, culture, and right to participate in U.S. democracy. By starting with the conflict over Latinx
migration in 2018, I do not seek to equate migrant experiences or erase
fundamental differences of race and social, economic, and political circumstances. In drawing a connection, however loose, I gesture toward
the stakes of understanding how our culture generates meanings from
movement by migrant bodies.

This book argues that performance served as a critical apparatus
through which movement was given meaning and therefore impacted
the ways the nineteenth-century United States debated migration, belonging, and citizenship. By giving power to divergent views of movement's meanings, mobility in performance played a foundational role in
the construction of class, race, and gender in the cultural imagination.
Since it is impossible to survey them all, the book centers on one primary space: variety theatre. The social, political, and economic circumstances of variety theatre after the Civil War until the mid-1880s made
it a focal point for working- and middle-class tensions over the Irish
and mobility. As a popular entertainment, it also was accessible to Irish
migrants and Irish Americans as performers and audience members,
which enables an examination of the Irish's acquiescent and transgres-
sive responses. I call the repeated narratives, strategies, and performative practices emerging from society's debates surrounding movement
and its meanings "dramaturgies of mobility."

Critical Interventions in Mobility

On the eve of the Civil War, a writer for the *New York Phoenix*, a New York Irish newspaper, faced a dilemma. Trying to write a history of "Irish clans" in the United States, he bemoans, "the immense majority of the later Irish immigrants are as yet but a mere floating population, migrating from place to place, wherever they may find a market for their labor."[9]

Noting the "floating" Irish's absence from city directories and official records, he concedes, "we have at present no means of finding out anything certain about the distribution of the remnants of our Irish clans in these floating masses."[10] As a result, he explains that his writing will address the experiences of the "fixed" Irish. The majority of the Irish thus disappear from his narrative. Persistent movement consigns them to the unknowable. Paradoxically, their movement marks them as an aberration, even as, he argues, it defined the U.S. experience for the majority of Irish and Irish Americans around 1860. *Irish on the Move* takes this paradox as inspiration for its study. When studying mobile populations, how do scholars need to think and imagine differently in order to trace and better understand their subjects' lives and experiences?

At the center of this book are questions concerning how to analyze mobility, its relation to systems of power, and performance's role in constructing and perpetuating the various meanings of movement. It is indebted to scholarship in Irish studies, American studies, and theatre and performance studies. Irish studies scholars, including Kerby Miller and Timothy Meagher, among many others, have examined the experience and impact of migration on identities, daily lives, and communities within local, national, and transnational contexts. Historians writing about migrant and urban communities, working-class life, and poverty, such as Kenneth A. Scherzer and David M. Emmons, have attempted to trace and analyze the peripatetic lives of many working-class Irish as they traveled in search of work.[11] While explaining how it is intrinsic to American studies, scholar Rüdiger Kunowm calls for a more systematic study of mobility. He claims, "mobility was a defining characteristic of all those that were not yet American but on their way, literally, towards becoming so."[12] This conceptualization set up a binary with sedentary life, signified by U.S. citizenship, while mobility defined the migrant experience and became a "*rite de passage* . . . as they become fully American."[13] At the same time, as scholar Ann Brigham has discussed, literary and American studies scholars have argued that "the Euro-American national imaginary has been profoundly shaped by the promise of mobility: the freedom to go anywhere and become anyone."[14]

Navigating these tensions, scholars explored white settler movement and colonialist projects that erased indigenous peoples and tethered the "American Dream" and social mobility to national expansion and manifest destiny.[15] Considering movement and (im)mobility certainly is not new for theatre, dance, and performance studies scholars, who consider movement a vital component of generating embodied knowledge.[16] This book follows the work of scholars Marlis Schweitzer, Fiona Wilkie, and Sabine Haenni in drawing on the "new mobility paradigm" in its analysis of theatre and performance studies to extend scholarly conversations around movement and mobility.

Emerging from sociology and cultural geography, the new mobility paradigm, according to sociologist John Urry, "enables the 'social world' to be theorized as a wide array of economic, social and political practices, infrastructures and ideologies that all involve or curtail various kinds of movement of people, or ideas, or information or objects."[17] Extending work by anthropologists such as James Clifford and Marc Augé, who pushed their fields to study travel and routes, scholars working within the "deliberately expansive methodology," as Schweitzer notes, center human and nonhuman agents' mobilities and immobilities as sites of study and theorization.[18] Although scholars have not ignored mobility and movement, studies have often focused on the places or sites between which people moved. For example, in immigration studies, the analysis typically concentrates on home and host countries as opposed to the movement itself. The mobility studies approach extends to and emphasizes how mobility plays a critical role in systems of power and the constructions of not only race, ethnicity, gender, class, sexuality, and citizenship but also vertical mobilities, such as social and economic mobility.

As general terms, movement and mobility invoke a range of possible meanings. Cultural geographer Tim Cresswell provides a framework for considering their conceptualization, difference, and relation to the production of meaning. While movement is "an act of displacement that allows people to move between locations" or "mobility abstracted from contexts of power," mobility is "socially produced motion" contingent on power and understood through relations between mobilities across different scales.[19] Mobility involves a consideration of meaning and how it is produced, including the "type, strategies, and social implications" of movement.[20] Cresswell illustrates the workings of "pervading *constellations of mobility*—particular patterns of movement, representations of movement, and ways of practising movement that make sense together" and his insistence that "these entanglements have broadly traceable histories and geographies."[21]

Political theorist Hagar Kotef critiques Cresswell for creating too stark a binary between mobility and immobility. Along with others who write on movement and governance, her arguments build on Michel Foucault's work on discipline and modernity. Referring to "[p]olitical orders" as "regimes of movement," Kotef argues for the emergence of the liberal idea of freedom and new forms of Western governance alongside increasingly restrictive conceptualizations of movement.[22] She claims that "rather than competing metaphysics" of movement and sedentariness, they are "complementary processes."[23]

Kotef describes this process and, similar to Cresswell, challenges nomadic and rhizomatic theories that link movement with transgressiveness and subaltern power: "The flux that is frequently celebrated as subversive has repeatedly served to restrict movement-as-freedom, to facilitate non free movements (expulsion, slave trade, denial of land tenure), and ultimately to preclude movement."[24] Migrants to the United States, including the Irish, have negotiated a process similar to that described by Kotef. In the nineteenth-century, laws made white migrants eligible for citizenship the moment they stepped foot in the United States. However, migrants and the working class's need to move from town to town in search of work added to the factors marking them as other to the supposedly more settled middle-class Anglo-Protestant American citizen. Irish-American movement and its implications for their class, race, and gender status acquired meanings in relation to Anglo Protestants and black Americans, beside whom they lived and worked in many urban northeastern cities. At the same time, as more Irish Americans entered the middle class and more stable home lives at the turn of the twentieth century, their social mobility helped facilitate their physical movement in new, accepted ways, such as the tourist economy.

Other writers critique theorizations of mobility for not acknowledging different levels of access and for reinscribing systems of power by idealizing movement as freedom. Several scholars, including Gilles Deluze and Félix Guatari and Michel de Certeau, have theorized movement as a method of transgression or resistance through nomads and city walkers, respectively.[25] Subsequent studies have critiqued the pitfalls of generalizing and valorizing movement and mobility, especially in the application of these theories that often elide historical circumstances and the gendered, racial, and colonial implications of who is permitted to move and how. As Kotef notes, some populations' freedom of movement served to restrict or reinforce the oppression of others. Disability studies scholars have long highlighted how the normalization of certain types of movement and ability define and restrict ideas of humanity, rights, and access.[26] Feminist critic Janet Wolff points out, "the problem with terms like 'nomad,' 'maps' and 'travel' is that they are not usually located, and hence (and purposely) they suggest ungrounded and unbounded movement. . . . But the consequent suggestion of free and equal mobility is itself a deception, since we don't all have the same access to the road."[27] Where and how differently abled, female, nonbinary gendered, LGBTQA+ people, and people of color move through public spaces is fraught with anxieties resulting from white, male, and cisgender assumptions and prejudices that may result in violence and government oppression. For example, as the murders of Trayvon Martin and Eric Garner, among many others throughout U.S. history, tragically highlight, the stakes for black Americans walking down the street or driving down a road are radically differently than those for white Americans. By situating Irish and Irish-American mobility in its historical circumstances, I aim to avoid reductive binaries and instead to flesh out how race, class, and gender relations inform mobility and vice versa.

Scholars in American studies and theatre and performance studies have adapted the new mobility paradigm to their fields. Kunowm works through its impact for American studies and advocates for "*mobility con-stellations* in which the sign 'America' is constituted and performed across different social and cultural spaces."[28] Over the past several years, inspiring work by theatre and performance studies scholars Fiona Wilkie, Sabine Haenni, and Marlis Schweitzer have demonstrated the new mobility paradigm's importance for theatre and performance studies and questioned how performance "engages with other mobile practices."[29] Wilkie's *Performance, Transport, and Mobility: Making Passage* analyzes how site-specific performance shapes our understandings and experiences of transport and debates about mobility in contemporary life. Considering film, theatre, and circulation in New York, Haenni's *The Immigrant Scene: Ethnic Amusements in New York, 1880–1920* explores German, Yiddish, and Italian immigrant cultures and how their social, cultural, and virtual mobility informed the development of mass-mediated leisure. Expanding the ways in which the field considers mobility, objects, and performance, Schweitzer's *Transatlantic Broadway: The Infrastructural Politics of Global Performance* investigates the development of transatlantic Broadway networks at the turn of the twentieth century and argues how the performance of objects helped facilitate major infrastructural changes.[30]

As *Irish on the Move* draws on these scholars' work, it looks across scales of performance and mobility from the bodily mobility of performers to cross-continental touring. I focus on one form, variety theatre, and one diverse community, Irish America, to consider mobility's role in cultural construction and class, racial, and gender formation. Analyzing one form and one diverse community offers an opportunity to understand the meanings of mobility that informed Irish-American life. This book explores not only how variety theatre intersected with mobility, but how performance operated as a process that perpetuated and transformed ideas of mobility. For decades, performance studies scholars have researched and analyzed how, as performance studies scholar Diana Taylor argues, "performances function as vital acts of transfer, transmitting social knowledge, memory and a sense of identity" through its reiterations.[31] Investigating performance's potential to convey, challenge, and embody knowledge, this book advocates for analyzing mobility in performance acts.

Dramaturgies of mobility translate systems of meaning emerging from movement into repeated narratives, types, images, strategies, and performative practices. Depending on the performance, dramaturgies of mobility enable movement's meanings to be received, resisted, and reformed by performers and communities as they circulate through the culture. In this study, "dramaturgy" does not refer to an intentional action practiced by a dramaturg, but to "structural particulars, whether it be finished or in process."[32] As structures created through live performance, analyzing dramaturgies of mobility necessitates attention to how they are produced, what is performed, and how they are received.

Sometimes fleeting, sometimes lingering for decades, dramaturgies may take on a range of forms, but they all rely on relationships to other groups to constitute their structures. For example, as examined in chapter 1, the comic tramp embodies and represents a specific constellation of mobility, class, gender, and race that emerged in the wake of the Panic of 1873. Its construction relied on the character's performance as well as its relationship to the audience, the Irish-American community, and the realities facing mobile black Americans. In contrast, chapter 4 analyzes dramaturgies generated by the touring of Irish-American variety companies, which relied on partnerships with Catholic parishes along their routes. These dramaturgies are produced by interaction as opposed to representation. The patterns created through the companies' repeated interactions shaped Irish-American Catholic identity and community.

The same movement does not always signify stable meanings or dramaturgies. For example, the perception of the Irish and Irish Americans as a mobile population in Ireland and the United States generated conflicting dramaturgies disseminated through popular song and entertainments. In some instances, the dramaturgy relied on mobility as a marker of Irish laziness, a lack of responsibility, and a peripatetic nature that nothing would calm until Ireland achieved independence. In a song performed on both sides of the Atlantic, William Carleton's popular "Rovin' Irish Boy" reflected nineteenth-century Irish stereotypes as part of this dramaturgy. "I'm a rovin' Irish Boy" who "thravelled [sic] many a mile" one stage Irish character sang before listing "all the funny things / In my thravels [sic] I have seen."[33] In a song thick with brogue, jokes at his expense, and comic details about his visits to

France, Germany, Russia, China, and Japan, the character explains, after "reach[ing] Columbia's [America's] shore . . . I'll never leave it more," only to leave for Ireland to fight for its independence in the next stanza.[34] "How Paddy's Represented," another variety song sung by an Irish comic, suggests a different dramaturgy for Irish and Irish Americans on the move in which mobility is an indicator of resilience and dedication to hard work. After arriving from Dublin, the character complains that the Irish are "not fairly represented, It seems to be a general rule to make poor Pat a rogue and fool."[35] He sings, "In public works through the country round in railway tunnels or underground, Or where hard work is to be found, you'll find the boys from Ireland."[36] In this context, the mobility of the Irish is tied to the technological advances of modernity, such as the railroad, as opposed to a "primitive" way of life. Mobility transforms from a blight and antithesis of U.S. middle-class values into a strategy for survival for Irish Americans and the nation.

A full analysis would consider not only the textual traces, but also lingering evidence of how these performances embodied the dramaturgies. One might investigate how these songs circulated as well as how audiences received them. Both these examples draw on Irish stereotypes, but dramaturgies of mobility move beyond stereotypical representation to historically locate mobility by considering how the representations were shaped by mobility, how the performance contributed to the constitution of movement's meanings, and how it was disseminated. Analyzing these dramaturgies surrounding Irish and Irish Americans reveals the tensions surrounding their presence in the United States and their efforts to be viewed as viable and welcomed American citizens.

Dramaturgies of mobility also offer a method for understanding social and economic mobility for Irish Americans. As I argue in this study, as Irish Americans gained more access to social and economic mobility, this mobility served as a complementary process to the disciplining of their physical movement, which performed their viability as U.S. citizens. This access to social mobility was not even or progressive across the diverse Irish-American population. Neither mobility or immobility alone were valorized or condemned; *how* one performed them helped facilitate access or the potential to access social and economic mobility.

Drawing on Kotef's theorizations of movement and freedom, *Irish on the Move* centers mobility and performance in a messy, nonlinear, and unevenly accessed process for Irish Americans. The book highlights the hierarchies surrounding mobility that discriminated against as well as privileged Irish Americans. In the process it troubles binaries of stasis and movement as well as resistance and oppression. Whether or not movement or stasis functioned as resistance rested on a range of factors, not limited to class, race, and gender. Its intersections with patriarchy and white supremacy further complicated its potential. The privileges mobility enabled in the nineteenth century shape this book's focus. This study mostly centers on Irish-American men within and outside the variety theatre since many of the privileges of freer movement were granted to them. Alice Elliot argues that investigations of gender and mobility aim to "capture how socially, culturally, historically constructed relations between the sexes inflect the texture of mobility, and vice versa."[37] She suggests "[G]endered relations are part and parcel of mobility, inflecting it, transforming it, activating it in multiple ways."[38] For the Irish, the gendered access to movement shaped the dramaturgies produced and the broader cultural and social fears tied to the Irish after the Civil War. Irish and Irish-American working-class women were less likely to take to the road for work than Irish and Irish-American men. This resulted in part from the types of work that hired Irish and Irish-American working-class and poor women, domestic service and the textile industry especially, but also, as scholars have speculated, from the dangers of transience for women. In the wrong neighborhood, simply walking down the street by herself could lead a woman to charges of prostitution or other criminality. This accusation followed women as they tried to access new spaces or spaces that the Anglo-Protestant middle- and upper-class culture believed respectable women did not belong. For example, even though efforts to attract women as part of variety audiences were increasingly successful, throughout these decades women's presence in the audience still led to accusations of prostitution by reformers.[39] Although examining Irish-American women's experiences in depth mostly falls outside of this study, I explore how gender relations inform the dramaturgies spread through variety performance.

Finally, an extensive debate surrounds the analytical use of "diaspora" in relation to the Irish. The debates in Irish studies revolve around the term's definition and use as a synonym for migration, the diversity of Irish migrants across the centuries, and how Irish migrants and their descendants identified. Not all Irish migrants left Ireland under conditions that warrant the specific use of the term, and the population's diversity is erased when diaspora is used to generalize about Irish Americans.[40] Dramaturgies of mobility might be used to explore other migrant or mobile populations, including diasporic ones. However, it is critical to historically situate the mobility and people under study. A mobility studies approach enables analysis of how movement impacted migrants who envisioned themselves as part of the diaspora and those who did not. During the two decades following the Civil War, the Irish's varied migration experiences and racial relations with Anglo-American Protestants and black Americans played a critical role in shaping their mobility and its meanings.

The Irish in the United States

In his introduction to *Irish Immigrants in the Land of Canaan: 1675–1815*, historian Kerby Miller discusses how "In the late 1700s . . . 'Irish' became — both in Ireland and in the United States — a more inclusive and more favorable appellation than ever before or since."[41] Yet, Miller claims, "the moment soon passed."[42] As the number of Catholic migrants increased, by the 1830s, their numbers almost equaled the Protestant migrants who dominated earlier Irish migration. In the United States, religious and political conflicts increased between Protestants and Catholics during the first few decades of the nineteenth century. Escalating mob violence led to the destruction of Irish Catholic homes and churches in several northeastern cities where the Irish settled in high numbers. Between 1845 and 1852, the large influx of poor, Catholic Irish migrants fleeing the Great Famine reinforced Anglo-Protestant anxieties and redefined the Irish's public image in the United States. Anglo-Protestant leaders described the Irish as the antithesis of ideal American citizens with incompatible characteristics that prevented them from assimilating. Tying the Irish to crime, religious leader Theodore Parker described the Irish as "ignorant, and, as a consequence thereof, [they] are idle, thriftless, poor, intemperate, and barbarian."[43] These negative stereotypes continued to define the Irish for decades after the Great Famine's end. As a result, as Miller notes, "[o]nce again 'Irish' became virtually synonymous with Irish Catholics alone, and among most Protestants, Irish and otherwise, once more the term designated a group laden with negative stereotypes."[44] Late nineteenth-century social conditions and perceptions of Irishness shape how the term "Irish" and "Irish American" are used in this book. Throughout this study, "Irish" and "Irish American" refers to Irish and Irish-American Catholics.

Between 1856 and 1921, over three million Irish migrants, mostly Catholic, impoverished, and from western and southern Irish counties, moved to the United States. After the Famine, the widespread adoption of "impartible inheritance" or primogeniture allowed only the eldest son to inherit and generally provided only enough extra money for a single dowry. As a result, the younger children of Irish families seldom had the land or money to marry and many chose to emigrate. Unlike the Famine migration, an almost equal sex ratio of male and female migrants in their teens and twenties characterized post-Famine years. Although German migrants surpassed the Irish in numbers post-1848, the Irish remained the second largest migrant group for decades, and its post-Famine gender balance made it unique among the groups entering the United States. Arriving with few marketable skills, they often started working as laborers, factory workers, and domestic servants, which required men to travel in search of employment. It is estimated that by 1880, half of Irish-American men remained unskilled workers. The Irish comprised the largest white migrant group among the nation's poor, with high percentages of Irish in city almshouses.[45] Historian David M. Emmons describes how "the Irish-American world consisted of three parts": "the settled of whatever class; the unsettled workers who moved along paths laid out by the ethnic communities and who hoped one day to settle and enter one of them; and the transient workers who either could not or would not fix themselves."[46] Settlers in working-class neighborhoods may not have traveled much on a daily basis, given the prohibitive cost of public transportation. However, the economy kept the working class on the move. Moving one or more times a year "adrift in New York's regionally based labor markets," historian

Kenneth A. Scherzer points out that "the extraordinarily high levels of mobility (estimated at between 44 and 70 percent per decade) make questions about the 'peregrinations of those who moved about' particularly difficult to answer."[47] Moving from place to place for work was a way of life for many post-Famine migrants as well as for the Irish-American working class and poor. Many of the city poor also worked in mobile occupations, including peddling, newspaper selling, boot blacking, rag pickers, and street sweepers. "By whatever name—out-migration, transiency, geographical mobility—the movement of people into and out of America's cities is recognized as one of the most important aspects of modern American history," Emmons remarks, "affecting everything from community stability to working class radicalism."[48]

During these years, Irish-American nationalism and Catholicism emerged as two major symbols and expressions of Irish-American identity. Although to some extent, Irish-American nationalism created a national bond, Irish-American communities followed their own local brand of nationalism and often disagreed on how to achieve independence. These local differences resulted from whether the community majority supported parliamentary or violent solutions to Ireland's problems. As Irish migrants fought for social mobility, many aspiring and middle-class Irish Americans disassociated from nationalism in an attempt to achieve respectability and out of allegiance to the Catholic Church, which opposed the movement's violent wings. In spite of anti-Catholic prejudice, many Irish viewed Catholicism as a safer and more respectable expression of their Irish identity, and the Church "provided a focus for unity in the Irish ghettos, creating an Irish-American community out of people who arrived in the United States with diverse loyalties to parish, townland, and country."[49] With public schools and services run by Anglo Protestants and typically anti-Irish and anti-Catholic, the Church also offered social services and assistance.

Discrimination shaped the Irish experience in the United States, especially after the Famine in the 1840s. Discrimination limited their occupational mobility, with Irish discouraged from applying for certain jobs by the sentiment "No Irish Need Apply." Anti-Catholic opinions intensified in the 1830s and 1840s as mobs burned convents and anti-Catholic riots occurred in northeastern cities. In the 1850s, the

Know-Nothing Party's platform linked Anglo-Saxon Protestant supremacy with nativism, and its members believed migrants, including Irish Catholics, were unfit for U.S. citizenship. Even after the Civil War, many Anglo-American Protestants continued to view Irish Catholics as unable to successfully participate in democracy because of their Catholicism and supposed penchant for drinking and violence. As fears of migrants intensified at mid-century, regulation moved from local to state levels, especially in Massachusetts and New York. Historian Hidetaka Hirota argues this shift led to stricter migration and deportation laws that disproportionately impacted the Irish. These state laws later influenced the writing of the first federal migration restrictions, including the Chinese Exclusion Act of 1882.[50] These actions and sentiments prompted the Irish to find refuge in the Democratic Party.[51]

The Irish and Race

Even as the Irish fought against discrimination, they participated in and, at times, violently enforced a system of racial oppression and discrimination in the United States. For many, Irish identity intersected with white supremacy and the denial of rights for black Americans, indigenous people, and Chinese immigrants. The Irish comprised a substantial part of the Democratic Party, which offered the Irish assistance, opportunities for social advancement, political positions, and an anti-abolition platform that spoke to their racial fears and prejudices. In 1863, racial tensions between the Irish and black populations in New York erupted into the worst race riot in the city's history. The New York Draft Riots started as a protest against a system that disproportionately targeted the working class, especially the Irish, but the riot soon transformed into racial violence that lasted days and injured and killed an unknown number of black Americans. After the war, the Irish continued to win elected office as Democrats, especially in cities like New York, Chicago, Boston, and Philadelphia. The Democratic Party's politics remained rooted in white supremacy, and they continued to fight Reconstruction-era efforts to guarantee equal rights for black Americans. Many Irish and Irish Americans worked to exclude black Americans and Chinese immigrants from emerging unions and

labor rights organizations as well as the occupations that they dominated, such as longshoremen. In California, white laborers rioted in
opposition to Chinese migrant workers, destroying and burning down
their businesses and communities.[52]

The Irish also played a major role as performers, writers, and musicians in popular entertainment that perpetuated and reinforced racist images, rhetoric, and narratives. From its origins in the 1820s and
1830s through the decades examined in this study, the Irish performed
in minstrel shows in the north that propagated racist and derogatory
caricatures of black Americans. In spite of the often-virulent racism on
display onstage, at times representation of black Americans was more
ambiguous. Variety afterpieces did not tend to portray them as villains,
and some sketches had Irish and black Americans teaming up to foil the
villain. As Susan Kattwinkel points out, these afterpieces "present[ed] a
positive, while humorous, image of the potential collaborative relationship between Irish Americans and African Americans."[53] Any positive
characteristics, though, "were tempered, of course, by the antics of the
blackface performers and the uneducated reasoning behind most of
their statements."[54] Considering many Irish and black Americans in-
termarried or lived and worked peacefully alongside each other in New
York and other cities, these stage representations highlighted the complicated racial relationship between the Irish and black Americans.[55]

Variety theatre also perpetuated racist Chinese caricatures in sketches
and songs, but without the ambiguity surrounding some black American representations. As American Studies scholar Krystyn R. Moon
analyzes, Irish and Irish-American writers and performers helped create these images, including Edward Harrigan's character Hog Eye. Variety songs explicitly represented the Chinese as job competition.[56] The
song "John Chinaman" complains, "For he's a nice, cheap Chinaman;
A meek submissive Chinaman, Who ne'er 'turns Turk,' or 'strikes' his
work, For more pay, like the Irishman."[57]

Over the past several decades, scholars have debated how Irish-
American connections to white supremacy impacted racial formation.
Early whiteness studies scholars, such as historians Noel Ignatiev and
David Roediger, argued for a process in which the Irish "became"
white by learning the behaviors and social performances tied to U.S.

whiteness. Pointing to the use of similar language to denigrate Irish and black Americans, Ignatiev argues that Anglo-American Protestants considered the Irish nonwhite. "Becoming" white involved learning the tenants of white supremacy and participating in the oppression of black Americans, which helped ally the Irish with Anglo-American Protestants and perform their fitness for U.S. citizenship.[58]

Scholars such as Timothy Meagher, Kevin Kenny, Thomas Guglielmo, Eric Goldstein, Eric Arneson, Eric Foner, and Cian McMahon have complicated and deepened whiteness studies beyond the early foundational works. As they have discussed, arguments for the Irish's blackness or nonwhite status often do not adequately accommodate the Irish's legal whiteness upon arrival. In spite of anti-Irish discrimination, U.S. law classified the Irish as white and sanctioned a clear route to legal citizenship, including voting and jury service. As a result, assertions of the Irish's supposed nonwhite status seemingly and falsely equate the discrimination they faced with the oppression, legal sanctions, and violence against people of color. These early studies presume almost a blank slate for Irish racial formation upon arrival and situate the Irish's new host society as the major force in their racial consciousness. These discussions ignored the Irish migrants and Irish Americans continued interactions with nations outside of the United States and the racial beliefs migrants brought with them from Ireland and passed on to their children. Finally, how early whiteness studies scholars conducted their analysis of the Irish and race has fallen under attack for their focus on what others said about the Irish as opposed to looking at how the Irish voiced their own racial conceptions.[59]

Refuting the notion that the Irish identified as nonwhite, Irish studies scholar Timothy Meagher argues that the Irish's racist actions did not reveal attempts to acquire "whiteness," but a "fear that once those groups [black Americans or Chinese immigrants] became free, they and their patrons, a powerful Republican Party and rich industrialists, would overpower the Irish and the Celts' own allies."[60] "[T]he Irish were not trying to become white," he suggests. "[T]hey were fighting to prevent the elevation of nonwhites to a new status that would render whiteness and its resources and privileges irrelevant."[61] In her study of performance, blackness, and transatlantic Irish identity, scholar Lauren

Onkey suggests a more nuanced understanding of simian imagery and other parallels between anti-Irish and anti-black rhetoric. She claims, "If African Americans are an available signifier for uncivilized, threatening behavior, then the comparisons with the Irish reifies that idea by calling on its power."[62] In her view, the similarities justified anti-Irish discrimination and the continued colonization of Ireland, as opposed to equating Irish and black Americans. In line with these prominent scholars, when discussing the challenges facing Irish and Irish Americans, my study rejects equating anti-Irish discrimination and the oppression faced by people of color. Even when facing discrimination, the Irish arrived in the United States as white migrants whose experiences remained shaped by their white privilege and not uncommon identification with white supremacy.[63]

As much as possible, this study approaches the racial formation and representation of the Irish through how they described and presented their own racial identification in the nineteenth century. This approach relies on the theorization of race argued by McMahon, who illustrates how Irish race operated at the intersection of color and nation. McMahon demonstrates how Irish Catholics brought a racial identity rooted in European racialism to the United States. Grounded in a centuries-long battle between the Celts and the Anglo-Saxons, European racialism assumed irreconcilable differences between these two primary races based in cultural and physiological differences. The Anglo-Saxon "reading of the races of humankind described Anglo-Saxons as rational, freedom-loving, self-reliant people. . . . Celts were imaginative, slavish boors dependent on leaders for direction."[64] This racial rhetoric also linked Irishness with Catholicism. The Irish might not have agreed on the denigrating images of their race rooted in this binary, but they supported the basic tenet of racial difference and viewed the fight for Irish independence as a battle of the Celts against the Anglo-Saxons. Instead of centering the Irish's racial formation primarily on their relationship to black Americans, McMahon argues that "American Anglo-Saxonism constituted a greater threat to these migrants than any alleged lack of whiteness" and that their continued transnational struggle against the oppressive forces of Anglo-Saxonism played a more formative role in Irish racial construction.[65] As historian James Barrett notes, the language of nativism often drew on differences in whiteness as opposed to nonwhite rhetoric. He explains how "[m]id-nineteenth century nativists began referring to a 'Celtic mind,' and 'Irish nature,' and something they termed 'Irishism'—a depravity characteristic of the immigrants and perhaps also of their children."[66]

Instead of performing whiteness, McMahon suggests that the Irish had to illustrate the compatibility of the Celtic race with U.S. citizenship, which had long been defined in Anglo-Saxon terms.[67] Focusing primarily on intellectual elites, including nationalist leaders and newspaper men, McMahon claims that "Irish immigrants expanded the boundaries of American citizenship by depicting themselves as members of what one exile termed a proud and noble 'world-wide race' of Celts" that fit the ideal conception of American civic republicanism.[68] Within this racial configuration, much of the Irish's support for white supremacy resulted from a desire to preserve their white privilege and its promises as opposed to a choice to align racially with Anglo-American Protestants over black Americans. The conceptualization of the Irish as white and Celtic does not erase the importance of racism in the Irish-American working class's interactions with black Americans, but reshapes the questions asked when analyzing the interactions between the two communities.

Acknowledging the diversity of the Irish and Irish-American population, this book does not assume that the beliefs of the Irish migrant intelligentsia, McMahon's primary focus, directly reflected working-class racial conceptualizations or politics. When considering race, however, I focus on the intricacies of whiteness tied to Irish Catholics' identification as Celts. As McMahon discusses, Irish-American newspapers read by the working class discussed race in parallel terms. Patrick Ford, editor of the New York *Irish World*, situated Irish Americans' racial identity within Celtic and Anglo-Saxon terms, stating in the paper's "cardinal principles," "Though American by nationality, we are yet Irish by race."[69] Ford applied this racial struggle to the stage when he denounced how "Our enemy the Saxon—on the stage, in the pulpit, and through the press—has persistently libeled us."[70] My analysis extends McMahon's racial argument to suggest how dramaturgies of mobility constructed and circulated these racial conceptions for working-class

Irish and Irish Americans. This book argues that mobility remained
fundamental to how the Irish and Irish-American constructed their
racial identities and how the Anglo-American Protestant imagination
racialized the Irish.

Variety Theatre and Irish-American Performance

Throughout my study I focus on variety performance because of its
importance to both working and middle-class audiences and the extensive participation of Irish and Irish Americans. Other forms of popular entertainment (such as vaudeville) have received extensive scholarly attention by Robert Snyder, M. Alison Kibler, David Nasaw, and
Andrew L. Erdman, among others.[71] By contrast, variety theatre, like
Irish-American mobility, presents a historiographical challenge, because it has left limited archival evidence of performance and received
little coverage in newspapers.

In her excellent study, theatre historian Jennifer Mooney examines
the development of Irish stereotypes on the U.S. stage in variety and
vaudeville, their connection to Irish and American identity, and their
relation to the Irish's shifting social positions. Although providing vital
context, I do not attempt to repeat that history here, but rather to further expand our understanding of Irish and Irish-American cultural
production through variety theatre and how mobility shaped it.[72] Other
scholars have also addressed the multifaceted functions of Irish popular performance in the late nineteenth century, and my analysis benefits from their work. Examining the afterpieces performed at Tony
Pastor's Opera House, Kattwinkel discusses how Irish variety types
were "more multidimensional, representing the complex negotiations
Irish Americans were navigating."[73] Stephen Rohs's *Eccentric Nation:
Irish Performance in Nineteenth-Century New York City* argues that although
nineteenth-century Irish performance utilized stereotypes, the Irish
used layered performances to construct a range of identities, especially
tied to diverse understandings of and identifications with a masculine
Irish nationalism.[74]

This book's focus on variety theatre alone across a range of spaces
and acts provides an opportunity to examine its distinct context and

form in-depth. As Gillian M. Rodger's foundational study of variety theatre, *Champagne Charlie, Pretty Jemima: Variety Theatre in the Nineteenth Century* illuminates, the context of variety theatre in the 1860s and 1870s impacted the type of material variety companies produced, who writers and performers targeted with their entertainments, the relationships they built with audiences and communities, and how audiences may have interpreted performances on stage. Its form, audience, and context also influenced how Irish and Irish-American variety performers and companies negotiated cultural conflicts with the Catholic Church and middle-class reformers. Rodger convincingly argues for how variety functioned as a provisional space where middle-class and working-class cultures intersected as managers attempted to expand their male working-class audiences to include the middle class and women. The class and gender tension over variety theatre, middle-class reformers' attempts to regulate it, and managers' efforts to expand their audience have received attention from many scholars, including Kattwinkel, Richard Butsch, Brooks McNamara, and David Monod.[75] Since these efforts led to the development of vaudeville, they are one of the most extensively discussed elements of variety covered in theatre scholarship. As a result of these theatrical developments, variety theatre became a staging ground for contests over mobility and Irishness in which working-class and middle-class conceptualizations informed emergent dramaturgies.

Performed mainly in saloons in the 1840s and 1850s, by mid-century variety shows increasingly moved into theatrical spaces. I investigate variety from after the Civil War until the early 1880s, when it becomes increasingly challenging to distinguish between variety and vaudeville. Influenced by minstrelsy in its structure and caricatures, variety started to be recognized as an entertainment distinct from minstrelsy by the end of the Civil War. It also began to expand out of the northeast along trade routes into the South and Midwest. Variety entertainments appeared in a range of performance spaces from saloons and theatres to church halls and basements. Many of these spaces had a raised stage. Audiences ranged in size depending on the performance space and location. Variety customarily had a two-act structure and often lasted around four hours. The olio featured singers, dancers, acrobatics,

sketches, and novelty acts. A comic, melodramatic, burlesque, or panto-
mime afterpiece filled the second act. Typically, no narrative connected
the acts. Variety theatre mostly operated on a stock company model
that allowed performers to gain familiarity with each other and draw
on individuals' strengths throughout the program, as opposed to vaudeville's later tendency to feature performers in only one act. It was not
unusual in variety to have a performer do her specialty and then perform in a sketch or afterpiece. Although some small companies toured
throughout the year, variety stock companies before the economic depression of the 1870s typically toured during the summer months. During the depression, companies increasingly toured throughout the year
when their cities could no longer support stock companies.[76]

Variety theatres had some success attracting more respectable female and middle-class audiences, as it increasingly split between sexualized and respectable, first-class houses. Sexualized variety typically
appeared in low-class theatres and saloons. It featured acts with lewder
humor and more scantily clad women. Reformers frequently accused
sexualized variety of enabling prostitution, selling alcohol, and corrupting young men with their unrespectable entertainments. Efforts led by
moral reformers, such as the Society for the Reformation of Juvenile
Delinquents in New York, contributed to the creation of licensing laws
throughout the country that restricted alcohol and the use of waiter
girls. In the 1870s, first-class variety appeared in theatres run by managers who wanted to clean up the entertainment to expand their audience beyond the male working class to women and the middle class.
Promising respectable entertainment free of bad language and alcohol,
first-class variety managers offered less crude entertainment and entice-
ments to women, such as food and sewing machines. Although Tony
Pastor is often credited with making variety respectable, as Rodger
documents, managers across the country participated in cleaning up
variety, starting as far back as the 1850s with Charley White.[77] First-
class variety managers started to make inroads into the respectable
theatre community during these years, but variety still struggled to be
viewed as legitimate.

The existence of variety stock companies allowed performers not only
to develop a relationship with each other, but also with their audiences,

many of whom lived in the surrounding neighborhoods. Evidence suggests that even first-class New York variety theatres like Pastor's Opera House or the Theatre Comique continued to draw primarily white working-class men during the 1870s, even if they attracted women for matinees and special offer evenings.[78] Most variety theatres explicitly or implicitly excluded black audience members. As a result, entertainments still played to white, male, working-class culture and conveyed strong themes of working-class solidarity.[79] Sexualized variety in saloons often did not charge for entrance; the shows made money from alcohol sales. In theatres, depending on the show, sexualized variety or first-class variety ticket prices could range anywhere from ten cents for the gallery to a dollar for the orchestra.[80]

With the high numbers of Irish and Irish-American working-class men in many cities and the placement of variety theatres near neighborhoods with large numbers of Irish and Irish-American residents, scholars have argued that Irish and Irish Americans comprised a large percentage of the audience.[81] Illuminating Irish audience members' presence as well as the continuing prejudice against them, a *New York Tribune* writer remarked that he had the "intrusive suspicion that two-thirds of the vast and enthusiastic audience had dined on beef-steak and onions" at the performance of a touring variety troupe.[82] In spite of these types of descriptions, Irish and Irish Americans who attended variety shows were by no means homogeneous. As part of the business model, variety accommodated for the shifting tastes and concerns of its working-class audience members and quickly reacted to many social and political developments to remain topical. With Irish and Irish Americans seemingly comprising a substantial number of variety audience members, it is likely managers and performers attempted to appeal to them.

The Irish performances viewed by variety audiences reflected stage Irish characteristics, which by the late nineteenth century were well-known on U.S. stages. Originating in England, the stage Irish type featured standard characteristics in the legitimate theatre's farces, comedies, and melodramas as well as in minstrelsy and burlesque. As defined by Maurice Bourgeois, the type "has an atrocious Irish brogue, makes perpetual jokes, blunders and bulls in speaking, and never fails to utter, by way of Hibernian seasoning, some screech or oath of Gaelic origin at every third word; he has an unsurpassable gift of 'blarney.'. . . His hair is of a fiery red; he is rosy-cheeked, massive and whiskey loving. His face is one of simian bestiality, with an expression of diabolical archness written all over it. He wears a tall felt hat . . . with a cutty clay pipe stuck in front, an open shirt-collar, a three-caped coat, knee-breeches, worsted stocking and cockaded brogue shoes."[83] Carrying a shillelagh, he is always ready for a fight. Many of these characteristics remained present in the stage Irish as the type developed, but, depending on the context, they softened or intensified. The creation of the Irish migrant type by mid-century translated the stage Irish character into a U.S. type. Much of this character's comedy resulted from his misunderstandings about U.S. society, but, especially in the plays of Irish migrant John Brougham, he was portrayed as honest and at times an ally for native-born Americans. Some Irish and Irish Americans credited the actor and playwright Dion Boucicault with improving the stage Irish type through his Irish melodramas. Boucicault's romantic nationalism often focused on stories that highlighted the lush green Irish landscape and portrayed heroic Irishmen, virtuous Irish women, and rogue characters that reflected many stage Irish conventions, but were loyal, clever, and kind.[84] As Dale T. Knobel's systematic study of terms describing the Irish in antebellum melodrama reveals, however, theatre still overwhelmingly referred to the Irish negatively, with references to the Irish's violent nature intensifying during the height of the Know-Nothing Party's popularity in the 1850s.[85]

In variety, a range of Irish characters filled the stage that drew on and expanded upon the Irish and Irish Americans presented in previous popular entertainments. The peasant Irishman still remained, but depictions of more respectable urban Irish Americans increasingly appeared. During the late 1870s and early 1880s, Edward Harrigan popularized this figure in his sketches and the *Mulligan Guard* series. In his analysis of popular song lyrics from 1800 to 1920, scholar William H. A. Williams discusses how Harrigan's lyrics "suggested the more positive qualities of Irishness: generosity, a sense of community, loyalty, and courage, and a simple pride in being Irish."[86] Part of Harrigan's achievement, he claims, involved "Americaniz[ing] and urbaniz[ing] Paddy" and how he "recogniz[ed] and . . . present[ed] a positive picture of one of the essential realities of Irish-American life . . . the Irish urban community."[87] Other variety sketches and songs depicted the social striving of Irish Americans through their portrayal of Irish and Irish-American workers, cops, Tammany politicians, grocers, and saloon owners.[88] The rise of the Irish-American type in variety did not eliminate the crude, reductive stereotypes. However, it reveals the complicated balancing act of playwrights, songwriters, and performers in adapting popular representations and managing the expectations of Irish and Irish-American audience members who understood the diversity of every day Irish-American life.

The number of Irish and Irish Americans who attended and participated in the creation of variety performance suggests it offered something more than insult. Some Irish Americans questioned why and what these performances offered Irish and Irish-American audience members. During several months at the beginning of 1875, the New York *Irish World* debated Irish caricatures on stage through a series of reader letters and editorials. Writers called out the English for developing the stage Irish stereotype and transporting it across the Atlantic. The main target of their critiques lived closer to home, however. Blaming Irish and Irish-American writers, performers, and audiences in variety on the continued success of "disgusting and abominable [Irish] caricatures," the writer of one letter aptly titled, "Who is to Blame?," complained, "the house is thronged . . . [with] Irishmen and Irishmen's sons."[89] He concluded, "when Irishmen's sons go to such places of amusement, applaud and take a delight in whistling such trash . . . doing all their power to popularize them, I do not think it any wonder we would be caricatured."[90] A writer for the New York *Irish American*, a middle-class Irish-American newspaper, concluded, the "play-going Irish public are strangely apathetic to the influence the drama can wield over popular feeling. If the Irish public not only tolerate, but liberally patronize theatrical performances that ridicule and insult them, we cannot be surprised that we fail to attain that place in the public esteem to which the virtues and talents of the Irish race entitle us."[91] The writer's connection between popular performance and the success or failure of Irish and Irish Americans demonstrates the importance Irish Americans gave to performance in how they navigated U.S. society.

Scholarship often reiterates these arguments about the negative aspects of Irish and Irish-American popular entertainments, which, while not inaccurate perspectives, erase the considerations of the performers and audiences who enjoyed or utilized these performances. These arguments also position popular entertainment in opposition to the serious concerns of the community. As a result, popular entertainment is assessed in condescending terms as quaint or frivolous and as an obstacle to respectability and assimilation. Arguments become framed ahistorically in terms of "realism," without considering how "accurate representation" was not necessarily the audience's criteria for acceptable stage performances.[92] With the number of Irish and Irish-American playwrights, composers, performers, and audience members in variety, it becomes impossible to categorize the entertainment as solely representative of Anglo-Saxon Protestant prejudices. As Miller explains about popular songs in the nineteenth century, "it is impossible to maintain the artificial distinction between the 'authenticity' of Gaelic materials and a supposedly synthetic quality often attributed to their English replacements."[93] Although the stage perpetuated problematic representations, these views of Irish and Irish-American performance do not encompass the entirety of the Irish and Irish-American theatre-going experience, and they should not prevent the exploration of the more complicated aspects of Irish-American popular entertainment in theatre and working-class history.

With the plethora of absent evidence pertaining to the majority of acts across the country, this book is not a broad history of Irish and Irish-American representation in variety, and it does not attempt to survey their representation. Most studies of Irish-American variety and performance, such as the work of Mooney, Rohs, Kattwinkel, and Williams, examine the role of stereotypes in relation to Irish-American identity. This book intervenes in these conversations by suggesting the importance of mobility in how Irish and Irish-American identity and representation functioned. Moving beyond exploring stereotypes, I analyze how variety developed dramaturgies that created distinct meanings for Irish and Irish-American movement that had the potential to influence the broader conversation about Irishness and mobility outside the theatre.

Microhistory, Variety Theatre, and Mobility

Similar to the challenge faced by historians writing about Irish mobility, the limited evidence left behind remains a challenge for anyone writing on variety theatre. As theatre historian Don Wilmeth details, variety entertainment "is almost invisible in the historical record because working-class entertainments received little press and left few archives."[94] Other than brief descriptions, the occasional review, and advertisements in the *New York Clipper*, few New York newspapers noted, let alone reviewed, variety performances. Some songsters (small books with song lyrics purchased by the working class), visuals, and sketches exist for the most popular performers and first-class variety houses. Two large collections of variety afterpieces and sketches from Tony Pastor's Opera House and the Theatre Comique provide a glimpse into how these pieces functioned in New York. Government archives offer some information about acts from reformers, police, and officials. The vast majority of variety performances are lost to the historian, however, especially non-text-based acts, acts in sexualized variety and saloons, and shows outside of urban centers.

As a strategy for navigating the tricky archival terrains of variety and the Irish-American working class, I draw on microhistory to structure this study. Microhistory offers an approach for considering broader cultural concerns and meanings, in this case mobility, citizenship, and belonging, from the perspective of groups and forms, such as the Irish-American working-class and variety, who left little behind. As historian Laura Putnam notes, microhistorians study telling examples to "challenge our understanding of the [historical] processes themselves, in 'the belief that microscopic observation will reveal factors previously unobserved.'"[95] I suggest the study of dramaturgies of mobility necessitates such detailed analysis in order to understand how they worked for performers and audiences as well as how they persisted in U.S. culture. *Irish on the Move*'s five microhistories center on distinct dramaturgies produced in or through variety, and they roughly progress from the end of the Civil War to the early 1880s. Collectively, I argue that these telling examples illustrate how dramaturgies of mobility functioned as a critical apparatus for constructing meanings, which held significance for how Irish and Irish-American culture, U.S. citizenship, and migrant belonging were constituted and imagined.

Within each chapter, I closely analyze key transformations in movement and how they influenced the creation of dramaturgies of mobility on the variety stage. Historically situating movement and its meanings, I juxtapose variety's archival evidence in hope that the fragments' proximity provides a picture, however fractured, of how mobility shaped and was shaped by Irish migrants, Irish Americans, and variety. I do not claim to write a seamless or totalizing narrative. My juxtaposition of evidence attempts to construct a web between the fragments to gesture toward speculations and arguments, while keeping the holes visible. Highlighting in Kotef's terms how "schemas of identity are formed in tandem with schemas of mobility," each chapter demonstrates the critical role dramaturgies played in constructing and propagating meaning tied to one form of Irish-American movement.[96]

Chapter 1 focuses on the emergence of the male comic tramp on the variety stage after the Panic of 1873. As the predecessor to the tramp act in vaudeville and Charlie Chaplin's Little Tramp, the Irish-American tramp character became a crucial battleground over working-class and Irish-American identity. After 1873, the rapid increase in the number of unemployed men traveling in search of work led to newspapers, novels, political speeches, and the theatre imagining a lazy, grotesque, petulant, and potentially dangerous figure: the tramp. The early comic tramp on the variety stage illustrates how dramaturgies of mobility navigated issues of race and gender as the nation increasingly debated who had the legitimate right to practice mobility. The development of the comic tramp as almost exclusively white and male and as often Irish erased black mobility, which white Americans increasingly feared during and after Reconstruction.

Chapter 2 analyzes two dramaturgies that emerged from fears and realities surrounding the mobile fighting Irish after the Civil War. Similar to chapter 1, even if these figures are not depicted traveling from

point A to B on stage, they embody ideas of mobility, and their characters, actions, and receptions structure their meaning. I examine how the
mobile transnational Irish freedom fighter demonstrated the male Celt's
suitability for U.S. citizenship and participation in Irish global nationalism. A more negative image of the mobile fighting Irishman arose
surrounding the Molly Maguires, a secret Irish organization accused
of murder in the coalfields of Pennsylvania. Creating a dramaturgy
through sound and absence, these performances linked Celtic male racial identity with violence and an inability to support democracy.

Chapter 3 analyzes the imagined mobility performed by the hibernicon, an Irish-American variety show and moving panorama. Widely
popular in the 1860s and 1870s, with dozens of companies touring the
United States and abroad, the hibernicon presented audiences with a
journey through Ireland filled with historical, religious, and scenic sites.
I argue that Irish migrant and Irish-American managers and performers used the dramaturgies produced by the show's imagined mobility
as a nationalist tactic for rewriting Irish history. This rewriting worked
against Anglo-Saxon, colonial histories of Ireland and used imagined
mobility to construct nationalist, Celtic histories of Ireland.

Chapter 4 moves the investigation of the hibernicon's mobility offstage. With the development of quick and relatively affordable transportation, variety touring expanded after the Civil War. Creating a
dramaturgy through their repeated interactions with Catholic parishes,
hibernicon companies illustrated how touring companies had the potential to function in commercial and community interests. Navigating
anti-Catholic discrimination, parish priests viewed hibernicon companies and their fundraisers as a crucial method of developing a church
community. The companies used their interactions with the church in
an attempt to appropriate its respectability and attract audiences beyond the male working class.

Chapter 5 explores the dramaturgies involved in competitive walking, known as pedestrianism, on and off the variety stage. In the late
nineteenth century, the culture of gentility shaped expectations of
bodily movement, such as walking. The chapter suggests how disciplined mobility, an embodiment of middle-class ideals of posture, movement, and physical form, became a method of social and cultural access.

Pedestrian performances may not have erased Irish stereotypes, and class, race, and gender complicated who could access respectability, but I suggest disciplined mobility became one way that Irish male pedestrians embodied values encouraged by genteel culture and gained access to social mobility. Through their performances, Irish-American men acquired the opportunity to demonstrate their racial equality or even superiority to Anglo-Saxons and their fitness for U.S. citizenship.

Throughout the five chapters, the elusive nature of variety performance and the transient Irish-American experience raises many more questions than it is feasible or possible to address in one study. In the epilogue, I raise several more pertaining to how for the Irish the dramaturgies discussed echo beyond variety's end. I then return to where I began this introduction—with the current conflict over Latinx migration to United States—and consider how lingering dramaturgies of mobility tied to the Irish inform today's national discussions of migration.

CHAPTER ONE

Wandering Menace

The Invention of the Comic Tramp

IN THEIR TATTERED CLOTHES and grotesque makeup, well over one hundred comic tramps staggered across the vaudeville stage at the turn of the twentieth century. One of the most popular stage types in vaudeville, comic tramps sang, recited monologues, juggled, rode bicycles, and performed in sketches. Starting in the 1890s, the comic tramp in vaudeville, scholars argue, reflected the broader transition and ideological tension inherent in tramp representations. Although lazy, dirty, and unwilling to work, the comic tramp had the capacity to elicit sympathy and question the status quo and social norms. Instead of a primarily negative caricature, they argue, the figure came to represent a more complicated portrait of working-class life. Scholars such as Kenneth Kusmer describe this shift as part of a broader cultural pattern demonstrated in literary culture. Through the work of writers such as William Dean Howells and Stephen Crane, the tramp in the cultural imagination transformed from a mostly negative construction to a more romanticized and rebellious figure.[1]

The tramp occupied a site of ideological struggle from its inception. Twenty years earlier, in the wake of the Panic of 1873, the specter of the tramp emerged as the nation debated how to deal with the new masses of mobile unemployed. The Panic reflected a turning point in how the nation imagined and considered mobility and the poor. The dialogues surrounding the emergence of the tramp implicitly and explicitly inform the investigations throughout the remainder of this book. To date, the variety theatre's distinctive role in this history remains unrecognized.

Although they may have become more culturally prominent in the 1890s, the tensions between the tramp's negative caricature and more sympathetic, positive connotations first emerged in performance culture in the 1870s. The comic tramp initially developed in first-class variety houses, which were navigating tensions between working- and middle-class culture. In spite of variety theatre's attempts to appeal to the middle class and women, they still attracted primarily working-class, male audiences who likely experienced (or knew someone who experienced) transient work. At the same time, through newspapers, laws, novels, images, and pamphlets, middle-class ideologies shaped the tramp image, which made its way into variety sketches. With a disproportionate number of Irish and Irish Americans among unskilled workers and substantial numbers of Irish and Irish-American performers and audience members in variety theatre, they became central figures in the struggle over the developing performance type.

American and European actors have performed variations on comic vagrants and beggars for hundreds of years.[2] However, tramps distinguished themselves from their predecessors through their scale and exceptional mobility. Transformations in mobility captured the popular imagination and offered variety theatre a way to appeal to their audience's fears and fantasies that accompanied the rapid economic and social changes sweeping through the country. In her study of road narratives, scholar Ann Brigham suggests moving past simply representing mobility to examine how representations "participate in imagining, recreating, and interrogating the term and terms of mobility."[3] This chapter examines the comic tramp's role as the nation increasingly debated who had the legitimate right to practice mobility. The comic tramp in variety theatre, I argue, became a prominent and enduring example of a dramaturgy of mobility.

Through a close analysis of the comic tramp, it is possible to trace its racial transformation in the 1870s. The comic tramp illustrates how variety comedic conventions naturalized Anglo-American Protestant middle-class notions about class, race, and gender connected to the mobile unemployed. Immediately after the Panic and during the early years of the tramp menace, variety actors performed the usually male comic tramp in both blackface and whiteface. They defined the figure and its role in the sketches' action through primarily nonverbal, physical performances. Other than their face paint, few differences between blackface and whiteface tramps are apparent from the figure's remaining performance traces. In both iterations, they exhibited lack of coordination, a penchant for drinking and fighting, and the inability to hold a job. As the decade continued, however, the comic tramp in variety transformed into primarily a whiteface, typically Irish American, figure. During and after Reconstruction, white anxieties arose surrounding the expansion of black rights. Since the Irish were white upon arrival and the comic tramp could be performed as white even during its early years, the transformation was less a whitening of the comic tramp than an erasure of black mobility. The white representation of the tramp maintained white rights to mobility, especially for migrant groups like the Irish who faced Anglo-American Protestant discrimination and viewed black Americans as competition. The Irish-American tramp may have reflected many of the negative characteristics of the tramp, including his wandering nature, his unemployment, and his drinking, but he also showed that the Irish-American comic tramp, unlike its earlier black counterpart, could be part of a community and in some instances, even a hero.

The Panic of 1873 and the Industrialized Worker

The failure of Jay Cooke's investment company triggered the Panic of 1873, the worst depression to date in American history. After word of Cooke's collapse reached the New York stock exchange, bank runs and brokerage firm closures rippled throughout New York, leading to the closure of Wall Street. Caused by the failure of the railroad boom, the Panic then moved to other industries that the nation's massive railroad expansion propelled, including coal, iron, and steam, as well as the insurance industry and real estate. Although it began in New York, the Panic quickly spread throughout the country and contributed to an international depression. The depression lasted until the economy entered a period of temporary recovery in 1879.[4]

The economic crisis hit the country during a critical turning point for the U.S. working class. On the eve of the Civil War, the traditional artisan system declined as industrialization increasingly eliminated skilled occupations, such as shoemakers, cabinetmakers, and weavers. Without the ability to learn and support themselves through a craft, workers lost a method of attaining respectability and passing it on to their children, who often followed them into their trades. Replaced by an ideology of individual responsibility, support networks and a social order based on trade, mastery, apprenticeships, and indenture disappeared. These developments accelerated after the war, permanently changing how the working class labored, the relationship between work and mobility, and conceptualizations of working-class identity and class pride. Industrialization eliminated craft symbols of working-class identification and replaced them with unskilled mechanized labor, destabilizing long-held notions of working-class identity. A significant percentage of working-class employment depended on emerging industries of transportation and manufacturing, which benefited from fluid, mobile labor. When the Panic hit in 1873, many workers did not have a craft to fall back on, and their fates depended on the whims of the market.[5]

Historians estimate that over three million people, and 25 percent of New Yorkers, lost their jobs over the next year. Those fortunate enough to retain their jobs saw their wages fall. Thousands slept in police station houses that gave free lodging to the homeless. Although the artisan system relied on mobility to some extent, with many younger craftsmen traveling for work or married men leaving families behind while they searched for seasonal employment, the Panic instigated a movement of unemployed workers previously unseen. In the 1870s, the nation's railroads gave unemployed workers the option of traveling faster and farther than ever. Rural areas were not unaccustomed to vagrants, but the numbers of the unemployed in the 1870s seemed to many like an urban invasion.[6] When mobile, unemployed strangers wandered through towns and cities across the country, people grew anxious over their inability to distinguish between who was unemployed and genuinely searching for work and who was idle and potentially a threat. The genesis of the tramp and the fear it inspired rested, in part, on how the industrial system erased ways of identifying an individual's means and willingness to work, which had played a central role in working-class identity under the artisan system.

FIGURE 1. Tintype of a butcher with his tools. Unidentified photographer [Butcher], ca. 1875. Collection International Center of Photography. Gift of Stephen Kasher, 2007 (2007.54.4).

FIGURE 2. A family of cobblers poses with their tools. Unidentified
photographer [Family of Cobblers], ca. 1870. Collection International
Center of Photography. Gift of Stephen Kasher, 2007 (2007.54.12).

Until the 1870s, "tramp" existed primarily as a verb in the American
lexicon and referred to a long walk or march. Throughout the Civil War,
newspapers, songs, and novels used the word in relation to the soldiers
marching across the nation to fight. Trade publications for various crafts
referred to traveling to another town in search of work as "tramping,"
but the word did not denigrate the craftsman; the papers conceived of
tramping as part of the job. When "tramp" emerged as a noun in the
1870s, it resulted from a collective questioning and effort to understand
the mobile spectacle of unemployed men. The emerging image focused
on an excessively mobile, idle, drunk, and potentially violent man, typically white. Although the tramp remained engaged in a decades-long
ideological struggle, it tended to reflect the Anglo-American Protestant
upper and middle classes' views of the moral deficiencies of the working
class and poor more than a realistic depiction of the men impacted by
the economic depression.[7]

Although historical studies highlight the economy and unemployment as the major causes for the wandering poor men traveling throughout the country, in the 1870s, middle-class reformers viewed poverty as the result of poor or deliberate choices and did not view economic factors as the cause for the social problem. The reformers' rationale reflected the long-held belief in the undeserving poor, who simply refused to work, as opposed to the honest poor, whose situation resulted from bad luck.[8] Reformer Francis Wayland succinctly summarized the tramp type in 1877 and made explicit how the figure actively opposed middle-class values:

> [A]s we utter the word *Tramp*, there arises straightway before us the spectacle of a lazy, shiftless, sauntering or swaggering, ill-conditioned, irreclaimable, incorrigible, cowardly, utterly depraved savage. . . . Having no moral sense, he knows no gradations in crime. . . . The strength and sacredness of family ties, the love of mother or wife, or child, have often restrained, and sometimes reclaimed a hardened criminal, to whom the idea of home was still a present reality. But this possible refuge of respectability is wanting to the tramp. He has no home, no family ties.[9]

Reformers' construction of the tramp demonstrates how they conceived of the mobile unemployed as immoral, and always male, criminals. Charity only enabled him to continue to refuse work and afford alcohol. The *New York Times* refuted attempts to blame the economy, stating, "It cannot be alleged that the cause is in lack of employment, and that a revival of business activity will correct the evil, for not one tramp in a hundred will accept any sort of situation."[10] Through the cultural production surrounding the tramp, dime novels, newspapers, literature, speeches, pamphlets, cartoons, and theatre, the tramp figure reflected views held by reformers that equated poverty with criminality.

Wayland's description highlighted reformers' fears that tramps' very existence challenged social norms by undercutting the free labor economy that many abolitionists advocated for before and during the war. If free labor could not provide for all workers, it implied problems with the system they had championed as the superior alternative to slave labor. Paradoxically, in an attempt to reinforce the contract labor system that supposedly relied on the individual's choice to enter and exit labor contracts at will, law makers, reformers, and capitalists supported legislation that criminalized poverty and forced the poor into labor contracts.

In the South, northern officials used these laws to "teach" former slaves about free labor, and southern officials utilized vagrancy laws after Reconstruction to impose a new system of labor imprisonment. Both efforts reinforced a racial hierarchy rooted in white supremacy.[11]

Imagining the tramp as a figure of mobile chaos, state governments designed the new tramp laws to stop him. Starting with the first tramp law passed in New Jersey in 1876, the new laws made tramping a crime of status as opposed to a crime of action, distinguishing between tramps and antebellum vagrants. A person only had to *appear* to be unemployed and mobile to be arrested. A person also could be arrested for living on public charity. New York State's 1880 law stated, "All persons who rove about from place to place begging, and all vagrants living without labor or visible means of support, who stroll over the country without lawful occasion, shall be held to be tramps."[12] By the early 1880s, most northern states had tramp laws that similarly criminalized men without "visible means of support" and excluded women, minors, and some disabled persons. In this way, the law gendered tramping as male and codified middle-class representations of the figure. Compared to previous vagrancy laws, the tramp laws drastically increased the punishment for those arrested, with most tramps sentenced to days or months of hard labor.[13]

The laws' vagueness permitted its liberal and discretionary application, which lay at the center of its "legal importance as a broad, overarching mechanism to control and punish a selective group of people."[14] Labor leaders and legal scholars highlighted this issue, which they argued led to the arrest not only of idle men, but also of honest men traveling in search of work. In his 1886 book on the limitations of police power, legal scholar Christopher Tiedemann questioned, "Is it a man's duty to the public to make his means of support visible, or else subject himself to summary punishment? . . . [W]hat amount and kind of evidence will be sufficient to establish . . . the case of invisibility of the means of support?"[15] Unlike the craftsmen before them, industrial workers did not have any tools or union cards to demonstrate their ability and willingness to work. Within the rhetoric of the tramp, performance became a crucial component in making the invisible, the absence of visible means of support, visible for the police and middle-class reformers. Placing them outside of social and economic causes for their circumstances, cultural representations construed tramps as consummate performers who survived and obtained charity through their lies. These performances presumed an audience; the tramp performed for people who were intentionally supposed to recognize and witness them in order to obtain food, drink, or shelter. For the Anglo-American Protestant upper and middle classes, the tramps' startling visibility comprised part of their central threat. Although the spectacle varied, it indexically signaled the absence of visible means of support and the individual's inability to successfully function as a citizen in postwar America.

The Man Who Tramps, a novel, reinforces the notion of tramps performing a character in an attempt to scam hardworking Americans. The book notes, "They were always ostensibly on the hunt for work, always bound for some special destination, and people believed their well-told stories."[16] A blatant example of the ability to identify a tramp on sight occurs in the first few pages of another novel, *A Tight Squeeze.* After a group of "gentlemen" friends debate what makes a tramp a tramp, coincidentally, "there appeared walking up the graveled walk, a being, whose every square inch of superficial surface indicated a bona fide, unadulterated specimen of the genus vagabond."[17] They might have a problem describing a tramp, but they know one when they see one. Among other characteristics, ragged clothes, a staggering and unsteady walk, and evidence of drinking all implicated a man as a tramp.

Another work of fiction, *The Tramp,* goes further, claiming each tramp had a specific character he or she prepared to perform to convince others to give them food or money. The central character does not become a tramp simply by losing his job; it is the choice to "become a Tramp" through his drinking and loafing.[18] He meets a group of tramps that live together in a forest camp while they beg for food and drink in the neighboring towns. The Perfessor [*sic*] is the leader of the group who helps each tramp reach his true potential. As the narrator explains, "Each Tramp had a peculiar character to perform; he was cast; like an actor, for a particular part best suited to his appearance and ability."[19] He lists the range of tramp characters one might select from: "The meek Tramp, with children, The bully Tramp, the ragged Tramp, the respectable Tramp, The Tramp who asks for work, The unwholesome

Tramp, The lubberly Tramp, The abject Tramp, the jolly Tramp, Mrs. Tramp and many others."[20] Unlike many other representations, the author includes female tramps and makes women equally degenerate and defiant of capitalist work expectations. The narrator takes pains to insist the tramps are not performing as actors, but simply highlighting their "natural character[s]."[21] This point is undercut by his subsequent outlining of how each tramp type is coached "artistically" by the Perfessor. For example, the unwholesome Tramp learns how to fake the symptoms of various illnesses, and Perfessor teaches the lubberly Tramp to whine.[22]

The tramp as performance is further reinforced by the ease with which reporters and investigators transformed into tramps. For example, Arthur Pember, a *New York Times* reporter, went undercover as a tramp soon after the Panic. He describes how he "proceeded to sprinkle my five-days' unshaven face with water and then to rub in some of the dust which, conveniently for my use, had been allowed to collect on the window-sill . . . then to array myself in a scarlet, poppy-colored flannel shirt, with a blue-and-yellow spotted pocket-handkerchief by way of neck-tie; then to don an old pair of trousers which had been artistically rent and mud-stained and patched on the seat and each knee, and to roll the bottoms of them up two folds."[23] As demonstrated by his employer's inability to recognize him on the street, the costume transforms him completely.

Tramps' mobility comprised a central component of their performance, contributing to their visibility and perceived menace to urban and rural communities across the country. In 1879, *Puck* magazine published a cartoon entitled "Tramp, Tramp, Tramp, the Tramp is Coming!," which illustrates the mobile threat presented by unemployed men. The cartoon depicts a giant tramp, in ragged clothes and carrying a walking stick, marching into a rural town. Towering over the farms, animals, and people, the tramp looks straight ahead as he takes another step, unaware of the frightened people and animals that scatter below. One woman clutches her child close to her chest as she runs. A man climbs over a fence to avoid him. A child, unfortunate to be in the road, attempts to outrun the giant's next step. The image literalizes the fear of the scale and mobility of the tramp menace (see figure 3).

FIGURE 3. A tramp causes panic and havoc as he walks
through town. James Albert Wales, "Tramp, Tramp, Tramp,
the Tramp Is Coming!" 1879, Wallach Division Picture
Collection. The New York Public Library, Astor,
Lenox, and Tilden Foundations.

Middle-class writers echoed these fears. Professor William H. Brewer
warned of the "warlike tribe" heading "towards a neighboring settlement
of peaceful, industrious, civilized whites."[24] Another writer warned, "we
heard of a force of five hundred of them approaching a Western city,
to the universal alarm of the inhabitants . . . how easy it is . . . to assemble
them by tens of thousands."[25] Many saw the only solution as arrests or in
the extreme, extermination. *The Chicago Tribune* suggested, "The simplest

plan, probably, where one is not a member of the Humane society, is to put a little strychnine or arsenic in the meat and the supplies furnished the tramp."[26] In the *New Englander*, Brewer similarly recommends that the "dangerous class" should "be throttled or—it will throttle us!"[27] As Cresswell notes, the tramp laws and these extreme responses demonstrated how the Anglo-American Protestant upper and middle classes saw the unemployed, wandering men "practicing something other than citizenship" through their mobility.[28] Even though police and reformers insisted that a person without visible means of support could be identified, exactly what visible qualities signaled the tramp varied. As the tramp emerged in the cultural imagination, Irishness became an easy, performative shorthand for identifying tramps, on and off the variety stage.

The Irish-American Tramp

Unlike the depression in the 1890s, when reformers conducted more systematic studies, no conclusive evidence exists about the identity of tramps in the 1870s. Many reformers assumed most tramps were migrants, however. Franklin B. Sanborn, secretary of Massachusetts's charity board, stated, "the two movements, as they show themselves in America—immigration and tramping—are but varieties of the same species."[29] Feeding anti-immigrant and antitramp prejudices, the conflation of migrants and tramps led to biological explanations for tramping and debates over migration, tramping, and citizenship. The connection imagined between the Irish and tramping provided one solution to identifying tramps. Building on long-held anti-Irish prejudices, reformers envisioned the Irish race as representative of the lack of means and desire to work.

Without a method for tracing the wandering unemployed, reformers tended to believe that tramps were primarily male and foreign born. They based their conclusions on the disproportionate numbers of Irish recorded in poorhouses and receiving outdoor relief (assistance given to the poor without requiring they live in poor- or workhouses). Although poverty and the need for aid did not necessarily signify someone lived as a tramp, reformers frequently conflated the two. In Octave Thanet's report for the *Atlantic Monthly* on paupers across several northern states, he concluded, "between half and two-thirds of them are of foreign birth."[30] In Queens County, New York, the county report on annual charity recorded all the aid recipients as foreign and highlighted the Irish as the largest migrant group receiving aid.[31] It was believed that migrants comprised half of New York State tramps by 1880, and records show half of the migrants came from Ireland.[32] Officials drew similar conclusions in Massachusetts, with one complaining, "nearly every inmate is of foreign birth or parentage—largely Irish."[33] The New York Association for Improving the Condition of the Poor denounced the "deteriorating effects of foreign immigration on the social and moral condition of this commercial emporium."[34] As historian Hidetaka Hirota notes, the association linked fitness for American citizenship directly to willing participation in the capitalist economy. It insisted on "the incompatibility of the foreign beggars with American capitalist society where people engaged in production and trade."[35]

The belief in the connection between migration and tramping led to a shift in the way northeastern states approached migration. In New York, the state legislature gave more power to the state charity board to regulate migration. Massachusetts also made efforts to regulate and deport poor migrants, which disproportionately impacted the Irish.[36] These efforts reflected reformers' beliefs that many migrants, especially the Irish, "the quintessential undeserving poor," "would remain permanently unfit for American republican society due to their innate predisposition to idleness and chronic dependency."[37]

Although the connection between poverty and the Irish was not new, scientific advantages in the late nineteenth century shaped reformers' biological arguments against migrants, tramps, and the Irish and their suitability for U.S. citizenship. Reformers blamed inherited characteristics and contagion for the rapid increase in the wanderers' numbers, which further emphasized their arguments' racial connotations. Although reformers still insisted that tramping resulted from individual choice, they argued that certain racial and ethnic groups were more inclined to make it. The Massachusetts State Board of Charities blamed "inherited organic imperfection, vitiated constitution, or *poor stock*" for paupers' condition.[38] Biological arguments led to claims that tramps reflected a primitive version of man, if writers recognized tramps'

humanity at all. The *New York Tribune* described the tramp as a "crea-
ture, midway between the vegetable and mineral world."[39] Many believed Catholicism contributed to the Irish's inability to assimilate and
learn the hardworking ways of the United States. As scholar Matthew
Frye Jacobson notes, "Ultimately such racial conceptions would lead
to a broad popular consensus that the Irish were 'constitutionally in-
capable of intelligent participation in the governance of the nation.'"[40]

These beliefs shaped how Americans visualized the Irish and tramping. A *Harper's Weekly* cartoon published in 1883 illustrates the intersection of migration, Irish poverty, and mobility. Depicting a poorhouse
transformed into a boat, the cartoon shows the ship sailing for America
and encountering a small boat from New York loaded with dynamite.
The caption reads, "650 paupers arrived at Boston in the Steamship
Nestoria, April 15th, from Galway, Ireland, shipped by the British Government." The cartoon reflected the belief that part of the pauper and
tramping problem resulted because Europe shipped over its poor. It
highlights the perceived menace through the looming threat of the New
York boat's dynamite, ready to blow up the Irish ship and prevent the
Irish poor from reaching America's shore. Sanborn highlighted the
fear of assisted migration's impact on the nation's number of tramps
and connected it to increased mobility, complaining, "so great now the
facilities given to the poor and vicious for migrating within our own
land, or from other countries to this, that it becomes important to . . .
consider them in their locomotive condition."[41] The Massachusetts
Board of State Charities also blamed assisted migration and reported,
"many paupers from foreign countries are unquestionably sent to America as paupers . . . in order to be rid of them."[42] As imagined through
the cartoon, part of the United States' issues with the poor stemmed
from an unending influx of other nation's unwanted paupers, not from
any social or economic condition in the United States (see figure 4).

Another cartoon, featured in *Puck*, is more explicit in connecting the
Irish with tramping and idleness. Entitled "Irish Industries," the cartoon is broken down into four panels. The first and third panels connect
the Irish to Irish nationalist violence, with one depicting an Irishman
building bombs and the other showing an Irishman lying in wait to kill
an Irish landlord. The second panel credits the Irish with corrupting

FIGURE 4. Highlighting the perceived menace of Irish migrants,
the cartoon illustrates Anglo Protestants' fears that Great Britain will
ship its poorest citizens to the United States. W. A. Rogers, "The
Balance of Trade with Great Britain seems to be still against us."
Harper's Weekly, April 28, 1883, 272. Library of Congress Prints
and Photographs Division, Washington, D.C.

democracy and is titled, "The Irish Vote Manufacturers." The final
panel, "A Never-Failing Irish Industry," shows an Irish tramp with his
hat out for coins while a personified globe throws coins into it. Behind
him stands a sign reading "Please Help the Lazy!" Taken all together,
the cartoon reinforces the notion that Irish laziness is hereditary and
a national trait. The globe man offering the Irishman money implies
that the Irish tramps are an international problem, not just a U.S. one
(see figure 5).

Although not all tramps were Irish, the connection between tramping
and Irishness lingered in the U.S. imagination. As historian Todd

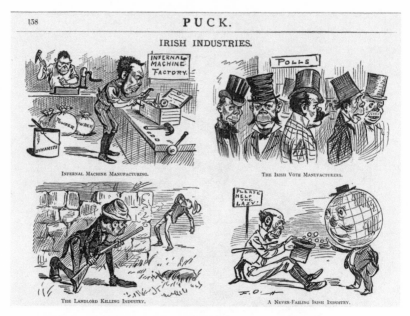

FIGURE 5. In its four panels, this cartoon characterizes the Irish as violent, corrupt, and lazy. Frederick Opper, "Irish Industries," *Puck*, November 2, 1881. Library of Congress Prints and Photographs Division, Washington, D.C.

DePastino notes, "the Irish wayfarer became a common Gilded Age stereotype. . . . Indeed, as new waves of immigrants from southern and eastern Europe poured into the country, the equation of Irishness and tramping became even more pronounced as the newcomers failed to take their places in the tramp army."[43] It is not surprising that as the nation struggled over the cause of the new wandering, unemployed masses, the comic tramp reinforced the connection between the Irish and tramps.

Racial Humor and the Tramp after the Panic

As the effects of the Panic rippled throughout New York City, they disproportionately impacted the city's legitimate theatres. Within weeks of the crash, Wallack's, Booth's, and others reported concerning drops in attendance. Newspapers complained that the decline resulted from high ticket prices established during and continued after the war. To deal with the economic challenges, some legitimate theatres cut their performers' salaries only a few months into the depression, and many handed out free tickets in an attempt to fill their theatres. In contrast, the variety theatre thrived and expanded its audience. Variety sold more affordable tickets and also presented more lighthearted acts that seemed to appeal to audiences during the current crisis. Reporting on the variety audience at the Olympic Theatre, one *New York Clipper* writer commented, "It was plainly discernable, while watching the faces of those in the lower portion of the auditorium, that the majority of them were not in the habit of attending variety theatres."[44] By February 1874, Booth's Theatre declared bankruptcy. Several months later, Josh Hart, manager of the Theatre Comique, and Tony Pastor, actor-manager of Tony Pastor's Opera House, boasted of record profits. According to the *Clipper,* Hart earned $60,000 over the 1873–1874 season. Pastor made $50,000 on his 1874 summer tour. The *Brooklyn Daily Eagle* bemoaned variety's continued success as the nation suffered: "the theatres are becoming variety halls."[45]

With its acrobats, dancers, singers, and comic duos, variety offered escapist entertainment, but it also incorporated local scams and scandals as well as national events and tragedies. Some theatres presented sketches and afterpieces seemingly based on recent events and their impact on its working-class audience members; examples included *Wall Street, or the Curse of Gold* and *The Rich and Poor of New York* at Tony Pastor's Opera House and *Rent Day, or Hard Times* at the Theatre Comique.[46] Some variety theatres, such as the Comique, held benefits for the increasing numbers of poor in their neighborhoods. Josh Hart, the manager of the Comique, organized a benefit for the fourteenth ward, which raised $1,134.25. Captain Clinchy, the police captain in charge of distributing the funds, explained that the benefit helped provide aid to eight hundred people in need. They distributed "a half ton of coal or two bags of flour" and helped pay local residents' rent. Hart received praise for his charity, with one paper hoping his example would "excite other managers to like worthy actions, and that the public will liberally respond to these appeals for aid to the distressed poor of our city."[47] With the variety theatres' tendency to appeal to novelty, include topical references, and recognize its audiences' hardships, it is not surprising that the comic tramp appeared on variety stages only a few months into the depression.

As a strategy for examining comic tramp performances in spite of the evidentiary gaps, this chapter primarily analyzes them at one of the few variety theatres to leave behind a comparatively fair-sized performance record, the Theatre Comique at 514 Broadway. This approach enables a close view of how the comic tramp developed at one of the most popular variety houses in 1870s New York. Managed by Hart at the start of the Panic and then from 1876 by the comic duo Edward Harrigan and Tony Hart, the Theatre Comique competed with Tony Pastor's Opera House on the Bowery only a few blocks away to offer working-class audiences respectable variety entertainment. As a result of Harrigan's children's efforts to preserve his legacy, an archival record of performance remains, in part, because of Harrigan's success and fame during his years at the Comique and later at the New Theatre Comique, which he established with Hart in the early 1880s.[48] The Theatre Comique's success also resulted in slightly more newspaper coverage, even if this commentary still remains sparse. Acknowledging the cracks in the narrative created through the lost archive and repertoire, I consider the remaining traces of performance within the scripts, along with newspapers, songsters, and sketches from other variety houses, to uncover the basic framework of the emerging tramp character. The comic tramp may or may not engage in travel on stage. By its definition, the tramp embodied an *idea* of mobility. Similar to Cresswell and others who have analyzed the tramp, I explore how tramp representations related to this mobile idea. By framing the comic tramp as a dramaturgy, I aim to highlight how the idea of the tramp became codified for working-class audiences and then perpetuated meanings about the tramp's mobility through its repetition.

At a time when variety theatres, appealing to novelty, changed sketches and afterpieces after only a week, the comic tramp appeared in songs, sketches, and afterpieces for weeks at a time. The comic tramp sketches with the longest runs and most revivals featured the Irish-American tramps, written by Edward Harrigan. Performing with his partner Tony Hart and writing the songs with composer and father-in-law David Braham, Harrigan began his ascent to variety stardom with his song and sketch, *The Mulligan Guard,* in 1873. As the 1870s progressed, Harrigan and Hart moved from valuable variety stock company members to the Theatre Comique's stars. Harrigan wrote the duo's most popular material, which focused on Irish-American and working-class life in New York. With their takeover of the first-class variety house in 1876, they became major players in New York's theatre scene. Harrigan's *The Terrible Example* premiered five months after the economic crash and ran from March 1874 until the end of the season in May. The Comique revived the sketch again, typically for several-week runs, in October 1874; March, April, and May 1875; October 1876; April 1877; and May 1879. After the Panic, minstrel and variety comedian Johnny Wild revived and revised his old minstrel sketch *One, Two, Three,* which he performed in May 1874, December 1874, and May 1876. Harrigan had a lasting hit with the *Mulligan Guard Picnic,* featuring several tramp characters, which he wrote as a sketch in 1878 and then expanded into a wildly popular early musical comedy performed in 1880 and 1883.[49] From its earliest appearances on the variety stage, the comic tramp navigated the fluid racial terrain surrounding the genesis of the tramp in the cultural imagination.

In each of Harrigan's comic tramp sketches and his own *One, Two, Three,* comedian Johnny Wild originated the character. Born in Manchester, England, to English and Irish parents, he was the third-ranked star at the Theatre Comique, after Harrigan and Hart. He made his name as a blackface performer in minstrelsy in the 1860s before moving into variety, where he played blackface characters in Harrigan's sketches and musical comedies. Performers in the variety stock companies tended to play a range of roles, and Wild also appeared on the Comique stage in stage Irish roles. Although it is difficult to say who performed the comic tramp first, people in the theatre industry remembered Wild's tramps as the predecessors to the comic tramp in vaudeville. William Ellis Horton remembered Wild as the "first tramp comedian . . . in a sketch called *A Terrible Example.*"[50] Upon Wild's death, the *New York Dramatic Mirror* explained, "In a *Terrible Example* he used to convulse audiences by his comicalities as a reckless tramp. It has been claimed that Johnny Wild's early tramp impersonations formed the model on which many subsequent characterizations of that type were founded both in vaudeville and farce-comedy."[51] Various newspapers and memoirs commented on Wild's choice to perform his tramps in whiteface. Referring to his appearance as a "white-faced tramp" and "white vagrant," papers cheered Wild's "marvelous sketch of the bummer, whom we now call a tramp."[52] The *Spirit of the Times* referred to Wild's Lemons as the "star" of the *Picnic*.[53] *Harper's Weekly* and James L. Ford in *Forty Odd Years* heralded his "remarkable success" with the character in which he "was never seen in better form."[54] It is possible Wild's performances made a major contribution to the comedic repertoire of the tramp as it transformed throughout popular entertainment for decades.

Unlike most representations in literature, newspapers, and song, comedians performed the earliest comic tramps in blackface and whiteface, which typically meant stage Irish. With Irish, blackface, and Dutch (German) acts dominating variety stages, the choice to perform Irish or blackface tramps resulted from the types' popularity with audiences and reflected distinct prejudices against black Americans and the Irish that made their racial types a clear visual marker of the tramp menace.[55] Even though the audience may have had personal experience with the hardships created by the Panic, these comic conventions translated middle-class ideologies surrounding the unemployed men's excessive mobility into a familiar, working-class framework. Drawing on standard comic conventions naturalized the idea of the tramp as lazy, drunk, and disruptive for variety audiences. Through an analysis of these early comic tramp figures, it is possible to see how variety theatre grappled with what Cresswell refers to as the "morally coded set of geographical suppositions about mobility" intrinsic to the tramp.[56]

The existence of blackface tramps in variety made it one of the few places to prominently imagine tramps as black. Although newspapers occasionally identified criminals as black tramps, in newspapers, novels, cartoons, and pamphlets, middle-class representations and rhetoric typically portrayed tramps as white and foreign. Less representation may have been due to the smaller black tramp population. Historians speculate that black tramps comprised less of the overall tramp population because of the effective use of vagrancy and tramp laws and the fear they instilled.[57] However, mobility remained a vital right that many black Americans claimed after the war. Black Americans left the South in search of economic opportunity, in the words of historian William Cohen, "voting with their feet."[58] Historian Peter Kolchin notes that this mobility "affirm[ed] their freedom, because free movement was one of the obvious earmarks of their new status."[59] Overseers of the Poor in Queens, New York, reported the reluctance of the black population to seek poor relief, which may have led reformers to believe they comprised less of the poor.[60] It is possible that the upper and middle classes could not envision, out of fear and racism, the mobile unemployed as comprised substantially of black Americans because they still imagined mobility as primarily a white right.

The black comic tramps portrayed on the variety stage worked against this trend. Although reformers may not have as consistently labeled black Americans as tramps, parallel concerns about black Americans joining the industrial economy circulated in postwar culture. After emancipation, officials worried that freed slaves would poorly adapt to contract wage labor. Northern and southern officials gave this justification when using vagrancy laws to force former slaves into labor contracts in the South. These actions related to anxieties about racial hierarchies shaken by emancipation, black reprisals for slavery, and the rights given to black Americans through the Thirteenth, Fourteenth, and Fifteenth Amendments. Propagating the idea that black Americans needed to be taught how to work in the industrial economy or inherently did not fit within that system placed them automatically below white workers and reinscribed doubts that they could successfully function as citizens.[61]

During the first few years after the Panic, blackface and Irish comic tramps were almost indistinguishable, other than by their face color. As scholars have discussed, print caricatures of black Americans and the Irish often reflected similar prejudices, making the parallels in stage representation not unusual. Political cartoons, newspapers, and middle-class reform literature offered biological justifications for the belief that both groups lacked the ability to be proper U.S. citizens. Simian caricatures portrayed black Americans and the Irish as having substandard intelligence, violent and alcoholic tendencies, and the lack of desire to work.[62] A famous 1876 *Harper's Weekly* cartoon shows black Americans and the Irish balancing each other on a scale. Although the scale labels the black American "black" and the Irishman "white," the image equates them as an issue for the regions labeled in the cartoon, North and South. Mocking charges of fraud in the 1876 election, the cartoon marked both black Americans and the Irish as equally unqualified to participate in democracy (see figure 6).

The close relationship between blackface and Irish stage representation started in minstrelsy. White migrants' and Americans' minstrel performances denigrated black Americans, sentimentalized plantation life, and mocked the ability of free black Americans to act as capable and responsible American citizens. Caricatures often included blackface makeup with exaggerated lips; ragged, ripped clothes; and malapropisms. As historian Dale Cockrell discusses, "minstrel shows became, to a certain extent, a product by and for Irish Americans."[63] Irish performers, musicians, and composers, such as Dan Bryant, Dan Emmett, and E.P. Christy, had long created and performed minstrel songs and acts, and the Irish and Irish-American working-class comprised a substantial part of audiences. Even though black and Irish Americans frequently lived alongside one another in northern cities, working-class Irish Americans did not support efforts for equal rights out of fear of losing the benefits and promises of whiteness. Minstrel performances undoubtedly played a role in asserting the Irish's white supremacy. As American Studies scholar Alison Kibler discusses, the "diverse group of whites" performing in minstrelsy "emphasize[d] their common whiteness to antebellum urban masses in the creation of an abject but fascinating blackness."[64]

Minstrelsy and variety remained closely linked around the Civil War, even as variety increasingly distinguished itself. Depending on the available jobs, a significant number of Irish and Irish-American performers worked in both minstrelsy and variety throughout their careers, which facilitated the forms' continued influence on each other.[65] Blackface and Irish caricatures also overlapped. American Studies scholar Eric Lott points out that in minstrelsy, blackface skits incorporated Irish brogues because "blackface, bizarrely enough, was actually used to represent all ethnicities on the antebellum stage prior to the development of ethnic types."[66] Even as more distinct racial and ethnic

FIGURE 6. Thomas Nast's cartoon equates black Americans and Irish Americans as obstacles to U.S. democracy. Thomas Nast, "The Ignorant Vote," *Harper's Weekly*, December 9, 1876, 985. Library of Congress Prints and Photographs Division, Washington, D.C.

types developed in popular culture, overlap in costume and behavior continued after the Civil War as raggedly dressed and frequently drunk blackface and Irish stage types appeared on variety stages. Lott and historian Robert Toll single out the sketches of Harrigan and Hart as representative of this performance trend, but they do not reference the comic tramp sketches.[67] This is not to say that every blackface or Irish character in variety was interchangeable, but the performance conventions presented a performance vocabulary with the potential to blur clear distinctions between blackface and Irish stage types. I argue that the early comic tramp reflects these popular entertainment conventions in which blackface and Irish types reflected similarities in character, costume, and comedy.

These similarities did not mean that audiences interpreted blackface and Irish characters in the same way or equated black and Irish experiences. In spite of the parallel character constructions, systematic oppression and everyday reality differed for the Irish and black Americans and likely influenced how audiences interpreted the blackface and whiteface tramp performances. With a significant amount of variety performance improvised or dependent on the actor playing the character, differences between blackface and Irish tramps likely emerged that are not apparent from the remaining performance evidence. In spite of these differences, both types were used to depict the early comic tramp, and the evidence suggests the differences were minimal at best.

During the comic tramp's early years, blackface and Irish comic stereotypes provided a visual vocabulary that offered a quickly recognizable stand-in for the tramp's seemingly invisible crime. The distinction between the performances of the rare native-born, Anglo-Saxon comic tramp and the blackface or Irish comic tramp demonstrates the important role of racial comedy in signaling a character's tramp status. Native-born, Anglo-Saxon comic tramps verbally identify themselves and their crimes or commit clear crimes on stage, highlighting the dangerous and threatening potential of their unemployed wandering. The majority of his comedy also emerges from his dialogue. The clearest example appeared in the sketch and longer musical comedy version of *Mulligan Guard Picnic*. Based on characters from his popular song and sketch "The Mulligan Guard," the loose plot of Harrigan's *Mulligan*

Guard Picnic and its expanded versions (1878, 1880, 1883) focus on the Mulligan Guards leaving the city with their families for a picnic, while dealing with the supposed death of a husband and friend. Mistaken identities, tramp robberies, new romances fated to fail, and boat hijinks fill the sketch. The 1878 version featured the native-born Anglo-Saxon tramp, a rural, wandering, violent vagabond named Gypsy Jack.

Whenever the tramp enters the stage or meets someone new, he confesses that he hates work with a variation of the lines, "I'm Gypsy Jack the mountain rover. I scorn work."[68] The repetition of this introduction, while comic, also reinforces the character's laziness. He explains that he "live[s] here on the classic Hudson" and is "the farmers' dread."[69] He reinforces his roaming lifestyle, explaining he is a "highwayman of the Palisades."[70] When Jack introduces himself to the two couples he intends to rob, he threatens, "another word, and your gore will redden the road."[71] The two couples, three Irish and one German, plead for mercy, but Jack rejects their claim to be "New Yorkers," retorting, "I never pity foreigners."[72]

During the first few years after the Panic, blackface and Irish comic tramps did not verbally identify themselves, if they spoke at all. In their startling visibility, other characters recognize them on sight. Performed by a cross-dressing man in blackface, the comedian John Gilbert, Mrs. Tramp in *Private Boarding* is instantly recognized as a tramp by the boardinghouse cook. First performed in January 1874 at the Olympic Theatre, William Courtright's *Private Boarding* features one of the few rare instances of a blackface female tramp on the variety stage, played by a cross-dressing man. The sketch is set in a boardinghouse, and comic characters enter, create chaos, and are then thrown out or leave. Although *Private Boarding* did not appear at the Comique, Courtright worked in minstrelsy and variety and did appear at the Comique on occasion. When Mrs. Tramp asks if the home is a boardinghouse, the cook replies, "What did you think it was? The station house, or the soup-house?"[73] There is no confusion over Mrs. Tramp's status, even before she begins her pleas for food.

Starring John Wild in the title role as Irish tramp Jimmy Lush, *Terrible Example* (March 1874) at the Comique focuses on a temperance meeting led by hypocritical Irish-American reformers trying to make a

quick profit off meeting fees. As the meeting progresses, various characters cause disturbances, and Lush is thrown out several times. The
sketch ultimately ends with many of the attendees drinking and a melee.
When Lush enters the temperance meeting in *Terrible Example*, no one
speaks to him or asks him for the fee to enter the talk. The president
of the temperance society, Moriarity, notices and recognizes him on
sight. He stands out automatically due to his makeup and demeanor.
The *Spirit of the Times* described the immediate effect of his appearance
on the audience, detailing how "Wild also came in for a good share of
the applause for his remarkable make-up as the Terrible Example. He
had only to look at the house to convulse it with laughter. His facial
expression is very grotesque, and he is an established favorite at the
Comique."[74] This review presents a range of questions concerning what
his grotesque makeup looked like and how his performance drew the
audiences' attention and laughter. Although the absent performance
record makes it impossible to know, the brief comment points out the
importance of the tramp's visual demeanor, the performer's construction of the tramp figure, and why it succeeded with audiences.

Unlike the native-born, Anglo-Saxon tramp who controlled his own
actions and his identity, other characters recognize the black and Irish
tramp through a visual vocabulary tied to their racial comedic stereotypes. The black and Irish comic tramps seem to be revealed as inherently tramps through their physical appearance and movement. The
comic tramps lack control over their bodies, in part due to drunkenness,
which plays a central role in these performances. Repeatedly, the black
and Irish comic tramps demonstrate their lack of bodily discipline,
whether standing, sitting, or walking. Wild originally wrote *One, Two,
Three* as a minstrel sketch in the 1860s and revised it for the Theatre
Comique in May 1874. Taking place at a dramatic agency for variety
actors, job-hunting performers come to the agency and inquire about
work. Similar to *Private Boarding*, as each person reveals his flaws, such
as drunkenness, the character Bounce, acting for the agent, Conner,
throws him out. Wild plays Tom Pepper, the blackface tramp, and the
only character to repeatedly come into the office and cause trouble before Bounce tosses him out. The sketch ends in a melee. Pepper enters
"very drunk, staggering, with an old segar butt in his mouth."[75] When

Pepper sneaks back into the office, the servant goes to remove him, but Pepper's legs go out from under him.[76]

Similarly, in the *Terrible Example*, Lush "staggers down" and falls against another character when he enters.[77] When the reformers decided to use Lush as their "terrible example" of alcoholism, they place him in a chair, but he slides off and falls, repeatedly, sometimes bringing other characters with him. The visual gag grows throughout the sketch, with the entire Thirteen Ward Glee Club falling over as a result of Lush's collapse.[78] Harrigan's *Down Broadway* (1875) at the Comique revolves around a moving panorama of New York sights and the journey of a character visiting the city for the first time. The sketch attempts to profit off the popularity of the comic tramp character Lush from *Terrible Example*, who appears directly involved or in the background of most scenes, played again by Wild. *Down Broadway* also includes business with Lush falling in the New York streets, along with a group of bummers.[79] Although most, if not all, the tramps are drunk, their bodies also appear inherently flawed. Aside from reflecting the physical comedy typically found on the variety stage, the comic tramps' physicality suggests that their flexible, floppy bodies cannot become disciplined enough for the regular, repetitive machine work increasingly dominating the American economy.

The chaos created by the comic tramps through their physical behavior also identifies them to surrounding characters. Reflecting the negative stereotype in the dominant imagination, the comic tramps present a violent threat, albeit a comic one. For Pepper in *One, Two, Three* and for Lush in *Terrible Example*, the comic tramps repeatedly fight other characters who try to remove them from the room. In *Down Broadway*, Lush fights with Roger, a tourist to New York, twice in Union Square and once outside Harry Hill's variety and dance hall. Lush threatens Roger: "I'm going to send you home in an express wagon as invalid. . . . You'll have to get a hearse, when I'm through with you."[80]

The fights' consequences are not minor in the sketches' overall structure. The comic tramps' presence creates chaos. It was not uncommon for sketches and afterpieces, especially those at the Theatre Comique or Tony Pastor's, to end with a melee. In these sketches, the comic tramps instigate the chaos that ends the scene or sketch. As the dramatic agent

tries to evaluate potential performers in *One, Two, Three*, Pepper enters again "with an armful of all the old poles, sticks and trash he can
carry, and lets it fall all about, while he himself jumps up on the table
and upsets everything. Confusion, bus[iness]. And quick close."[81] When
Private Boarding's cook decides Mrs. Tramp is taking advantage of her
generosity, the cook goes after Mrs. Tramp with a broom.[82] The *Terrible
Example* ends when "Example comes on fights Moriarity at the back and
is whipping him badly when *omnes* join in. General melee."[83]

As a result of their disruptive presence, other characters actively attempt to throw out the comic tramps in an effort to minimize the chaos.
These actions highlight a key aspect of the tramp figure: the tramps
have no place in contemporary society. In *Private Boarding*, Mrs. Boar-
dem chases Mrs. Tramp around the stage, hitting her with a broom and
eventually forcing her out the door.[84] The title *One, Two, Three* references
the centrality to the sketch of throwing people out. It is a reference
to "one, two, three bounce," a count before the "muscle" throws the
tramp out. Pepper enters, is noticed, chased, and either thrown out or
exits on his own five times throughout the sketch.[85] In *Terrible Example*,
the reformers attempt to toss Lush out a minimum of four times.[86] In
Down Broadway, Roger explicitly states that the tramps do not belong:
"I can't see why a big city like New York will let those poor men die in
the streets without giving them a home in the States Prison. Of course
the world will say they drink but what won't the world say about a poor
man."[87] Neither Roger nor any of the other characters in *Private Boarding, One, Two, Three*, or *Terrible Example* offer to help the tramps find a
job as a solution to their issues, because they are seen to live outside the
contract labor economy. Through his fall, fights, and disruptions, the
comic tramp makes his lack of means of work visible through the racial
caricatures of the variety stage. On sight, it is clear that the comic tramp
is lazy, drunk, and disruptive, which many in the audience intuitively
assumed about black and Irish Americans in American society.

Mrs. Tramp in *Private Boarding* points to a critical gender exception
in the comic tramp's representation. Female impersonators were common in minstrelsy and variety, so her existence would not seem unusual.
However, she is the only female comic tramp that I have traced through
either scripts or brief references in the *New York Clipper*. In comparison to

male comic tramps, her comedy emerges more from verbal banter. For example, she does offer a reason for her poverty, stating, "I'm a poor lone widow, with a sick husband at home."[88] The contradictions in her statements point to a poorly constructed tramp performance meant to elicit sympathy and food. Her continuing list of nonsensical reasons and ludicrous demands for fancy food eventually convince the cook to throw her out.

Her appearance offers a rare glimpse into female agency and working-class mobility in variety representation. With few differences between Mrs. Tramp and the other early tramps in terms of stage behavior, she seems to enjoy the same privileges of excessive mobility that mark them as societal pariahs. However, inherently gendered middle-class ideologies surrounding women and public movement likely contributed to the lack of widespread female comic tramps on stage and in the United States. Walking down the street and traveling for work presented different dangers for men than for women. As historian John H. Kasson discusses, the middle-class culture of gentility expected respectable women to maintain their "privacy in public" when walking down the street through self-restraint, "minimiz[ing] bodily contact," and ignoring "potential offenses."[89] Not maintaining this sense of privacy, working-class women often acted in opposition to middle-class norms through their brightly colored clothing and gregarious promenading with working-class men.[90] Their behavior opened them up to reformer and police accusations of prostitution and immorality. In addition to the implications of respectability, a woman traveling alone risked the danger of harassment or violence, which limited opportunities for mobile work or traveling in search of new job opportunities. As historians discuss, in the 1870s, reformers and writers assumed the tramp to be male, which more detailed surveys of tramps in the 1890s later seemed to confirm.[91]

In its focus on the most prominent middle-class and working-class ideologies that primarily viewed mobility as a male privilege, an in-depth examination of women's representation and connections to mobility and immobility fall outside this book's purview. However, I want to briefly point to how Irish women working in mobile occupations were performed in these comic tramp sketches as well as in others performed alongside them or a few blocks away at Tony Pastor's Opera House. The sketches highlight how working-class women went against middle-class norms to earn their livings in nineteenth-century New York and violated gendered expectations of mobility. In their poverty, mobility, and penchant for violence, they paralleled Mrs. Tramp in performance conventions, but they differed from her in their willingness to work and their potential to use violence for good, moral causes.

Street selling often required women to navigate the city streets. Urban reformers viewed street selling as disruptive and unhealthy for city life. In the sketches, Irish-American working women demonstrate their potential for chaos while plying their trade. *Down Broadway* and two sketches performed at Tony Pastor's, *High Life and Low Life in New York* (1869) and *The Match Girl of New York* (1873) featured Irish female street sellers, Mrs. Delaney who sells fruit and juice, Bridget who sell apples, and Bridget who sells peppermint and lemons, respectively. All three women show a penchant for violence. Mrs. Delaney beats Roger after he complains about the juice he purchased from her.[92] In the two sketches performed at Tony Pastor's, the Irish women fight with black-face male street sellers with little provocation. Similar to other poor and working-class characters on stage, including the tramp, their violence became a central part of their character and comedy.

The two Irish women named Bridget explicitly highlight racial tension in their fights. Bridget in *High Life* refers to the black whitewasher as a "black leprechaun," a jibe at his similarities to Irishmen and also possibly a metatheatrical reference to an Irish performer playing the character in blackface.[93] The Irish woman in *Match Girl* is more explicit in her racist disgust, stating, "Do you think a high born lady like me would demean herself by trafficking wid a" person "like you!"[94] Using a racial slur, she attempts to distinguish herself from the blackface street seller, Bob, and gives herself more social value through her claim that she is highborn. Bob makes clear that he does not like Bridget but responds, "I don't despise you on account of your color."[95] These fights reflected the racism and animosity between black Americans and the Irish, with which working-class audiences would be intimately familiar. Paradoxically, in marking their differences, the Irish women actually highlight their similarities with the blackface men through their abusive banter, violence, and disruptive behavior.

Bridget in *Match Girl* illuminates a more positive direction for her disruptive behavior. After Alice, the Anglo-American match girl, is targeted by a lecherous man, Bridget springs to her defense, and her violent nature becomes Alice's saving grace. Highlighting the dangers faced by women alone working on the streets, Bridget tells the predator, "that girl is not alone" before attacking the man and taking her to safety.[96] When the man catches up to Alice later in the sketch, Bridget again defends Alice, threatening that he will "feel the strength of her muscle."[97] Although she has many negative characteristics, Bridget draws on them to serve a noble cause. On two occasions, Bridget works with or convinces Bob to help her defend Alice. The positive role played by Bridget and Bob is not unusual in variety sketches, which provided more complicated, if negative, racial depictions, as Kattwinkel has argued.[98] However, the possibility of a moral center and putting the stereotype's "negative" characteristics toward a positive, moral end eventually became incorporated into the male Irish comic tramp on stage as well. The ultimate exclusion of women and blackface characters from this transformation highlights how middle-class ideologies surrounding unemployed men and mobility shaped the tramp, even as the variety stage demonstrates the possibility of imagining the tramp and mobile workers in other, more diverse ways.

The Irish-American Comic Tramp on the Variety Stage

The differences between blackface and Irish-American stage types ultimately did matter in how variety imagined the tramp. As the comic tramp developed, it became racially distinct and rejected the ambiguity that could surround blackface and Irish types. I suggest that different racial expectations and fears surrounding mobility influenced how variety imagined who had the right to mobility.

As each sketch developed the comic tramp, his evolution paralleled that of Harrigan's other stage characters. Contemporaries and scholars have credited Harrigan with improving the representation of the

Irish and Irish Americans on stage as well as for creating a predecessor of musical comedy. Even though his Irish and Irish-American characters portray many negative stage Irish characteristics grounded in nineteenth-century stage comedy, including the penchant for drink, blarney, and fighting, Harrigan downplayed these negative characteristics and related them to the pursuit of noble causes, such as family, community, and patriotism for Ireland and the United States.[99] In the same way, the comic tramp hinted at a more complicated situation for tramps. However simplistic, the comic tramp embodied the tension between the negative middle-class stereotype and the economic realities facing variety's working-class male audiences. Although the negative associations remained, each subsequent sketch increased the positive connotations of the comic tramp, making him more verbal, better integrated into the New York and Irish-American community, and, on occasion, heroic. Irishness may not have occupied the top of the whiteness hierarchy in the United States, but the popularity of the Irish-American comic tramp solidified its white representation on the variety stage, erased black mobility, and reinforced the superiority of a white mobile identity.

Harrigan's and Wild's portrayals of the tramp reflected more nuance, likely in acknowledgement that many in the audience experienced mobile unemployment. People working closely with the mobile unemployed recognized the disjunction between the statements of legislators and reformers and the situation on the ground. Labor newspapers advocated for the mobile unemployed and argued that tramps did not give up their citizenship when they lost their jobs. The *National Labor Tribune* and other labor newspapers pointed out that many tramps were men down on their luck and reiterated calls to acknowledge tramps' humanity and the circumstances that led to their condition.[100]

On the ground, government officials also confronted realities that contrasted with middle-class explanations for the large numbers of mobile men tramping throughout the country. William O'Gorman, an Irish Famine immigrant, served as Overseer of the Poor for Newtown, Queens. In the 1870s, Newtown, with its country homes, served as a retreat for the middle and upper classes, but it also provided a range of occupations for German and Irish migrants on farms, in factories, and at refineries tied to the expanding Long Island Railroad.[101] O'Gorman's daybook records his increasing disbelief over the numbers of poor and wandering men coming to him for aid. "This long continued poverty," he writes, "I cannot find power to check."[102] He complains, "strangers . . . seem now to over-run the roads."[103] He is amazed at the distress and famished state of the people coming to him for aid and compares them to his experiences with poverty in Ireland. He explains that he "was strongly reminded of the poverty and misery which in my young days in 1847 and 1848 I saw in the county Galway when I was employed as a Engineer under the government to lay out work to relieve the famished people"[104] He also discusses his internal conflict over the contrast between middle-class theories of the poor and the people he encountered daily. He explains how "Most Everyone says 'Let them freeze'; well I don't believe that that alternative falls under the head of the overseer of the Poor's duty. Still must be careful."[105] After a series of articles in the local press attacking overseers for giving aid that supposedly enabled people not to work, O'Gorman used his experiences to counter predominant theories of tramps as lazy in a letter to the editor of the *Newtown Register*. He protested that all "tramps are not worthless. I meet plenty of good mechanics among them, particularly moulders."[106] This conflict between the middle-class cultural imagination concerning the unemployed and the reality on the ground played out in Harrigan's sketches.

With each new sketch, the Irish-American comic tramp became more verbal and assertive about the causes of his condition being other than poor judgment, laziness, or alcoholism. In *Terrible Example*, Lush is primarily a physical character. Unlike the blackface tramps, his lack of physical control extends to his voice. When Lush asks to sing, the temperance president, Moriarity, says they should "Let him sing, give him a chance to reform."[107] When he starts singing, the other characters put their "hands to their ears as if horrified at his singing."[108] Lush controls his voice as well as he controls his body, poorly. This is a popular joke that Harrigan continued in *Down Broadway*. Harrigan's character Moriarity provides the only commentary on the condition of the poor, with his song, "When the Soup House Comes Again." Moriarity sings, "When the snow begins to fall, your landlord he will call,

You must have your money ready when for rent he calls your name, So let ye's bear in mind, don't spend your pinnies blind, Or you surely will be hungry when the soup house comes again."[109] Although the song recognizes the hardship of the poor, acknowledging "Last winter was so hard from alleyway to yard," it also places the responsibility solely on the individual to support himself as opposed to the economic system.[110]

In *Down Broadway*, Lush is more vocal, but his dialogue is primarily confined to begging for money or a drink or threatening fights. Lush and the other bummers are given a song in which they have an opportunity to describe their own situation to the audience. According to the manuscript, the scene opens in Union Square with a "view of Park and benches with four characters very raggedly attired," including Lush.[111] The song presents the tramps as lazy, petty thieves, and drunks. It also describes them as a spectacle within the city. They sing, "We sleep out on the benches, And sometimes on the grass; We're bums of the dirtiest water, Policemen let us pass; We brighten all the railings Of the Public Parks; you know Its there we set 'till a heavy wet compels us for to go."[112] Conveniently for others, they ask to be locked up on Blackwell's Isle, singing "Oh! Send us up to Blackwell's Isle. . . . We ask you in a heartbroken voice, To give us all Ten Days!"[113] With this sketch, Harrigan started to make a distinction between the deserving and the undeserving poor. Before the entrance of the tramps onstage, beggars have their opportunity to make their case. In the chorus, the beggars implore the audience to "Pity the beggars, oh do! Unable to work, not willing to die, Watching the rich walk proudly by, We wouldn't steal the weight of a pin—Have pity on these beggar min."[114] Even though the song states that "The blind, the lame, the sick, the sore" beg on the street, the last lines hint at the performative nature of these ailments and that the whole song possibly is based on a lie.[115] Even though they claim they are starving, somehow the beggars are "always fat and never thin—Its peculiar to these beggar min."[116] Lush separates himself from the character in *Terrible Example* by actively seeking out small opportunities to make some money, such as when he challenges a clog dancer to a dance competition.[117]

Harrigan continued to give his comic tramp more lines and direct plot involvement with the addition of Lemons to the expanded *Mulligan*

Guard Picnic in 1880 and 1883. He also builds on the notion that tramps are not inherently lazy. Lemons is the most vocal of all three Irish-American comic tramps. This allows him to tell the audience about his employment history in a dialogue with the Mulligans' black servant, Rebecca Allup, played by Hart in blackface. Lemons explains that he first met Dan Mulligan when he arrived from Ireland. He gave Dan a ride in his cart when he worked as a peddler.[118] He also explains that he worked as an inspector, "a jailor . . . and sailor boarding house runner. And I've played in the old Bowery Theatre."[119] By listing a bunch of working-class jobs, Lemons places himself in the same category as many of the men in the audience, who also moved from job to job. Lemons might be a tramp now, but his current situation does not mean he never worked for a living. Lemons brags to Rebecca, "I stood high once," even though the dialogue makes clear he likely did not succeed in his many professions.[120] Lemons also is willing to work to get what he wants: to join his friends on the picnic. He offers to work on the ship washing glasses if they will let him come along. This action reinforces the reformers' argument that tramps chose not to work, but, at the same time, demonstrates that Lemons is willing to work for the right reasons. In this case, his rationale does not tie directly to drink, which is the common reason why other comic tramps volunteer for work.[121]

Although negatively portrayed, the Irish comic tramps outsmart and outmaneuver the other characters throughout the sketches. Blackface comic tramps earned laughs through similar bits. For example, after Pepper enters a third time in *One, Two, Three*, the other characters are not able to catch him. The stage directions instruct Pepper to fall *"down and Bounce falls over him, but jumps up quickly, and before he gets hold of him Pepper has just slipped out in time."*[122] In this instance, Pepper does not achieve what he wants, to remain in the office, but he successfully escapes having Bounce throw him out. The sketch manuscripts often label stage fights "business," omitting staging details, but the comic tramps frequently outwit the people trying to get rid of them. They might not always avoid having other characters toss them out, but in multiple instances, all of Harrigan's Irish-American tramps escape before the other characters catch them. In *Terrible Example*, Lush sneaks back into the temperance meeting, sits under the table, and smokes his pipe. He remains undetected until the characters trace the smoke.[123] At the close, Lush is winning the fight when chaos breaks out, with the stage directions stating, "*Example comes on fights Moriarity* [the temperance president] *at the back and is whipping him badly.*"[124] In *Down Broadway*, Lush might not conclusively win the fight with Roger, but he leaves Roger with a black eye that he sports throughout the rest of the show.[125]

Even though *Terrible Example* does not present a flattering portrait of the tramp, it also does not portray middle-class reformers positively. The sketch is based on the premise that two Irish temperance reformers hold a meeting in an effort to make money from the tickets they sell to their audience. It is clear from the opening dialogue that they are holding the meeting only to make money. The reformers also do not follow the advice they give to their audience. When one audience member cannot pay the fee, they agree that he will buy them drinks at the bar later. In a later gag, the president, Moriarity, reads the by-laws, which state that any member who dies will receive fifty dollars. Everyone at the meeting falls down and plays dead. Then the president offers anyone who makes a recovery a drink. The crowd rushes to the front for their drink, but Moriarity explains, "I've drained every drop of it."[126] The characters' hypocrisy is tied to their Irishness, which may have led some to dismiss the critique. The reformers portray the basic drunk, full of blarney, and a politically corrupt Irish caricature. However, in the world of the sketch, there are no good guys.

Unlike the image of the tramp as a stranger invader, Harrigan's Irish-American comic tramps are New Yorkers with local ties. Through their portrayals, mobility does not eliminate the possibility of having a home. *Terrible Example* provides little information about Lush. The characters' recognition of Lush implies he might be a regular fixture in the neighborhood, but his exact status is unclear. *Down Broadway* starts to flesh out the Irish comic tramp in more detail. When the bummers leave Blackwell's Isle, they return to New York, their home. Harrigan also marks Lush's presence through his mobility along with the moving panorama. As the scene changed to a new sight in New York—Union Square, Harry Hill's, the Battery—Lush moves with it. The *New York Clipper* highlighted Wild's appearance as the "drunken bummer who figured in every scene with great fidelity to nature" as one of the show's main attractions.[127] Through this depiction, it is implied that New York is his city, and Roger, the tourist, is the stranger.

In the *Mulligan Guard Picnic*, Harrigan makes Lemons's ties to the Irish-American community explicit. He also indicates the tramp's capacity for loyalty and compassion, even if the expression of these emotions is inherently silly. When trying to convince Rebecca to give him the food from her basket, he claims a long-standing friendship with Dan, whom he refers to as a brother, and the Mulligan Committee, which planned the picnic. When he runs into Dan, he pleads for a ticket, which Dan denies him because he is a drunk and a tramp. In spite of his rejection, Lemons remains loyal to Dan stating, "So long Dan—No harm done. You can count on Lemons all the time."[128] Later, Dan hits Lemons because he will not go away, but Lemons remains steadfast telling him to "Slug me . . . I'm with you jist the same."[129] After jumping onto the boat and following the Mulligan crowd on their picnic, he learns about Dan's fight with the tailor, who cut off his pants' leg, and promises revenge on the tailor for Dan. Although this is a ludicrous mission, Lemons does not cause trouble because he is depraved, but because he wants to help his friend. The people at the picnic also defend and help Lemons as one of their own. Even when he causes trouble by stealing the milk can, some of the Mulligan Guard cheer for him to avoid and win the fight with a farmer. When Rebecca picks on Lemons by giving him soap instead of food to eat, one of the Mulligan Guard tell her to leave him alone.[130] Over Dan's objections, Cordelia, Dan's wife, and Bridget, their neighbor, insist Lemons join everyone at the picnic table because "The poor man is hungry!"[131] They even save him when he starts to choke on food. Throughout most of Lemons's scene, he jokes with the other characters and generally is accepted. They might not condone his drinking or his silly actions, but he is part of the community. This depiction of the tramp is not radical, but it portrays a nuance missing from previous representations. The tramp is not an evil stranger; he is someone you might know.

By making Lemons a hero, Harrigan makes the distinction between the Irish-American comic tramp and the native-born, white tramp.

Although Lemons drinks, fights, and steals, he never attacks anyone on the side of the Mulligan Guard. In contrast, Gypsy Jack holds up the picnic at gunpoint, taking clothes and food from the group. Lemons sees him, the "Jersey sneak," and realizes that he robbed his friends. Lemons attacks him, easily wins the fight, and gets the food and clothes back.[132] For all his faults, Lemons saves the picnic and the others cheer his heroism.

The increasing prominence of the Irish comic tramp through the popularity of Harrigan's and Wild's depictions implicitly tied whiteness to mobility. By reinforcing the tramp image as white, these images suggested that the ability to travel in search of work or idleness remained a right of white Americans. Performers like William Hoey and Lew Bloom continued the connection between whiteness and the tramp in variety performances during the 1880s, bridging the popular performances of Harrigan and Wild and the phenomenon of tramp comics at the turn of the century. The alignment of whiteness with tramping did not mean that laziness, drunkenness, poverty, and violence remained the province of only white or Irish representations in variety and vaudeville. Blackface comic characters continued to appear on variety and vaudeville stages, but performers, managers, newspapers, and historians tended to not label them tramps. As vaudeville historian Douglass Gilbert acknowledges, often in variety and vaudeville "blackface acts were brother comics of the tramps and it is no step at all into their dressing rooms where the grease color and occasional accent will be about the only changes found."[133] This quote follows a section on tramp comics that omits any major reference to race or ethnicity, implying the characters' whiteness. All the major stars highlighted in the section performed tramp comedy in whiteface. The whiteface comic performed tramp comedy; the blackface comics performed something else. The word "tramp" tied to mobility; terms like "poor" or "homeless" did not have the same mobile connotation.

Arguably, this representation of whiteness reflected the major Anglo-American Protestant middle-class images of tramps, who continued to be portrayed primarily as white in newspapers and novels. Officials and reformers may not have wanted Irish and Irish-American tramps, but they implied less of a threat to the racial and social structure than did notions of wandering black Americans. The comic tramp first stepped onto the stage in 1874 in the midst of Reconstruction and the continued struggle to install Southern state governments that would uphold black rights. Especially since the South continued to rely heavily on black labor, the ability to move not only asserted black Americans' freedom, it also indicated their ability to cripple white business through their economic choices. After Reconstruction ended in 1877, vagrancy laws, imprisonment, and forced labor curtailed black mobility, reinstating a racial hierarchy through different means. In both the North and the South, racism and discrimination continued to be pervasive in black Americans' daily life. Although it may not have been perceived as a victory for the Irish to be portrayed as tramps, it arguably further solidified their whiteness, privilege, and superiority, even as Anglo-American Protestants continued to perceive their Celtic racial identity as inferior. In the following chapter, I examine how the specter of the mobile Irish, its threats and its opportunities, formed in relation to Anglo-Saxon/Celt racial conflict.

CHAPTER TWO

The Two Faces of
the Mobile Fighting Irish

I N THE WAKE OF THE Civil War and Irish-American participation in it, opposing notions emerged of male Celtic identity and its relationship to mobility and violence. From one perspective, Irish Americans were envisioned as mobile fighters traveling the world to battle for freedom and democracy. The rhetoric of Thomas Francis Meagher, Young Irelander and general of the Irish Brigade in the Sixty-Ninth Regiment, helped shape this image as he recruited and rallied his troops by reminding them of the Irish Celts' military past. He framed their actions on behalf of the Union as part of a "glorious legacy bequeathed to them from a long line of military ancestors, dating . . . as far back as five centuries."[1] Meagher's speeches recalled the long battle for independence against the Anglo-Saxons as well as Irish participation in the War of Spanish Succession and wars on the side of Pope Pius IX. Meagher repeatedly mentioned the Battle of Fontenoy in 1745, in which the Irish fought for the French.[2] As historian Cian McMahon posits, the rhetoric of Irish-American leaders during the war "portrayed Irish Celts as a race of universal soldiers whose storied reputation for bravery and honor had been earned on countless battlefields across time and space."[3] Viewing themselves as "agents in the universal human struggle for freedom and democracy," the Irish Brigade even linked their fighting to this long tradition with the phrase "Sixty-Ninth, remember Fontenoy" on their regiment flag.[4] In their battles for freedom in the United States, Ireland, and beyond, "Celtic pride scuffled for equality with American Anglo-Saxonism."[5] Meagher told his soldiers that they could "look him [a U.S.-born soldier] straight and sternly in the face, and tell him that he has been equal to him in his allegiance to the Constitution."[6] The Irish believed that their military valor in the war demonstrated their suitability to be U.S. citizens.[7]

After the war, these sentiments laid the groundwork for a broader historiographical and cultural effort by Irish-American middle-class writers, historians, and newspaper editors to highlight the Irish's contributions to the development of the United States and its democracy since the Revolution. These narratives, writers hoped, would counter long-held anti-Irish stereotypes and nativist voices that argued against the Irish's compatibility with American values. McMahon discusses how these expressions constituted a global nationalism that "portrayed the Irish as an international community capable of simultaneous loyalty to their old and new worlds. Yet by laying claim to this identity, the Irish joined other migrant groups in expanding the modern parameters of citizenship and mobility."[8] When famines, economic discord, and British oppression prevented the Irish from remaining in Ireland, the Irish created a new multivalent identity grounded in and strengthened by their mobility.

At the same time, Irish-American military valor caused Anglo-American Protestant anxiety. Aside from reflecting prejudices against migrants and the poor, the tramp figure conveyed middle-class anxieties concerning former soldiers. Although some writers and officials argued that military life taught soldiers discipline, others worried that the men lacked the skills to settle down and dedicate themselves to a profession. The war trained men in military fighting and acquainted them with a mobile lifestyle, including introducing many to their first railroad experiences and to foraging in groups for survival. In his discussion of tramps, Pinkerton reserved disdain for veteran tramps in particular. "Our late war created thousands of tramps," he observed. "Hundreds upon hundreds became demoralized by the lazy habits of camp-life, and were suddenly turned loose upon society without any regular employment, or desire for any."[9] With the postwar army drastically reduced in number, the government providing limited veterans' benefits, men facing severe and permanent disability, and few jobs available due to the recession, many veterans faced limited choices in the war's wake.

Prison records across the northern states suggest that more than half their charges were veterans, and veterans continued to contribute to the number of homeless and unemployed throughout the 1870s. These numbers reinforced the worst fears of some middle-class reformers. Not only were tramps inherently violent, but a number of tramps were potentially trained in effective and dangerous killing methods.[10]

During the 1870s, the intensifying labor movement and strike action exacerbated these fears about the Irish and led many writers, reporters, and government leaders to conflate labor with violent, mobile Irishness. How Anglo-American Protestants described the Molly Maguires, a secret Irish society, incorporated long-held stereotypes of the Irish as violent and also drew on the emerging tramp image. The Molly Maguires operated in the coalfields of Pennsylvania, and the state executed members for labor violence in 1877. As labor unrest spread throughout the country, newspapers, government leaders, and business owners speculated that the roaming Molly Maguires initiated it, bringing unrest to their otherwise peaceful towns.

Both the patriotic, noble, Irish freedom fighter and the violent Irishman tied to labor quickly made their way to the variety stage after the war. Variety performance negotiated what I am referring to as a Janus-faced fighting-Irish image through its dramaturgies of mobility. The tension between these opposing dramaturgies implicitly asked audiences to consider the role of the Irish in the United States. Did either side of the violent Irishman have a place in the United States during peacetime?

This chapter examines how dramaturgies of mobility participated in perpetuating these meanings tied to and constituted through Irish-American male movement. In both instances, the movement occurs offstage, but it plays a central role in representing an Irishman who could act as a savior or a saboteur of U.S. democracy. The chapter extends McMahon's arguments about global nationalism from Irish-American nationalist leaders and newspapermen to the Irish-American working class. While McMahon focuses on the press as the vehicle for global nationalism, I suggest variety theatre created another conduit for these ideas' circulation. In addition to their dual loyalties to Ireland and the United States, the dramaturgies depicted the Irish as transnational, mobile freedom fighters and helped convey these ideas to a working-class audience. Through their mobility and freedom fighting, the dramaturgies illustrated the male Celt's suitability not only for U.S. citizenship, but also for exporting U.S. values to other nations.

In contrast, the dramaturgies surrounding the Molly Maguires connected Irishness, mobility, and violence to the potential downfall of American capitalism and democracy. The dramaturgy denigrated the fight for labor rights and detached it from democratic action. The Mollies' secrecy and stealth movements became not only part of their image in the broader imagination, but also emerged as a foundational component of the dramaturgy's structure. Unlike the dramaturgy tied to noble Irish freedom fighters rooted in plot, character, and action, the variety afterpieces featuring the Mollies created a dramaturgy structured through sound. Through its theatrical use, sound created movement's representation and meaning in the absence of the Mollies' physical presence on stage. Although this dramaturgy is revealed through the remaining texts, its existence illustrates the crucial role of live performance in its construction. Through its afterpiece depictions of the Molly Maguires, the dramaturgy perpetuated the idea of the violent Irish Celt as a faceless mob of heathens willing to stir up violence, no matter the cause, and unable to fulfill the duties of American citizenship.

Patriotic Heroes in Faraway Lands:
Mobile Irish Celts as Revolutionary Freedom Fighters

Negative Irish and Irish-American stereotypes had long incorporated violence as a central characteristic. Drunk and uncivilized, these stereotypical Irishmen often fight with little provocation and carry a shillelagh, a traditional Irish weapon. Their penchant for violence supposedly resulted from their lack of self-control and their premodern culture. Stage Irish female caricatures also included this inclination for violence, which served to masculinize Irish women and further separate them from Anglo-American middle-class feminine ideals. In the theatre, the tendency to brawl and carry a shillelagh became key components of the stage Irish type, but it did not make the Irish automatic villains. Although violent, stage Irishmen and women often provided comic relief as opposed to any real threat.[11] The positive images of the Irish-American soldier helped transform the negative stereotype, even as the representations maintained many of the same caricatured elements. The image of the Irish-American soldier helped shift the Irish's mobile, fighting nature from an indicator of their inability to be American citizens to a justification for their belonging as defenders of democracy. Through these fighters' historicization within a transnational, mobile freedom-fighting tradition, Irish movement played a critical role in the creation of these meanings. The fragments of variety performance suggest that songs and afterpieces conveyed global nationalism to working-class audiences. The afterpieces of Irish freedom fighters outside Ireland and the United States extended representations of global nationalism by demonstrating that the Irish Celt's dedication to freedom and democracy was intrinsic to their race, no matter where they traveled.

Typically performed by Irishmen for a primarily working-class and substantially Irish-American audience in New York, the Irish-American soldier quickly spread to the variety stage during the war. Songsters offer a glimpse into how these performances operated in New York. These small books became a vehicle for circulating these images within the working-class community outside the theatre. As Irish folklorist and musician Mick Moloney discusses, variety songwriters found an enthusiastic audience for songs about Irish-American soldiers. "The Irish Volunteer" (1864) by Joe English, a variety writer and performer, typifies the genre and demonstrates several key functions of the Irish-American soldier in highlighting a tradition of patriotic valor and linking mobility and violence with justice. The song begins by situating the narrator as an Irish migrant who comes from a long line of Irish freedom fighters. "I was born among old Erin's bogs and left when but a child," he sings, "me granddad fought in '98 for liberty so dear, he fell upon old Vinegar Hill as an Irish volunteer."[12] The following verses and choruses emphasize the soldiers' mobile life and their capacity for gruesome violence in the nation's defense:

Now when the traitors in the south commenced a war-like raid
I quickly then laid down me hoe, to the divil went me spade!
To our recruiting office that I went, that happened to be near

And joined the good old 69th as an Irish volunteer
Then fill the ranks and march away! No traitors do we fear;
We'll drive them all to blazes says the Irish volunteer. . . .
Now if the traitors in the south shall ever cross our roads,
We'd drive them to the divil as St. Patrick did the toads;
We'd give them all sharp nooses that come just below the ears
Made strong and good from Irish hemp by Irish volunteers . . .
May Erin's Harp and the Starry Flag united ever be;
May traitors quake, and rebels shake, and tremble in their fears,
When next they meet the Yankee boys and the Irish volunteers![13]

Other songs in this vein framed the Irish's sacrifice not only as an Irish tradition, but also an Irish American one by highlighting the Irish's participation in the American Revolution and the Civil War. The song illustrates the Irish's dual loyalties to freedom both in the United States and in Ireland. The lyrics also make the claim for the Irish as patriotic Americans not by arguing that they have become like the Anglo-Saxon "Yankee boys" but *because* of their Irish and Celtic identity and history.

Songs further developed these images by placing the Irish's fight within a global context. Songs, such as the popular "Pat Murphy of Meagher's Brigade" sung by Tony Pastor at his Opera House, framed the Civil War experience as a training ground for creating mobile freedom fighters who would then travel back to Ireland to free it from Britain. One verse from "Pat Murphy of Meagher's Brigade" explains, "How nobly those brave Irish volunteers fought, / In defense of the flag of our Union / And if ever old Ireland for freedom should strike, / We'll a helping hand offer quite freely / And the Stars and the Stripes will be seen alongside / Of the flag of the Land of Shillaly."[14] Notably, the verse recognizes that the Irishmen will return not only as Irishmen trained to fight but also as Americans. The return trip remains in the future, as opposed to being manifested on stage. Drawing attention to the Irish living around the world, a song selling itself as a response to the infamous "No Irish Need Apply" celebrated "What Irish Boys Can Do" and conceived of the Irish as an internationally mobile people. The song states, "If you want to find their principles, go search the wide world through, And you'll find all things that's noble the Irish folks can do."[15] Tying the fighting Irish in the United States to these Irish across the world, shifted the context of the mobile, violent Irish. It situated Irish violence, noble or otherwise, as a continuing phenomenon after the war and essential-izes the characteristics as Irish. When the Civil War ends, the songs do not imagine the soldiers returning home to their families and jobs. They envision them as continuing to live on the move, fighting for freedom.

Perhaps out of an anxiety that the Irish were in the country to stay, popular culture struggled to imagine a place for these soldiers in the postwar United States. The afterpieces from Tony Pastor's Opera House provide an opportunity to examine how the fighting Irishman trans-formed after the Civil War. Alongside his main competitor, manager Josh Hart at the Theatre Comique, Pastor attracted large audiences of working-class men while attempting to expand his audience to include women and the middle class. Along with Hart, he is credited with push-ing variety toward more respectable vaudeville.[16]

Kattwinkel argues that Pastor featured a large number of Irish char-acters because of the composition of his company and his audience. Pastor employed a substantial number of Irish and Irish Americans as writers and performers. Irish migrants and their descendants lived in substantial numbers in the sixth and the fourth wards, which were located only a few blocks away. Kattwinkel argues these factors encour-aged Pastor to play to this audience and create more complex Irish and Irish-American characters.[17] She explains that there were predomi-nantly two types of Irish representation at Pastor's. First, in the after-pieces "Ireland and/or its people is at the thematic and narrative center of the play. Many of them are little more than Fenian battle cries, call-ing for freedom of Ireland from the tyrannical rule of England."[18] She considers the second major grouping "characters in plays that revolve around the actions of a young American."[19] Various scholars, including Kattwinkel and Jennifer Mooney, have discussed the afterpieces focus-ing on the Irish fighting for freedom in Ireland and expressing their dual loyalties to their home country as well as to the United States.[20]

This section focuses on the afterpieces that imagined the Irish as continuing to fight for the noble causes of liberty and justice outside of the United States and Ireland. Kattwinkel considers these a subcategory "dealing with the Irish abroad" within her first grouping.[21] She and

Mooney briefly summarize them and consider their relation to U.S. and Irish loyalties.[22] However, the afterpieces complicate the representation of the Irish beyond simply calling for freedom from Britain and establish dramaturgies that further develop meanings of Irish movement. Although still a stereotypical stage Irishman, his international movement signified meanings tied to global nationalism. Unlike productions set in the United States and Ireland, these dramaturgies demonstrated a commitment to freedom beyond his old and new homes, which reinforced a racial argument for Irish Celts' suitability for U.S. citizenship. It presented "the Irish Celts' duty as transnational agents of liberty" as intrinsic, not dependent on a personal attachment to the political situation.[23] Paradoxically, the dedication illustrated through their embodiment of transnational mobility made them more suited to make the United States their home.

Three remaining afterpieces performed at Pastor's, *Americans in Turkey* (December 1866), *Irishman in Greece* (April 1867 and March 1872), and *Irishman in Cuba* (March 1870), featured the Irish fighting abroad for freedom, in various guises. Frequently featuring afterpieces with topical relevance, Pastor produced each afterpiece while the show's location filled U.S. headlines. His company first performed *Americans in Turkey* and *Irishman in Greece* as violence broke out in the Mediterranean. Prevented from joining the new Greek state in the 1830s, Crete remained under the control of the Ottoman Empire and revolted in 1866. *Irishman in Cuba* premiered during the Ten Years' War (1868–1878) between Spain and Cuba, the first of three late nineteenth-century wars for Cuban independence. The newspapers in the United States covered the violence. The *New York Herald* referred to Crete as "a little Ireland in the Mediterranean" and explained, "the bulk of the people remained Greek in heart and sentiment."[24] The state of United States' neutrality preoccupied newspaper debates as the war in Cuba continued for ten years off the American coastline.[25] Although the afterpiece scripts only provide one fragment of the performances that would have been shaped significantly by the performers, the afterpieces give a glimpse into how these dramaturgies functioned for variety audiences.

The afterpieces only ran for a few weeks each, but the repeated dramaturgies reflect a narrative pattern tied to the mobile, fighting

Irish and suggest character threads popular with audiences.[26] All the shows have the same basic plot involving separated lovers, a kidnapped woman, and evil foreigners. Structurally, the dramaturgy involves an Irishman telling the story of his travel to the foreign country, a battle in freedom's name, and a pattern of repeated fight victories by the Irishman that ultimately lead to the Irishman helping rescue women in distress. Reinforcing the underlying belief in the Irish as transnationally mobile, these "patterns of mobility have functioned, and still do, to convert" and frame identities and politics.[27] Instead of Kotef's focus on how these patterns helped shape "punishable practices," the patterns of mobility that framed the action informed the creation of a more positive, Irish identity that "[t]ake[s] form via im/mobility," even though the movement itself occurs offstage.[28] As Urry notes, it is "in these mobilities that social life and cultural identity are recursively formed and reformed."[29]

Each afterpiece introduces an Irishman who has traveled to the show's location by way of the United States. The audience does not see the journey, but each has a scene where the Irishman relates his adventures to another character. It is through these stories that the Irishmen's mobility frames their actions and begins to inform their identity within the piece. Their journeys all involve a misunderstanding. While living in New York and walking around drunk, Dan Driscoll, from the *Irishman in Cuba*, runs into a man who asks him if he wants to "join the patriots" and fight for independence in Cuba.[30] Dan immediately agrees, but since he is drunk, he gets on a Spanish gunboat instead of a privateer with pro-Cuban volunteers.[31] As a result, when the audience first meets him, he has been pretending to support the Spanish to stay alive, which places him in the perfect position to help the Cuban rebel leader's wife escape capture. Dan characterizes himself through his travels and refers to himself as a "wanderer of the world."[32] In *Irishman in Greece*, Looney O'Leary randomly shipwrecks on the island and has to take an oath of loyalty to a group of smugglers to save himself. Similar to *Irishman in Cuba*, this positions Looney perfectly to gain information and help a woman in distress. It is not entirely clear why Looney was on the ship to begin with, and the shipwreck seems to have interrupted his wanderings. Finally, Pat O'Doyle, in *Americans in Turkey*, is the only Irishman directly associated with American forces. He arrives intentionally with an American vessel and on a mission to free Christian slaves from the Turks, not necessarily the show's main couple.[33]

Even though not all three Irishmen's journeys or destinations were planned, their Irish nature compels them to fight for freedom. Each character has at least one moment in the show when they justify their actions by pointing out that they are Irishmen. After another character calls him names for beating up the "wrong" men, Looney proudly declares he did it because he's "an Irishman."[34] Dan ties his violent ways in his support of freedom directly to his race. "I'd be a mighty poor man and no Irishman at all," Dan explains, "if I left you in the hands of that black [illegible] thief."[35] Linking this fighting nature to his racial lineage, he justifies his rescue of a female character by stating, "Ye was a woman in distress and that's a claim on any o' the Driscolls."[36] Pat characterizes his violence as linked to his race, threatening to use his "Irish fist."[37] He refers to himself as a "rattling Irishman" and defends a woman by proclaiming her "under the protection from a boy from Paddy's Land."[38] If their race explains their fighting nature and dedication to liberty across the world, this conceptualization also essentializes negative stage Irish characteristics, such as violence, drinking, and womanizing.

Their masculinity is constructed in two primary ways: their boldly heteronormative relationship to women and their use of violence. As Rohs discusses, Irish-American working-class masculinity "came [with] an attitude of swagger and bravado—and the unrestrained masculine expression of sexuality at odds with bourgeois norms of sexual restraint in men."[39] Anglo-Saxon Protestants often used representations of Irish-American working-class masculinity to illustrate their unfitness for American citizenship. For example, Rohs analyzes one 1850s ballad that portrayed Meagher as a womanizer. Through his inability to conform to Anglo-Saxon middle-class Protestant norms of masculinity and marriage, the ballad used this portrayal to mark Meagher as unwanted in the United States and a failed leader.[40] All three afterpieces show the Irish freedom fighters as womanizers who flirt with most women they meet, regardless of their marital status. These moments are played for comic relief, however, and the only married women they flirt with are wives to the oppressors, which seems to justify the Irishmen's attempts. When the Irishmen try to woo the women, it is not shown in a negative light, but as a comic attempt to save the women from their evil husbands. In this warped way, even their womanizing is framed as part of their dedication to liberty.

The Irishman's propensity for violence also is justified through the noble causes he fights for throughout the pieces. Dan attempts to help the Cuban rebel leader and his wife unite and hopes to support the cause of Cuban independence. He draws parallels between the Cuban and Irish fights for liberty when speaking with the rebel leader's wife, stating "[Y]e're the wife of a noble patriot that's trying to free Cuba what ould Ireland's waiting for, freedom from a foreign yoke."[41] When he realizes how the colonial situation has impacted people in Cuba, he declares, "I wish I could help all the poor craytons to escape from the blaggard Spanish tyrants."[42] He also offers a pointed critique of the United States' willingness to supply either side. When telling the rebel's wife about his trip to Cuba, he explains, "I was on one of the damned Spanish gunboats that's a disgrace to New York and to America were ever built there [sic]."[43] When the rebel leader complains, "even the American government . . . should have been the first to encourage our struggle for freedom," Dan corrects him and makes a distinction between the government and the sentiments of the American people.[44] "[S]ure the people is one thing," Dan argues, "and the ould offices that govern them another."[45] By allying with the people who value freedom and democracy, Dan places himself in line with the sentiments of U.S. citizens, even if they sometimes conflict with government policy. Dan tells the audience how he wishes violence on the show's antagonists, remarking "I'd give three or four of the eyes out of me head just to have him at the end of me shillelagh for five or ten minutes."[46] Pat similarly arrives in Turkey to fight oppression in *Americans in Turkey*. The Turks enslave the afterpiece's central characters, two Americans, a Christian and a Jew. Pat and Captain Harding arrive with American firepower to demand the release of Christian slaves. While they wait to strike, Pat tells Harding how he wishes they could act, condemning the Turks' treatment of the slaves. When Harding asks him what he would do if he led the men, Pat explains that he would "upset the divils own hornets nest, blow their bulwarks, set their city ablaze."[47] Harding remains the main deterrent to Pat's violent actions. Looney is the least politically motivated. After realizing that he did not help in a lovers' quarrel, but rather assisted in a woman's kidnapping, he pledges his soul that he will help save her and nobly fights alongside others to rescue her from Greek bandits.[48] He ties his methods directly to his racial identity stating, he will "give these blaggards a taste of Irish strategy."[49]

The rhythm of fights led and often won by the Irishmen sets the structure of the afterpieces. During these years, fighting and physical comedy were typical for variety theatre, but the patterns set up an expectation for the Irishmen. Although he reflects the stage Irish stereotype in his use of blarney and love of drink and women, his clumsiness does not impact his ability to effectively fight. In all three, the Irishman becomes an essential ally for the afterpieces' heroes. At one point after Dan has already given them a beating, he is cornered by the Spaniards, who happily taunt him for not having his shillelagh to defend himself. He then pulls his stick out from behind his back to distressed cries of "Oh lord, he has it!"[50] Even though he is only a man with a stick and faces several men, some with pistols, Dan easily wins. Similarly, Looney and Pat win battles with their shillelaghs.

Although the afterpieces imagine the Irish victoriously winning fights abroad, the afterpieces end the action with a spectacular exit. After the main couple is reunited, the characters express their goal to return to the United States for its unparalleled freedom, but the audience never sees it on stage. *Irishman in Cuba* and *Americans in Turkey* end with the entrance through the upstage wall of a U.S. vessel with guns visible to help the characters escape. Then the Irishman comes out waving the U.S. flag. In some ways, the gesture implies the arrival of American freedom as part of the show's victory, aided in part by the Irishman.[51] The shows end with the Irishmen on the move again, off to continue their fight for freedom in the United States, Ireland, and beyond.

It seems possible that this dramaturgy extended beyond Pastor's afterpieces, but the lack of remaining scripts limits this analysis. Reports of other sketches set in Cuba especially imply a similar dramaturgy and its circulation beyond Pastor's. For example, J. Z. Little's *Santiago Avenged!* performed as part of a variety show at Hooley's Opera House

in Brooklyn depicted the events surrounding the Cuban war in order
to, the *Brooklyn Daily Eagle* suggested, "hit the public temper."[52] With the
Cubans' similarly presented as victims, the American "nobly sacrific[es]
himself in the interest of liberty, justice, freedom and Cuba" and "of
course, there are virtuous Cuban girls, beloved by Cuban soldiers and
seized by Spanish officers . . . whose alternate capture and rescue make
the great interest of the play."[53] The progression of the plot is aided
by a freedom-fighting Irish person, only in this case, it is a woman.
The paper describes "a comic Irish woman [who] outwit[s] the Chief
of the Spanish forces."[54] This gender change raises many questions. In
what ways does mobility frame her freedom fighting? How are Irish
race and violence in the dramaturgy shifted in relation to her gender?
Considering global nationalism's male-centered ideology, how does her
gender disrupt constructions of citizenship and military participation,
two areas where women remained excluded from full rights? On these
questions and others, the archival record is silent. The show was a hit
with the working class in the gallery, however, and the newspaper commented, "It was essentially a gallery play, and kept the boys in a state
of boisterous enthusiasm."[55] These fragments leave tantalizing glimpses
into how variety theatre perpetuated global nationalism as well as its
seeming success with working-class audiences. A few years after these
afterpieces premiered, the other side of the Janus-faced fighting Irishman gained new prominence as the labor movement and Molly Maguires made headlines in Pennsylvania.

The Roaming Molly Maguires and Sonic Aesthetics

In 1880, Michael Mooney led a twenty-three-day nonviolent miners'
strike in the booming silver mine town of Leadville, Colorado. Even
though no evidence suggested that the strike involved the Molly Maguires, men of capital used the fear associated with the Mollies to intim-
idate striking workers, unions, and communities. The Leadville strike
remained nonviolent, but newspapers ran stories entitled, "Mob in the
Mines: The Molly Maguires Take Actual Possession of Leadville."[56]
Demanding better wages and an eight-hour day, the striking miners
returned to work only after the governor sent in the state militia to

force the reopening of the mines. Unsatisfied with the lack of arrests, the anti-labor vigilantes committee threatened to lynch Mooney and other labor leaders, who fled to Denver.[57] In spite of lingering tensions, in 1881, Mooney returned to Leadville, and during his brief visit, he attended a variety show with an afterpiece entitled, *The Molly Maguires,* at the Grand Central Theatre.

Outraged at what he saw on that November evening, Mooney wrote a letter to the editor of the *Leadville Daily Herald.* "The manager of the Grand Central [Theatre] may call his production of Monday night a struggle between capital and labour," wrote Mooney, "but I call it a ridicule and a slander to the Irish element of Leadville generally."[58] He condemned the conflation of Irishness and violence that led to a simplistic portrait of labor as inherently evil. Mooney expressed his horror that the actors through "whose veins courses the same Celtic current that flows through mine" gave "their talent to such an infernal production as was given to us on Monday night."[59] Mooney believed in respectable radicalism, which "was rooted in sobriety, honesty, nonviolence, Irish nationalism, and ethnic pride."[60] As a result, it is not surprising that in one of his last public statements on labor, Mooney called for the citizens of Leadville to boycott the production that violated the values he held dear. However, the myth of the Molly Maguires and the draw of theatrical productions featuring them were already well established by the 1880s. The production continued and Mooney left town soon after.[61]

The Molly Maguires played a prominent role in how Americans imagined the threat of the mobile Irish, the resurgent labor movement, and violence on stage and off. The connections between the tramp and labor magnified the threat presented by the Molly Maguires. The specter of the tramp haunted Americans, especially rural Americans, who feared tramps would steal, kill, and attack women. As labor unrest escalated after the Panic, the Irish tramp became linked to strikes and labor violence and was constructed in opposition to American values. A cartoon in *Puck* personified this idea in 1882. Entitled "Uncle Sam's Lodging House," the cartoon pictures a boardinghouse filled with poor lodgers from all over the world with bunks labeled with their nationality or race. Most of the lodgers sleep peacefully except for the Irishman, who angrily gestures and rants at Uncle Sam and Lady Liberty, who

FIGURE 7. As other migrants and black Americans try to sleep, an Irishman disrupts the quiet of the lodging house. Uncle Sam scolds, "Look here, you, everybody else is quiet and peaceable, and you're all the time a-kicking up a row!" Joseph Keppler, "Uncle Sam's Lodging House," June 7, 1882. Library of Congress Prints and Photographs Division, Washington, D.C.

cover their ears and glare. The caption, a line of dialogue for Uncle Sam, reads, "Look here, you, everybody else is quiet and peaceable, and you're all the time a-kicking up a row!" As the scattered bricks with words like "Agitation" and "Irish Independence" near the Irishman indicate, the chaos he causes is triggered in part by his politics (see figure 7). The cartoon contrasts starkly with the image propagated by Irish-American communities that the Irish Celt's dedication to freedom in Ireland made them ideal American citizens.

Although not always depicted as tramps explicitly, the emerging cultural images of the labor movement depicting violence, mobility, and Irishness extended the Mollies' threat beyond the coalfields of Pennsylvania. In 1877, the state of Pennsylvania executed twenty men and sentenced another twenty to lengthy prison terms for the murders of sixteen mine officials and their associates. The court believed the men, who were all Irish immigrants or Irish Americans, to be part of the Molly Maguires, a secret organization that originated in Ireland. In spite of historians' studies, no hard evidence has emerged to confirm that the Molly Maguires ever existed as an organized group in Pennsylvania. The trials and newspaper coverage presented the Irishmen as evil terrorists who acted with no real motivation other than their own depravity. As historian Kevin Kenny notes, this lack of motivation became the core of the Molly Maguires myth, with the murders solely "explained in terms of a natural Irish propensity toward violence and savagery."[62] As a result, the Molly Maguires' myth made their violence and degeneracy a direct result of inherent Irish racial characteristics. The prosecution and newspapers speculated that the labor movement and Ancient Order of Hibernians (AOH) also supported the Molly Maguires and therefore were complicit in their crimes. Implicating the AOH, an international Irish fraternal organization, implied that their network could spread the violence anywhere the Irish lived. The extent of any collaboration with the AOH or the Workingmen's Benevolent Association remains unclear. However, "lumping labor activists and unruly Irishmen into a single conspiratorial category" motivated authorities "to destroy the power of both."[63]

In the first American "red scare" after the Paris Commune of 1871, many Americans feared a violent, communist uprising. Although the association started earlier in the decade, the narratives surrounding the Great Strike of 1877 solidified the connection between tramps, labor, and communism in the national imagination. Triggered by the Baltimore and Ohio Railroad's wage cuts, the railroad strike began first in West Virginia before spreading to New York, Pennsylvania, Maryland, Missouri, and Illinois. It is estimated that over 100,000 people participated in the strike, which created transportation stoppages, property damage, shootings, and looting before the police and National Guard suppressed it.[64] For many, the perceived connection between labor and communism tainted labor leaders' claims that their fight for an eight-hour day and better pay was not opposed to capitalist or democratic values. For the many Anglo Protestants, migrants' association with labor, including German Jews and the Irish, among others, weakened their claims to be suitable American citizens.

Allan Pinkerton, a detective involved in both the Molly Maguires investigation in Pennsylvania and the Great Strike of 1877, directly linked tramps to the Great Strike. In his book, *Strikers, Communists, Tramps, and Detectives*, Pinkerton explains he will give "an account of those classes and organizations most extensively represented in the great strike of '77."[65] Four chapters on tramps follow the introduction. Newspapers made the connection between tramps and the strikers during the July 1877 strike as well. The *New York Evening Telegram* explained, "It is said that but few railroad employees are in the mob, which is composed almost exclusively of outsiders and tramps."[66] Highlighting the specter of the tramp menace, newspapers detailed the lingering threat of the tramps seemingly involved in the strike. "[L]arge numbers of tramps . . . [were] escorted out of the city by police last night," the *Evening Telegram* reported, "and to-night they are said to be assuming a threatening attitude outside the town."[67] The connection between tramps and socialism remained after the strike's conclusion, with the *New York Tribune* claiming that tramps were influenced by "communistic literature which flatters the indolent with the assurance that the world owes them a living."[68] However prevalent these images in contemporary accounts, Kusmer suggests they existed as "inventions of the imagination."[69] Although tramps participated in the strikes, "their behavior was as haphazard and unplanned as that of most strikers," and no solid evidence indicates tramps were organized or motivated by a specific political or economic ideology.[70] In spite of the seeming historical reality, fears about tramps and labor persisted in the dominant imagination.

Soon after the Great Strike, novels quickly incorporated the intersection of the tramp, violence, and labor. *The Tramp* (1878) by Frank Bellew describes how the tramp's organization is "political and revolutionary."[71] Contrasting the tramps with strikers who genuinely fight to improve working conditions, the novel attributes sinister and selfish motives to the tramps and their secret society. Bellows explains how the "Tramp's object is, when any trouble takes place, to aid the revolutionary party, strikers or what not, and reap a large harvest of plunder."[72] In *The Man Who Tramps* (1878), Lee O. Harris creates an image of "political tramps," "refugees from all the despotisms of the world," that plague American society and helped start the unrest and violence of the Paris Commune and Great Strike.[73] Political tramps "talked their inflammable doctrines on all occasions, and were arrogant and insolent as

well as vicious . . . a pestilence which permeated society, and threatened
the very life of the nation."[74] Depicting the Great Strike of 1877, Harris details the tramps walking among the strikers, "prompting them to
deeds of violence."[75] In these imaginings, tramps, typically migrants,
roam, spreading their dangerous ideology and inciting violence against
the state among honest, usually native-born, workers.

Spectacle played a central role in establishing and circulating negative notions of labor and Irishness even before the story of the Molly
Maguires reached the theatre. Although Pennsylvania banned public
executions in 1834, the Molly Maguires' deaths still created a public
spectacle. On Black Thursday (June 21, 1877), ten of the twenty men
died by hanging. As the militia and police patrolled the streets, hundreds of elite guests witnessed the Mollies' deaths before the prison gates
opened and allowed the thousands who waited outside the opportunity
to inspect the scene. Newspapers printed detailed and sensational accounts, which allowed the entire nation to participate in witnessing the
men's deaths.[76] The spectacle of the day became a powerful instrument
of social control. Kenny writes that these "the rituals of execution sent
a stern warning to the residents of the anthracite region, proclaiming
the triumph of order over anarchy. They also consolidated the notion
that the Molly Maguires were inherently depraved and had represented
a conspiracy of enormous proportions."[77] In subsequent years, newspapers often accused the striking workers of Molly Maguirism, regardless of the workers' actual ethnic or racial composition or the presence
of violence. Molly Maguirism "became a label used across the nation
to apply to all working-class Irish workers who resisted the industrial
status quo in any way."[78] After the well-publicized executions, newspapers often characterized the Molly Maguires as in hiding and roaming
through the countryside, stirring up trouble wherever they traveled.

After the trials and executions of the Molly Maguires, they captured
the popular imagination.[79] Reports from the trials, accounts from
Pinkerton about his agents who infiltrated the Mollies, pamphlets, serialized stories in newspapers, and dime novels created an image of the
Mollies as violent and without legitimate motivation. These stories typically fell into two narrative categories. The early serialized stories and
dime novels focused on an honest mechanic and a Pennsylvania strike,

typically the Long Strike of 1875, and offered an ambiguous image of labor that acknowledged some justified reasons for the laborers' complaints. The second main Mollies narrative reflected the detective genre and followed an undercover Pinkerton agent. As Denning discusses, in both narratives, "the Molly Maguires remain a multiaccentual sign, at one time the vengeful arm of the miners, at another time a criminal organization for the personal vengeance of the villains, at yet another time in league with millionaires and monopolists."[80] The novels incorporated more ambiguity than many contemporary accounts, but even the rare novel that acknowledges the Mollies had concrete reasons for their actions, such as David Doyle's *Molly Maguires the Terror of the Coal Field*, does not represent the Mollies' violence as justified.[81]

Historians have extensively analyzed the Molly Maguires in U.S. labor history. Michael Denning and Kevin Kenny have examined the Molly Maguires' myth as it appeared in serialized stories and dime novels. Little discussion has taken place about how the theatre participated in creating and revising the Mollies' mythical image in the U.S. cultural imagination. The Molly Maguires afterpieces illustrate the importance of reconsidering the Mollies in terms of cultural history, a project started by Kenny and Denning.[82] Such a reconsideration illuminates the vital role played by touring variety in establishing and perpetuating the Mollies as a mobile Irish menace, especially among the working class, as noted by Mooney's experience in Leadville. The afterpieces featuring the Mollies transformed the violent, mobile stage Irish into a social menace. The evidence for these afterpieces is sparse. Most of the scripts are not extant and even coverage in newspapers is limited. However, by juxtaposing the fragments that remain while acknowledging the gap, this section reveals patterns in how the afterpieces defined the Molly Maguires through their mobility and utilized theatrical tactics to convey that movement and menace in spite of their frequent physical absence.

Often conflating the labor movement and the Mollies, the afterpieces create a specter of a mob of heathens controlled by selfish, Irish socialists willing to stir up violence no matter the cause. They appear unable to participate in rational democracy and to be unsuited for citizenship because they choose violence over the vote to create change. The convicted Mollies included miners as well as better off pub and grocery owners, but, through their repeated performance, the afterpieces inscribed violent Irishness as an unskilled working-class characteristic. The afterpieces utilized a dramaturgy rooted in regular patterns of physical absence and sonic aesthetics to create a dehumanized, disembodied mobile Irish threat on stage.

The Molly Maguires melodramas and afterpieces developed along the serialized stories' and dime novels' two narrative strains: the detective story and the adventures of the honest mechanic. Allan Pinkerton's semifictional volume, *The Molly Maguires and the Detectives* published in 1877, inspired a melodrama that first appeared under the title *Secret Service or McPharlan [sic], the Detective* at Philadelphia's Walnut Theatre in August 1877. The theatre tried to lure audiences to the production by promising to provide a "complete review of the secret workings and lawless acts of the Mollie Maguires."[83] The 1881 variety afterpiece produced in Leadville and critiqued by Mooney, *The Molly Maguires,* appears to have been based on the same storyline. Although scripts do not remain for either show, newspaper accounts indicate that the productions followed Pinkerton's story rather closely. Both shows claim to depict the historical events that led to the Mollies' arrests and convictions. The hero is Pinkerton agent James McParland, who went undercover in the mid-1870s and became the main witness in the Molly Maguires' trials.

Newspaper accounts of *Secret Service* seem to corroborate Mooney's summary of the detective story narrative as anti-Irish and antilabor.[84] According to a review in the *Philadelphia Inquirer*, the audience took the side of the authorities and cheered for McPharlan. "It was pleasing to hear how loudly the 'gods' cheered on the right side," the writer reported, "how they encouraged the laboring McParlan [sic] as he championed the law and groaned at the enormities of the reckless 'Mollies.'"[85] Complimenting the show for its historical accuracy, the writer explained that the spectacle drew the audience to the show. They wanted "to see trains pitched into chasms, collieries burnt, policemen and bosses murdered; they desired to make the acquaintance of the Mollies at home, to follow the adventures of 'McParlan' [sic], to see the rogues brought to justice."[86] At least from the reviews, the play painted a picture of good versus evil, in which labor and the Mollies unquestionably acted in the wrong. In showing McPharlan among the Molly Maguires, by necessity, it seems the shows likely had actors playing the Mollies on stage, but, from the available evidence, it is unclear to what extent. The *Secret Service* and *Molly Maguires* afterpieces toured, but they had limited long-term success.[87]

Although the narrative trend in the Mollies novels transitioned from the honest mechanic narrative to the detective narrative, in the theatre the honest mechanic narrative held the stage for decades. Over a year before *Secret Service*'s debut and months before the Mollies' executions, a touring variety show, the Great Aiken Combination, first produced *Black Diamond, or The Molly Maguires of Hazelton*. Its performances and their variations over the next thirty years conveyed a conflicted and ambivalent portrait of Irishness and labor, but they reinforced a dehumanized, disembodied theatrical portrait of the Molly Maguires as mobile menaces. In the midst of the Molly Maguires' trials and before McParland was outed as an informer, Albert Aiken, brother of *Uncle Tom's Cabin* playwright George Aiken, wrote a serial story for George Munro's *Fireside Companion: The Molly Maguires; or The Black Diamond of Hazleton*. The story appeared in installments through the spring and summer of 1876. Not long after the story's debut, Albert Aiken, who was a playwright and actor as well as a prolific dime novelist, began touring a melodramatic adaptation as his variety show's afterpiece. The popularity and timeliness of Aiken's show immediately inspired several imitations. By July 1876, Aiken published notices in the *New York Clipper* staking claim to the piece as the hit's author.[88]

However much it infuriated playwrights and companies, the appropriation of shows was not unusual. Jerry Cohan, father of George M. Cohan, appeared in the original Aiken production of *The Molly Maguires*.[89] Not long after, Cohan and his family took the afterpiece on the road with their variety show, and it proved to be one of his family's biggest hits on tour during the 1870s and 1880s. Based on reviews detailing the same plot and characters, it seems that Cohan bought his show from Aiken, but Cohan also complained that his play "was widely plagiarized and the principal characters imitated and butchered by all the barnstormers in the country. I found a Chicago play pirate selling manuscripts of my 'Molly Maguire' under the title of 'the Black

Diamond.' I tried to catch the cheerful burglar, but he was too slippery."[90] The notice seems a bit disingenuous, considering Cohan was well aware of the original production by Aiken, but his comments point to the continued popularity of the piece in various forms decades after its original debut.

It is thanks to this "cheerful burglar," Alex Byers, that the scripts for Aiken's melodramatic afterpiece and its variations remained in circulation into the early twentieth century. Byers was a well-known play pirate who established the Chicago Manuscript Company, a lucrative play piracy business that existed from 1880 to 1922. Taking advantage of weak copyright laws, Byers changed the title, tweaked the plot, or changed the character names before taking out new copyrights for many popular plays.[91] The Molly Maguires afterpieces' popularity seemed to wane on the eastern seaboard by the late 1880s, which aligns with variety's shift into vaudeville and the decline of the afterpiece as the standard second half of variety. However, they remained popular enough as sketches in vaudeville and as extended standalone melodramas that Byers took out new copyrights for the Molly Maguire scripts in the 1910s.

It is not possible to know if Byers or others made major changes from the original afterpieces first performed in the 1870s. *The Black Diamond*, copyrighted in 1914 with Charles Morton listed as the playwright, appears identical in plot and character to the available descriptions of Aiken's original afterpiece and the Cohan performances. Its structure also reflects the basic structure of melodramatic afterpieces. It is not possible to know whether this precise dialogue was performed, but Cohan's complaints about Byers's script suggest it was almost, if not completely, identical, in terms of its major elements. A consideration of the Byers text alongside the productions' newspaper record suggests an emergent dramaturgy surrounding the Mollies and violence that played a role in attracting audiences for decades.[92]

The story of Aiken's adaptation focuses on one thread of his serial story about Hazleton, Pennsylvania, centering on the exploits of a noble mining engineer, Mark O'Dare. The major conflict emerges from the attempts by Nathan Lyfford, a wealthy friend of Dychink, the owner of the Black Diamond mine, to force Dychink's daughter, Diana, to marry him. Aware that Father Dychink is facing financial troubles,

Lyfford and the local corrupt, socialist Irish migrant politician, Bernard McTurk, decide to start a strike to close the mine and make it an unattractive investment. At first, Lyfford asks McTurk to accelerate the spread of the Molly Maguires' labor unrest, which McTurk claims is headed their way from eastern Pennsylvania. Then Lyfford suggests violence and murder will help spread the chaos. McTurk explains that the Mollies hate O'Dare and will not need much provocation to murder him. When Dychink cannot find investors for his closed mine, Lyfford plans to bail out Dychink, but only if Diana agrees to marry him. Throughout the course of the afterpiece, Diana falls in love with O'Dare, who is loyal to Dychink and anti-labor. A bunch of failed attempts to sabotage the mine and kill O'Dare ensure. O'Dare avoids death repeatedly through the assistance of his friend and the loyal blackface mine worker, Banty Bob. In the end, O'Dare and Banty Bob defeat the Mollies, Lyfford, and McTurk. O'Dare and Diana reunite. The mine remains in financial peril until a mystery investor bails out the Dychinks. After declaring his love for Diana, O'Dare reveals that he was born wealthy, gave up his inheritance to take care of his sister when their parents died, and recently became a wealthy man again when his sister paid him back upon her marriage. He then reveals that he is the mystery investor who saved the Dychinks from financial ruin.[93]

The heroic mine engineer's race changed in the adaptation of Aiken's serial to the variety afterpiece. In the serial, the mine engineer is British and faces off against the evil Irish Molly Maguires, restaging a centuries-long battle between rational Anglo-Saxons and supposedly primitive Celts. Irishness is one-dimensional and directly connected to labor violence and community instability.[94] Through its depiction of O'Dare as a champion fighter, descriptions of O'Dare maintain the long-held connection between the Irish and violence, but as an admirable facet of his character. When talking about the mine workers' loyalty to O'Dare, Lyfford remarks, "Probably his prowess as a fighter is what makes him so popular with the men."[95] O'Dare is antistrike, but beloved by his men. Repeatedly, the politician McTurk preys on this connection and attempts to convince O'Dare to join the strike. At one point, he uses O'Dare's race as motivation. McTurk explains that O'Dare should join because "over half the boys" are Irish too.[96] Lyfford also tries to use O'Dare's Irishness against him to convince Diana to marry him. He questions how she can marry a "man of his caliber, an ignorant Irishman."[97] Diana responds by describing O'Dare's good, honorable character. At no point is O'Dare's character in question.

By transforming the show's hero into an Irishman, the afterpiece provides a more complicated version of Irishness that reinscribes the specter of violent mobile Irishness as an unskilled working-class characteristic. This class connection is reinforced when the noble O'Dare is revealed to be wealthy and not working class. This is a common trope in melodramas with working-class characters. In the case of *The Black Diamond*, the corrupt Irish politician's evilness furthers the relationship between class and morality developed through the performance. At one point, McTurk explains to Lyfford how he started out "carry[ing] the hod for a dollar and a quarter a day" before becoming a politician.[98] McTurk's selfishness and his willingness to turn to violence and accept bribes seem tied to his working-class background. It is possible that the creation of an Irish hero contributed to the afterpiece's success by not entirely relegating Irishness to evil. The Irish and Irish-American working-class audiences that attended variety in large numbers, especially on the east coast, could cheer for the hero without indicting all Irish.

The dramaturgy of mobility surrounding the Molly Maguires contrasted with the portrait of the noble O'Dare. Through its use of physical absence and sonic aesthetics, the afterpiece created a dramaturgy reliant on dehumanizing the Molly Maguires and portraying them as a mobile menace. Throughout most of the show, the Mollies operate as the show's dark matter, a concept theorized by performance scholar Andrew Sofer. Sofer defines dark matter as *"whatever is materially unrepresented onstage but un-ignorable."*[99] Sofer distinguishes between dark matter and more traditional indexical signs or material presence, which also appear in the piece. The Molly Maguires primarily have presence through their absence, however, and it is this absent presence that creates terror. Sofer marks this difference noting, "It is dark matter that produces the difference between horror and terror, for example. Horror is what we see; terror is what we know is there though it remains unseen."[100] Although a Molly Maguire makes one appearance on stage, the Mollies' mobility never materializes. However, the production makes it "unignorable" and a critical aspect of how violent Irishness is constructed onstage.

From the first scene, the other characters construct an image of the Molly Maguires as a mobile threat without strong connections to Hazleton. When first hatching his plot, Lyfford asks Banty Bob if the strike has spread to the Black Diamond mine from the east, and Bob replies, "I shorely spect it will fore long."[101] McTurk links the Mollies to the spread of chaos as well, telling Lyfford, "There's going to be merry hell through the coal regions before long."[102] In these instances, the characters conflate the Mollies with the labor movement, especially through McTurk's position of influence over them and his self-identification as a labor representative. The idea of the Molly Maguires as a mobile, untraceable, constant threat is further reinforced by Banty Bob. Detailing how he or O'Dare always monitor the breaker, he explains how the Mollies are "dem imps of de devil . . . just couldn't say nuffin' politer 'bout dem to save my soul. If we don't watch dey steal de mine."[103] Opening the show with these conversations quickly sets up the Molly Maguires as the show's antagonists and highlights their wandering, yet persistent, threat to Hazleton.

Throughout, the characters refer to the Molly Maguires as a group, and the show avoids any individualization of character or motivation for their violent actions. These tactics contribute to a dehumanizing portrait of the organization and its Irish and Irish-American workers. Repeatedly, characters refer to the Mollies as "the boys" and a "bunch of thugs."[104] O'Dare declares them to be "crowd of cowardly ruffians, who are masquerading under the guise of honest working men."[105] They create a lingering threat as McTurk suggests to O'Dare, stating, "I warn you that if you hold out agin the boys, we'll get you, and we'll get you right."[106] In the only instance where a Molly Maguire appears on stage and plants dynamite, he enters masked.[107] Denying the Mollies their individuality reinforces their mystery as well as makes them less relatable to the audience. The men are never given an opportunity to give the audience an alternate impression. The script also plays on racial tensions to degrade the Irish and the Mollies. O'Dare tells a story about how he became trapped in a mine. Everyone gave up on him except for Banty Bob, the blackface character. O'Dare talks about how Bob's courage and nobility surpass those of the other workers. In spite of his loyalty, Bob is still a standard racist stereotype of the drunk and violent blackface comic character. By creating an absence of the Mollies as individual characters through their representation as a mass, the audience is left to imagine how bad they must be if the hero proclaims Bob as superior.[108] The risk is low that the audience will sympathize with the Mollies when the show provides no individual character or story explaining how or why they act.

Even though the theatrical representations do not condemn the Irish overall as a racial group, they do reinforce the image of the Mollies as an unthinking, violent, mobile mass. When Lyfford suggests violence or murder will help his cause, McTurk quickly offers that the Mollies would murder O'Dare without pay because he defied them when he did not go along with their labor demands.[109] In spite of their connection to labor through their involvement in strikes and connection to McTurk, no specific labor issues are mentioned as motivation. The strikes are characterized only as disruptive, and good workingmen such as O'Dare and his mine workers recognize the damage strikes cause. "My men have agreed to stick by me," O'Dare informs Diana Dychink. "They understand the misery a strike now would entail."[110] In other instances, it is stated that the Mollies only strike when manipulated by politicians or the capitalists. In this way, unlike the depictions during the trials, the capitalists share some of the blame. An ad for the Cohans' tour boasts, "the play abounds in sentiment, elevating in its nature, showing how political intrigue, wire pullers and capitalists, used the secret order of the Molly Maguires to carry out their wicked and tyrannical designs."[111] *The Black Diamond* explicitly makes this connection in performance. At one point, O'Dare scolds McTurk stating, "You call yourself the workingman's friend. It is political rascals like you who breed discontent among the laboring classes, not to better their condition, but to make them worse that you may profit by their poverty."[112] Contrasted with the honorable workingman O'Dare, the afterpiece leaves no ambiguity about who the workingmen in the audience should cheer for throughout the performance. The Mollies are the antagonists of the noble, American citizens and of the relatively settled Irish O'Dare, and no path is opened for redemption.

How the afterpiece constructs the Molly Maguires' presence on stage further removes them from the audience, decreases any chance of identification or sympathy, reinforces the group identification and individual identity erasure reflected in the dialogue, and generates the Mollies as disembodied, threatening, mobile figures. Yet they still play a pivotal role in the action. Although never seen, they participate through their aural presence, creating a mobile threat through sonic aesthetics, which forms the heart of their repeated dramaturgy. Throughout the afterpiece, the audience know by the increasing volume of their offstage voices that the Mollies are traveling toward the action onstage.

The Molly Maguires join the action aurally multiple times during the afterpiece, but the two most spectacular examples illustrate how the sonic operates to create the Mollies as a mobile threat. The audience never sees the Mollie march on Hazleton or physically threaten the characters through their movement. However, the sonic aesthetics mark their mobility and the threat it presents. Both examples point to a narrative pattern of violent approach and then defeat and retreat. The Mollies first sonic manifestation occurs after Lyfford insults Diana's honor and O'Dare strikes him. Lyfford calls for McTurk and the Mollies to help him. As noted in the stage directions, the audience follows their approach through the increasing "loud murmur of voices."[113] In addition to their voices, the other characters' increasing fear at their approach signals the Molly Maguires' movement closer to the breaker. Then Banty Bob starts shooting at the Mollies as the curtain falls. The audience does not see the fight between Bob, O'Dare, and the Mollies. When the curtain rises again, the characters describe how Bob's shooting scared them off, and he sings about defeating the Mollies remarking, "Dey's sneaking away."[114] The other major incident with the Mollies occurs after the dynamite is planted. Bob discovers the dynamite and puts out the lit fuse. Confused about why the breaker has not exploded, McTurk sneaks up to the break to relight the dynamite. O'Dare and Bob catch him. McTurk triumphantly declares, "You fool, do you hear that? (*Yells.*) Those are the Molly Maguires. They're coming for you and

in five minutes they'll string you up like a dog."[115] The audience hears
the approaching yells of the Mollies offstage. In an attempt to halt their
approach, O'Dare threatens to throw McTurk off a cliff, and his speech
to the Mollies is punctuated by yells. Lyfford offers to give the Molly
Maguires $10,000 if they close the mine. They cry "Yes." Bob relights
the dynamite and throws it offstage as the Mollies shout "No, no."[116]
There are "yells" and "sounds of retreat."[117]

The Mollies' repeated construction, primarily through the sonic,
helps magnify their threat as well as serving as a tactic for conveying
sweeping movement in the confined space of the stage. Without the
Molly Maguires' physical manifestation on stage, the audience is freed
from visual guidelines or restrictions and forced to use their imagina-
tions to define the Mollies' numbers, appearance, and movement. Since
the audience cannot see the scale or magnitude of the Mollies' threat,
the imagined specter holds the possibility of instilling heightened fear
because the threat cannot be visually defined. The Mollies never speak
as individuals, only as a mob, and often in unison, which further implies
a lack of individual agency. Practically for a touring variety company,
the use of aural cues becomes a way to evoke a mob without having
to hire a large cast to act on stage. The use of the sonic as the Mollies'
defining theatrical characteristic creates a sense of movement and an-
ticipation of the conflict that will occur upon their arrival. In each scene
in which the Mollies are heard offstage, they march toward the central
characters. They never reach the stage, and therefore they seem never
to stop moving. Their threat is comprised of the connection between
mobility and violence created by the offstage voices.

The scale of their threat is further emphasized through the show's
ending. Although absent from *The Black Diamond* text, Cohan and
Aiken's productions ended with the spectacular entrance of the state
militia. Ultimately, the governor did not call in state militia to crush
the Molly Maguires during the crisis in the 1870s. However, states often
forced the end of a strike and the reopening of the mines with the dec-
laration of martial law and the dispatching of the state militia. In a
display that collapsed reality and fiction, Cohan often recruited the
local town's actual militia to squash the fictional strike of the Mollies.
In moments like this, the theatrical spectacles of the Molly Maguires

had the potential to similarly act as instruments of social control by reminding audience members of military force they would face if they challenged the status quo.[118]

The dramaturgy of mobility created by Aiken's *The Black Diamond* and its variations was repeated on U.S. stages for decades.[119] As a result, it continued to reinforce the notion of the Molly Maguires as a violent Irish specter in the U.S. imagination. In effect, it reminded audiences why the Irish were unsuitable for citizenship: because of their mobile violence. Events surrounding the Molly Maguires afterpieces also continued to reinforce these negative images. When *The Molly Maguires* returned to Leadville, Mooney was no longer around to lead the nonviolent protest. Men, supposedly ex-Mollies, disrupted the performance in protest, threw rotten eggs at the actors, and caused a small riot. In their attempt to perform their disgust at the lies presented onstage, the men merely reinforced how, according to the *Leadville Daily Herald*, "a good deal of unpleasant realism" in the play "is proven."[120] As labor struggled to establish a stable foothold in the United States and the Irish strove to move up the social ladder, this circular logic of the Molly Maguires' myth helped keep it alive well into the twentieth century. In this depiction, the Irishman still appeared too out of step with U.S. values of restraint, middle-class morality, and hard work.

Viewed together, the Janus-faced fighting Irishmen presented an ambiguous view of the Irish in America. On one hand, variety theatre presented the mobile, violent Irishman as the dedicated defenders of American democracy and freedom. On the other, he seemed to convey the antithesis of an ideal American citizen. Anglo-American Protestants' lingering uncertainty about Irish Americans created continuing challenges to advocacy for Irish-American communities and championship of Irish nationalist causes. Although mobility contributed to the denigration of the Irish, it also held potential as a strategy for reimagining their histories, building community, and climbing the social ladder. The remaining chapters consider how dramaturgies of mobility also served as a tactic for Irish-American survival and community.

CHAPTER THREE

Imagined Journeys

The Hibernicon and the
Culture of International Travel

I N THE 1860s, the culture of international travel contributed to the rise of a new entertainment called the hibernicon, a hybrid of an Irish-American variety show and a moving panorama. From its debut in 1863, *MacEvoy's Hibernicon* drew on British travel literature, Irish landscape prints, Irish moving panoramas, and Irish comedy in variety to lure spectators into a virtual trip to Ireland. The hibernicon offered homesick immigrants a glimpse of home. It gave Irish Americans a link to the land many had heard of but had never seen. It also presented Anglo Protestants with an idealized image of a sometimes troubled Ireland. *MacEvoy's Hibernicon* inspired the entertainment's popular name, and the form became a national and international phenomenon for two decades.

Although wildly popular after the Civil War, today the hibernicon is little more than an obscure reference in theatre history. It came to my attention when I was reading nineteenth-century newspapers. When a writer commented on its ubiquity and the entertainment's essential Irish-American nature, I assumed the short paragraph was a puff overselling its production to draw audiences. Not expecting much, I searched for "hibernicon" on the newspaper database. A glimpse across the surprising number of hits revealed multiple companies touring throughout the United States. Intrigued, I moved my search to theatre histories in hope of finding a more concrete description. The hibernicon received brief, vague mentions. Scholars refer to it as "a sort of Irish minstrel show," "a sort of Irish variety show," "an all Irish version of vaudeville," and as a title for a variety sketch.[1] Although these studies' goals are not to analyze the hibernicon, their failure to provide a clear idea of the entertainment further obscured it. In the only analytical work dealing directly with the hibernicon, theatre historian Laurence Senelick provides a glimpse into the entertainment's comedy. By comparing Jerry Cohan's 1880s variety repertoire book, including his hibernicon sketches, to an earlier variety gag book, Senelick illustrates how Cohan participated in the trend to clean up variety comedy in the late nineteenth century. Senelick also provides a general description of the hibernicon's basic narrative: "a wealthy American couple hir[es] a pert young Irishman to chauffeur them on a motor-trip through the Emerald Isle. . . . Episodes could be added or subtracted, depending on the strength of the company and the needs of the manager."[2] Senelick's work starts to provide a clearer picture of the hibernicon, but how the show functioned, why it became wildly popular, and how and why newspapers recognized it as a specifically Irish-American entertainment remained unexplored.

Writing about the hibernicon, I confronted many of the same challenges as other scholars studying popular entertainments, especially those that mainly thrived through touring. Little performance evidence seemingly existed, especially outside northeastern urban centers. However, advances in digital newspapers opened up possibilities to trace the entertainment in ways not previously available to scholars. Digital newspapers made it possible to ascertain the scale and longevity of the entertainment and to gain information on various companies. This information provided a framework for tracking down performance evidence across the country, including songsters, sketches, sheet music, and images. The moving panorama paintings that constituted the performance's heart no longer remain, but some direct performance evidence, in combination with accounts in newspapers, lecture notes, government records, and memoirs, offered enough fragments to start to piece together the hibernicon's cultural history. Similar to this study's other chapters, I place these fragments in juxtaposition, not in pursuit or expectation of a seamless narrative, but in an attempt to create a web between them that begins to develop an understanding of the hibernicon's significance and operation. The holes within the web remain.

This chapter and chapter 4 move along the web's various segments to argue for the hibernicon's importance as an Irish-American phenomenon. Although this chapter focuses on the hibernicon in the United States, companies eventually toured Canada, Australia, New Zealand, and India. Albeit at the same time they reinforced prevalent, romantic Irish stereotypes, the hibernicon became a forum for Irish migrant and Irish-American artists to assert their perspectives about Ireland. The dozens of companies provided an unrecognized training ground and life-long career for many Irish and Irish-American performers. As a result, the hibernicon's creative impact influenced the next generation of Irish-American performers and stars. This chapter explores the entertainment's history and onstage performances; chapter 4 analyzes the hibernicon's operations mostly offstage through how it created critical partnerships with the Catholic Church while on tour. Ultimately, these chapters argue for the fundamental importance of mobility to the entertainment's success on and off stage.

In this chapter, I argue that Irish migrant and Irish-American artists used the hibernicon's imagined mobility as a nationalist tactic for rewriting Irish history. According to scholar Daphne Brooks, a "radical unframing of the [moving panorama] genre" through the troubling of conventions "offer[s] a critical point of possibility."[3] Investigating this critical point of possibility, I explore how the show's dramaturgy broke the moving panorama's naturalizing framing and therefore transformed British colonial narratives. This transformation resulted in a deviation from portrayals in colonial Anglo-Saxon travel literature and constructed Irish nationalist ideologies rooted in land, history, and the Celtic race. The dramaturgy suggested a multitude of histories that held the potential to undercut a singular colonial vision of Ireland.

Moving Panoramas, Visual Technology, and Imagined Mobility

The hibernicon combined a moving panorama depicting a trip to Ireland's scenic and historic sites with an Irish-American variety show. The moving panorama functioned as the heart of the shows and played a critical role in how they operated as a vehicle for ideology, representation

of mobility, history of Ireland, and visual technology. Before discussing
the hibernicon in more depth, it is important to discuss how scholars
have theorized moving panorama's visual technology and its ideological
implications. These theories illustrate how moving panoramas potentially naturalized colonial ideologies through their imagined mobility.

Invented around 1810 in Europe, moving panoramas were comprised
of small, flat strips of canvas that a mechanist unrolled across a pro-
scenium stage. Some moving panoramas portrayed one continuous
view, while others depicted a series of thematically connected scenes
that moved through time and space without any necessary logical justification. Starting to appear in the United States around 1828, moving
panoramas' standard company included a lecturer who described the
scenes, a musician who provided background accompaniment, and a
company member to crank the panorama. Some moving panoramas
featured dioramas, which Frenchman L. J. M. Daguerre invented in the
1820s. By coordinating cutouts in the panorama canvas with machinery,
lights, and fog, dioramas created spectacular effects like full moons or
sunlight shining through cathedral windows. Compared to the popular
circular panoramas performed in special rotunda performance spaces in
Europe, moving panoramas offered a convenient alternative that trav-
elled easily and functioned in a range of performance spaces, including
minstrel and variety houses. Although audience composition depended
on the theatre and town, the more affordable moving panoramas held
the potential to draw cross-class audiences, with the spectacle appealing
to the working classes and the middle classes supporting the panoramas'
presumed educational value.[4]

Moving panoramas toured the United States by the late 1830s, but
they did not become an entertainment for mass American audiences
until John Banvard debuted his Mississippi panorama in 1846. During
the first peak of moving panorama popularity in the late 1840s and
1850s, Banvard created a craze for American Western moving panoramas. For years, other companies imitated his paintings in an attempt
to replicate his financial success. Banvard also helped popularize the
comic lecturer, who offered jokes and performed in character while lec-
turing about the paintings.[5]

Reacting to the increasing commercial viability of panoramas depicting foreign landscapes, during the early 1850s, companies started touring Irish moving panoramas, among other foreign locations. The increasing number of Irish migrants after the Great Famine created a growing audience for Irish entertainments. Irish moving panoramas also appealed to non-Irish audience members, who were drawn to the idyllic and exotic landscapes. In 1859, the *New York Times* applauded the decade's shift away from moving panoramas of the American West and the panoramas' ability to encourage audiences to imagine themselves as "global citizens" through their fictional travels.[6]

These moving panoramas emerged as part of the broader "culture of international travel." As the nation's railroads rapidly expanded and faster, more efficient steamships raced to beat the Atlantic-crossing record, revolutions in transportation not only transformed who and how people traveled, but also how people imagined travel. In spite of advancements in transportation, decreasing travel costs, and increased accessibility, transatlantic tourism remained outside of the realm of possibility for the working class and poor migrants. The middle class continued to accrue leisure time and expendable income, but transatlantic travel presented challenges and sacrifices even for many middle-class families. For people who could not afford international travel, an imaginative culture of travel emerged that fulfilled similar desires. As described by scholar Kristin L. Hoganson, the "culture of international travel" refers to "a culture permeated with reports and images of foreign travel, a culture rife with ersatz travel experiences."[7] The culture of international travel was "a culture in which the sum was greater than the constituent parts. . . . [It] resulted in a sense of living in a time and place marked by mobility and touristic encounters."[8] The culture of international travel became a discourse in which people could participate without ever leaving home.[9]

The culture of international travel emerged from the nation's long-held interest in travel and foreign culture. Although the middle and upper classes had read travel literature since the beginning of the century, after mid-century, the interest in travel culture became increasingly commercialized. The number of travel books published in the United States more than tripled after 1851. Some lecturers who previously toured the country speaking about their travels expanded their

travel business involvement by selling imaginary study tours. The popular press also ran features by journalists like James J. O'Kelly and Nellie Bly about international travel and treated their travels like special
events. Middle-class women participated in imaginary travel clubs. Department stores, restaurants, and hotels offered customers opportunities
to purchase foreign goods.[10] The imaginary culture of travel also found
a flexible medium for its ideas and values in popular entertainment.

Moving panoramas attempted to replicate reality and provided their
customers with a view of what most could not afford to see in person.[11]
Scholars of nineteenth-century popular entertainment have long argued
about the moving panorama's relationship to reality while questioning
how spectacle serves as a method of conveying authenticity, realism,
and ideology. Brooks discusses how moving panoramas had a "para-
doxical goal of validating the 'truth' of history via spectacular theatrical
illusion."[12] Angela Miller argues that moving panoramas' spectacular
realism naturalized colonial, national expansionist, and white supremacist ideologies. Miller explains how the "mechanically controlled narrative with a definable beginning, middle, and end encouraged a view
of history as a series of unfolding scenes fluidly connected with one another, giving to audiences the illusion of mastery over random, distant,
or otherwise incomprehensible events."[13] For example, the Mississippi
river panoramas depicted the American West as lying in wait for white
settlement, naturalized slavery by representing it as part of the landscape, and erased the histories of indigenous people who continued to
live on the land by primarily presenting them in the context of ancient
traditions and passed ancestors. In creating a position of "mastery" over
the landscape for the mostly white audience, the performances reinforced white settler and manifest destiny sentiments.[14]

Drawing on the same tactics, moving panoramas of foreign countries held the potential to make colonized territories "both accessible
and visible" while at the same time "glorifying the imperial state, and
imposing the illusion of order."[15] The panorama's scrolling pushed the
audience toward a preordained destination grounded in colonized nations' picturesque landscape, the erasure of colonized people, and colonialist victories that transformed supposedly primitive cultures into
modern civilized nations. In the hibernicon's case, by presenting scenes

of lush, timeless western Irish landscape, the productions ran the risk of dehistoricizing and erasing the hundreds of years of colonial conflict that shaped who lived on the land and the continuing battle over native Irish's land rights. It also opened up the possibility of portraying an empty landscape and "premodern" people who would be helped and not harmed by colonial intervention.

Mobility is an implicit, if not explicitly theorized, component of these discussions. Analysis of imaginative mobilities became foundational to the new mobilities' paradigm through the work of sociologist John Urry, who considers how imaginative travel constitutes one of five "interdependent" mobilities. Examining mostly television and radio, Urry argues that imaginative travel is "effected through the images of places and peoples appearing on and moving across multiple print and visual media."[16] Across disciplines, scholars have centered mobility in discussions of imaginative travel across various media, including photography, film, and digital culture, and of how imaginative travel motivates physical tourism.[17] Scholar Shanna Robinson calls for expanding the two imaginative travel parameters defined by Urry, that it inspires physical travel or operates alongside someone physically taking a journey. Advocating for a closer examination of how imagination functions in relation to imaginative travel, her work highlights that one benefit of approaching imaginative travel from a mobilities perspectives is that it "allows for consideration of both the representational and the embodied, particularly in terms of contextualizing travel imagination and vicarious experience."[18] This approach involves a focus not only on what is represented through the mobility, but also on how mobility's relationship to space and time constitutes its meaning.

Teasing out how mobility works within Miller's moving panorama theories prompts an investigation of how the panoramas' interdependent physical and imaginative movement contributes to the construction of progressive, colonial histories. If the movement is the imagined journey from one location to the next, it gains meaning through the fluidity of the movement, which offers a (false) sense of connectedness. The fluidity of the narrative and visual imagery is dependent on the panorama's scrolling canvas, on the lecturer's and supporting entertainer's avoidance of disrupting the flow's sense of connectedness, and on a narrative with a clear beginning, middle, and end. As a performance, the panorama's meaning also depended on how the audience *saw* the mobility. Within arguments for colonial histories' construction, these ways of seeing depend on the audience gaining a position of mastery. Viewing the moving panorama from a mobility perspective, scholars must consider how movement contributes (or does not) to the creation of this mastery.

In combination with the visuals, part of the panorama's construction of reality relied on replicating prevailing modes of perception. It is possible to consider how these modes intersected with physical and imaginative movement and supported a naturalized, mastered view of panorama visuals. During her trip to Ireland in 1885, tourist Evangeline Bense described how she viewed the Irish coast from the steamship's deck. She recorded in her diary how "the sturdy rig bore us into the harbor . . . the yellows and dull reds of the changing foliage, and the ivy . . . formed an ideal picture never to be forgotten." She watched the "moving panorama until we reached Queenstown, picturesque with its high vine-covered walls and streets rising tier above tier."[19] In detailing the ship's picturesque entrance into the port, Bense's use of the term "moving panorama" to describe her viewing experience was not unique to the period. Scholar Wolfgang Schivelbusch argues that such observations reflect a perception shift resulting from the incorporation of quicker motion into visual perception. Schivelbusch writes: "[T]he train's speed separates the traveller from the space that he had previously been a part of . . . [A]s the traveller steps out of that space, it becomes a stage setting, or a series of pictures or scenes created by the continuously changing perspective. . . . [T]he traveller sees the objects, landscapes, etc., through the apparatus which moves him through the world."[20] As a result, he concludes, "motion of vision . . . becomes a prerequisite for the 'normality' of panoramic vision."[21]

By replicating the motion of vision, moving panoramas such as the hibernicon forced audiences to use these newer methods of perceiving visually that were developing outside the theatre. As a result, moving panoramas are a potentially effective media for ideology, propaganda, advertising, and history not only because of how the visuals reflect the appearance of real locations, but because they replicate a particular method of vision that was becoming more commonly viewed as natural. If moving panoramas achieved the fluid and cohesive performance argued by Miller, these new modes of perception may have worked in tandem with the performance to support colonial ideologies.[22] The hibernicon's adaptation of British travel literature operated within and against these dynamics.

Following the Beaten Path: Print Culture and Irish Travel

Upon entering the theatre for an 1870s performance of *McGill and Strong's Mirror of Ireland*, a hibernicon, the female patrons received a hand-colored souvenir print, Currier and Ives's *The Cove of Cork*. Depicting Cobh Harbor, then officially called Queenstown, the lithograph portrayed rolling green hills, a picturesque stone cottage, sailing ships gliding through the harbor, and several well-dressed, faceless people enjoying the weather. The audience may not have been able to afford a journey to Ireland, but the souvenir promised that beautiful scenes of local Irish life lay ahead of them. The lithograph reveals the close relationship and tension between the emerging culture of international travel, travel literature, travel prints, and the hibernicon in the late nineteenth century (see figure 8).

When the patrons received the print, they might have recognized the image, which circulated through British and American culture for decades. Originally engraved by William Henry Bartlett, a popular British artist in the 1830s, *The Cove of Cork* appeared as a black and white engraving in Coyne, Willis, and Bartlett's *Scenery and Antiques of Ireland* (1842) and in Mr. and Mrs. Hall's *Ireland, Its Scenery and Character* (1841–1843). For the next seventy years, new travel books such as *Picturesque Ireland: Historical and Descriptive* (1890) and various reprints of the antebellum guides kept the image of Cove Harbor in circulation. *McGill and Strong's* bragged about using Bartlett's sketches as a template for its moving panorama. The company boasts about Bartlett's worldwide "reputation as an artist" for his "graceful and truthful" sketches made "on the spot."[23] British travel literature and prints created the germinal source for the hibernicon and helped establish the hibernicon's credibility, standard narrative, and visual lexicon. Travel literature and

FIGURE 8. A hibernicon souvenir, *Cove of Cork: Presented to the Lady Patrons of McGill & Strong's Mirror of Ireland,* features a sketch from a popular travel book from New York printers Currier and Ives. Hand-colored lithograph print. N.d. Library of Congress Prints and Photographs Division, Washington, D.C.

prints also embodied the tensions between colonial Anglo-Saxon and Irish Celtic nationalist perspectives and demonstrated how writers and artists mobilized the same imagery in support of opposing ideological viewpoints.

British travel literature depicted a tourist's journey throughout Ireland. The tourist visited natural wonders and local sites, often while providing historical information about major political and military events as well as some contemporary issues facing the Irish people. As scholars have discussed, in writers' descriptions of landscape, culture, or people, the attention to difference frequently framed the colonial relationship between Ireland and Britain as a cultural and racial conflict between premodern Celtic and modern Anglo-Saxon societies. Even when British writers detail Ireland's troubles, the narratives reinforce British superiority and lay the blame for Irish problems on their "primitive" lifestyle, which is assumed to result from their racial inferiority. Throughout the nineteenth century, travel literature's representation of

Ireland shifted while retaining many of these basic characteristics. For example, as scholar William H. A. Williams discusses, for a brief time after the Great Famine narratives became more optimistic about Ireland's future. Some British writers believed that Ireland's devastation would allow its remaining people to finally build a modern culture. Others emphasized how the British labor force could benefit from the Irish exodus and hoped that the trauma would quell political unrest. The representation of the Irish landscape provided a dual motive for the British to travel to Ireland. The picturesque and idealized depictions appealed to tourists who wanted to escape the increasingly industrialized Britain. Recurrent descriptions of the Irish landscape as empty also seemed to justify the British colonial presence; if the nation was mostly empty, British colonization simply occupied unclaimed territory.[24] These narratives were not homogeneous, and the approach to Ireland continued to shift as the century progressed. However, certain conventions remained fairly constant. In support of an authentic experience for readers, writers traveled the "beaten path," used two narrator figures—the tourist and a local Irish guide—and drew on romanticized, "on-the-spot" Irish landscape in descriptions and visuals.

British travel writers validated the accounts' authenticity and helped create a popular lexicon of Ireland through the "beaten track." As scholar James Buzard discusses, the idea of the "beaten track" was "one dominant and recurrent image in the annals of the modern tour."[25] Even if readers never visited Ireland before, British travel literature created and reinforced a lexicon of Ireland by visiting the well-known tourist sites throughout the country, such as the Lakes of Killarney, Giant's Causeway, Blarney Castle, and St. Patrick's Cathedral. Even if writers interpreted their experiences differently, the repetition in travel literature and later travel prints created a relatively consistent group of images associated with Ireland.[26] Similar to Miller's theorization of moving panoramas, the mobility's predictability established conventions and ideologies emphasizing Anglo-Saxon superiority.

British travel literature reinforced the beaten path's authenticity through its convention of two narrators. The first narrator was the tourist, typically the writer, constructed within the narrative as a mostly objective outsider. These tourists state that they simply report what they see, supplementing their experiences with scholarly and statistical sources.[27] Even though the writers promise to give their readers an accurate depiction of Ireland, they also are aware of the need to tell a good story. Travel literature invariably included "incidents, descriptions, legends, traditions, and personal sketches."[28] As S. C. Hall stated in his preface, this combination of elements served the audience demands. He hoped that the more personal sketches and legends "might serve to excite interest in those who are deterred from the perusal of mere facts, if communicated in a less popular form."[29] These testimonies served to reinforce not only the writers' authority, but also the idea that readers gain a thorough picture of Ireland through the narratives.

The Irish tour guide and jaunting-car driver was British travel literature's second narrator, and his image developed alongside travel literature's transforming depiction of the Irish peasant. Starting in the 1850s, the Irish peasant transformed from a drunk and violent barbarian into a new stereotype that emphasized the Irish as good-natured and hospitable. This new stereotype involved expectations that their Irish tour guides act and sound like stage Irishmen, especially in terms of their humor. The jaunting-car driver was typically hired by the tourists to take them throughout the country to see the sights. On the way, the driver provides details about the passing landscape and landmarks along with plenty of amusing anecdotes.[30] British tourists continued to be cautious and critical of their guides' perceived trustworthiness, talkativeness, tendency to exaggerate, and inclination to scheme.[31] Regardless of their suspicions, the use of a local Irish guide helped confirm the authenticity of the sites.[32] Even though tourists ultimately selected what made it into the narrative, the Irish jaunting-car driver supposedly gives tourists access to the "back area," the "true" story behind the Ireland staged for outsiders or the "front area."[33]

Finally, the romantic landscape's representation comprised a central component of travel literature. According to scholar A. Norman Jeffares, "the physical entity of Ireland is an integral part of the atmosphere of much Anglo-Irish writing."[34] As an aspect of romanticism that shaped nineteenth-century poetry and music as well as literature and theatre, the aesthetic influenced artists to convey the "visual realization of poetic beauty."[35] By mid-century, these "realizations" often involved rolling landscapes, quaint peasant folk, and thatched cottages.[36] Improvements in print technology made it easier and cheaper to print images, which led to an explosion of Irish travel books with Irish landscape images in the 1830s and 1840s. As scholar Michael Booth notes, through these books, "for the first time the interested reader could, from a variety of publications, gain a visual impression of Irish scenery without leaving his fireside."[37] Travel writers emphasized the "on-the-spot" nature of the drawings as evidence of their accuracy and equated the romantic imagery with the "true" Ireland.[38] Taken together, these images and British travel literature's conventions ran the risk of creating a tourism imaginary, as defined by scholar Noel B. Salazaar, which "propagates historically inherited stereotypes that are based on the (colonial) myths and fantasies."[39]

The ability to print more affordable images contributed to a market for Irish landscape and local life prints. Currier and Ives, a major printmaking firm based in New York, sold more than one hundred thousand copies of two hundred different Irish prints. Although the majority of Currier and Ives prints presented American views, the company printed more Irish prints than any other foreign country. The prints depicted a romanticized, positive view of Ireland and offered an affordable way for people to obtain Irish images to display in their homes. Romantic landscape prints seem to have sold best. Others featured images of saints and holy places, battles with Britain, Irish nationalist leaders, and Irish-American religious, military, and sports figures.[40] Sheet music also took advantage of the appeal of Irish landscape. Although landscape covers comprised about 26 percent of antebellum song covers, the number skyrocketed in the 1860s and 1870s.[41] *How* the images were mobilized by writers, artists, and consumers structured their meanings and potential. These landscape images may have been used to reinforce a premodern idea of the Irish for some. However, outside of the narrative frame of British travel literature, they held the potential to reinforce pride in rural Ireland, which increasingly became tied to nationalist expressions of Celtic racial identity through the Young Irelander nationalist movement in the 1840s.[42]

As travel culture expanded post–Civil War, the market for Irish travel literature and imagery in the United States grew. Americans and the

FIGURE 9. A Currier and Ives print depicts the picturesque lakes of Killarney. *Lakes of Killarney.* New York: Currier and Ives, 1868. Hand-colored lithograph print. Library of Congress Prints and Photographs Division, Washington, D.C.

Irish started writing travel narratives in larger numbers and contributed to a booming Irish travel literature business by the early twentieth century. Yet these American and Irish writers often replicated many of the British writers' motifs and imagery. The Irish knew that they could profit from the stereotypical associations with their country. Travelers might be inspired by their narratives to visit an idyllic landscape with quaint, kind people, thereby boosting the local economy. Expressing the reality of Irish lives—including cycles of famines, political unrest and violence, and widespread poverty—would not attract visitors. The Irish who wanted their country to profit from the expanding tourist business saw their success as resting on perpetuating centuries-old stereotypes.[43]

Nineteenth-century Irish and Irish-American theatre artists faced a similar challenge when producing, writing, and performing in the theatre. Popular performance remained rooted in stage Irish stereotypes. The romantic imagery held the potential to continue to conflate the land with the Irish people and to erase daily challenges. Replicating the movement of British travel literature in combination with the moving

FIGURE 10. In their attempts to appeal to Irish consumers, Currier and Ives printed lithographs that celebrated Irish nationalist leaders. *Charles Stuart Parnell, M. P., president of the Irish Land League — addressing a meeting.* New York: Currier and Ives, 1881. Lithograph. Library of Congress Prints and Photographs Division, Washington, D.C.

panoramas' visual technology held the risk of replicating colonial ideologies. However, by presenting an opportunity for Irish migrant and
Irish-American artists to rewrite narratives and histories of Ireland, the
hibernicon's mobility also operated as a site of revolutionary potential.

The Emergence of the Hibernicon

When it debuted in 1863, the hibernicon combined the popular moving
panorama and variety show with print culture's prevalent Irish lexicon and conventions. Its emergence as a popular entertainment phenomenon occurred after a decade of struggle by the show's creators,
the Irish migrant MacEvoy family, as performers and musicians in the
Midwest. Tracing the development of the hibernicon demonstrates how
the MacEvoy family exploited novel performance forms to repackage
imaginative travel for cross-class audiences.

Presenting a trip through Ireland, Irish moving panoramas combined depictions of the urban and the rural to appeal to a variety of
aesthetic tastes. Through imagined movement, the audience retreads
the beaten path in performance; it visits Ireland's key historical, political, and religious sites and scenes as well as natural marvels. *Nagle's
Grand Panorama of Ireland* and *O'Reilly's Original Grand Panorama of Ireland*
among others enjoyed a short period of popularity between 1851 and
1853. Reviews detailed how the lecturer told stories and jokes about
Ireland, its history, and its people as music played and the panorama
scrolled. Some panoramas occasionally hired a well-known Irish musician to play during the performance. For example, Charles Ferguson, a
blind Irish union piper and well-known Irish musician, played a series
of shows with *O'Reilly's Original Grand Panorama of Ireland* in 1852.[44]

John MacEvoy, an Irish migrant and Chicago music instructor, developed the longest-running Irish panorama before creating the *Hibernicon* through over a decade of experimentation.[45] From 1852 to 1856, he
reworked his Irish moving panorama and attempted to combine it with
other popular entertainment trends in the hope that its novelty would
appeal to audiences. Aside from promising high-quality paintings of
Ireland, MacEvoy's panorama was a family business and featured his
children Charles, Mary, and Kate as the "Young Irish Minstrels." With

the addition of his children, MacEvoy combined two popular performance trends, the moving panorama and the infant phenomenon.
Charles played violin and Mary played the Irish harp. The performance's star was nine-year-old Kate. Dubbed the "celebrated INFANT
POWER" and "the only youthful delineator of Irish character," Kate
performed the role of "Barney Brallaghan, the Irish Guide and Car
Driver."[46] Unlike the previous panoramas of Ireland, "vocal music"
performed by the children played a regular role in the performances.[47]
Although it is unclear to what extent the shows introduced a narrative,
Kate's Barney added a variety character that drew on contemporary
notions of Irish comedy.[48]

In 1860, the MacEvoy family returned to the stage and adapted
travel literature conventions that defined the hibernicon around the
world for decades to come. Although the overarching narrative of a
trip to Ireland remained, the MacEvoys personified the trip by adding
the character of a tourist and his female companion. The male character was typically referred to as an Irish, Irish American, or American
gentleman, and he reflected the travel literature writer personified onstage. In some instances, the lecturer played the tourist, which gave him
a narrative reason to appear onstage. The show started with the tourists
boarding a ship in New York and depicted their journey across the Atlantic. During the ocean voyage, the ship ran into a storm, a common
nineteenth-century spectacle scene, which used sensational scenic and
lighting effects. After the tourists' arrival in Ireland, Barney, MacEvoy's
version of travel literature's tour guide, joined the lecturer in explaining
the sites, and the tourists became involved in a romantic and comic plot
involving Barney and his love Nora. The additional plot usually introduced various obstacles, such as an overprotective mother, other suitors,
political events, and mistaken identities, that threatened to separate the
couple. At the end of their visit, the tourists once again board their ship
to return to New York and Barney and Nora are reunited. Sometime
between the second half of 1862 and 1863, the MacEvoys renamed their
new show the *Hibernicon*, a title that soon defined the genre.[49]

The MacEvoys adopted a variety structure to their performances,
with an olio of songs, dances, and sketches loosely connected by the
travel narrative during the scrolling of the panorama and an afterpiece

with the main comedic plot at the end. Within the presentation of the loose narrative, MacEvoy experimented with an early form of musical theatre by connecting the songs and performer specialties to plot and character points. For example, upon his entrance, Barney often sang a song, such as "Barney the Jarvey" or "Barney the Driver Lad," that introduced his character. He sings, "I wish to introduce myself and tell from where I came, I drive a Dublin Jaunting Car and Barney is my name, I'm always ready for a job to drive you near or far, So try the value of my words by jumping on my car."[50] Reviewers recognized MacEvoy's productions for their novel use of music. One newspaper claims, "What renders the whole thing particularly interesting is the accompaniment. . . . Each scene has its song . . . as it passes before the gaze of the audience. . . . The Whole is explained by a rollicking young man, styling himself 'Barney the Guide.'"[51] Even if this notice is a puff piece, it shows the company's belief that its approach of matching songs with scenes and characters was novel enough to be used as a selling point.

With his children now adults and the infant phenomenon no longer at its height, MacEvoy's restructuring of his moving panorama as a variety entertainment reflected his skill at adapting popular performance trends. Irish music and dancing became increasingly popular on variety and minstrel stages during mid-century, especially Irish jigs performed by male performers. His show also emerged at a time of increasing popularity for Irish comedy, and it benefited from the central role Barney provided male Irish comedians. Male variety comedians typically rooted their acts in character songs that allowed the performer to create "a central character, a narrative full of comic events, and an opportunity to interpolate longer comic monologues or commentary within the songs."[52] The hibernicon's acceptance by the Catholic Church, discussed in chapter 4, suggests that many hibernicon companies developed a more family friendly variety entertainment while still drawing on popular entertainment forms.

The limited remaining visual evidence illustrates the hibernicon's more respectable stage Irish representations. In a photo from the 1875 Australian tour of *Howarth's Hibernica,* Barney and Nora reflected muted stage Irish characteristics[53] (see figure 11). Barney and Nora do not wear grotesque or exaggerated makeup. They wear stereotypical, but

FIGURE 11. *Howarth's Hibernica* performers in costume during a tour
of Australia and New Zealand. Photographer unknown, Miss Marie
Poinier and Mr. Tim Cohan of *Howarth's Hibernica*, 1875,
State Library, New South Wales.

romanticized versions of peasant clothing, and they appear neat and clean. In a portrait of Mary MacEvoy posing with her harp, her dress and makeup similarly do not reflect stage Irish characteristics but a more genteel Irish womanhood. She stands poised, ready to play her harp, dressed all in white. Although it is not possible to know whether these staged portraits always accurately reflected hibernicon performances, the images illustrate that while the show reinforced certain stage stereotypes, it also offered more respectable Irish representations. Similar to first-class variety companies throughout the country, the hibernicon's more respectable entertainment became a tactic for expanding audiences across gender and class lines. The choice also likely resulted from companies' attempts to cultivate favor from Irish-American communities.

In its adaptation of the tourist narrator, Irish tour guide, and romantic landscape, the hibernicon replicated key components from print culture while making some crucial changes. As will be discussed later, these changes were important for how the hibernicon functioned in performance and constructed its dramaturgies of mobility. The moving panorama lecturer and tourist character split the narrative responsibilities of travel literature's travel writer. The fragmented evidence of hibernicon lectures suggests the narrative situated the audiences' location in the geography, conveyed anecdotes, described the location's beauty, and provided historical information about sites and key historical figures. With lecturers typically referred to as Professor, the productions automatically placed the lecturer in a position of authority. Lectures appeared in songsters, and newspaper articles described the lecturers' performances. The lecturer often reinforces the picturesque aesthetic of the images. For example, for the "Beautiful Lakes of Killarney," one *Gavin and Ryan's Emerald Isle* lecturer describes how "[b]y Killarney's lakes and fells Emerald Isles and winding bays, Mountain paths and woodland dells, memory ever fondly strays, Bounteous nature loves all lands, beauty wanders everywhere."[54] This romanticism is tempered by factual and anecdotal information. Like travel literature narrators, the lecturer had the potential to reinforce the authenticity and validity of romanticized, stereotypical Anglo-Saxon images of Ireland.[55] Although the evidence is not always consistent, it seems that in some instances the

FIGURE 12. Mary MacEvoy, John MacEvoy's daughter, pictured with her
harp, which she was known for playing during hibernicon performances.
"Miss Mary MacEvoy," clipping in J. S. G. Hagan, *Records of the New York Stage,
1860–1870*. Extended and illustrated for Augustin Daly by Augustus
Toedteberg (New York: New York Dispatch, 18??), vol. 11, 178,
Harvard Theatre Collection, pf TS 939.5.4.

same performer played the lecturer and the tourist. There exists even less evidence pertaining to the performance of the tourist character. Only a few hibernicon sketches written by Jerry Cohan survive. These sketches suggest that much of the power dynamic from British travel literature between the tourist and the Irish remained. The tourist occupies a more knowledgeable position compared to the Irish characters, whom he helps with advice, and he plays the straight man to the tour guide's comedic antics.[56]

Often played by an Irish migrant or Irish American, the local tour guide, typically called Barney the Guide or Dublin Dan, served as an additional narrator as well as a stage Irishman who engaged in variety comic sketches. Aside from explaining the sites and performing in comedic bits, Barney explains how he will continue the same type of narrative as the lecturer, describing "my own darling Isle, The nate [sic] Emerald gem of the Ocean, About the kings and the bogs, the priests and the frogs."[57] He implies that he will pass down his memories and the testimony of the Irish who came before him. The potential for Barney to act in this manner highlights the stage Irishman's multifaceted function, which is often downplayed. Unlike his role in travel literature, his perspective here is not filtered through the writer. Although the character reinforces stage Irish stereotypes, the character's embodiment on stage and his job of informing not only the tourist but also the audience about Ireland opened up possibilities to destabilize the romanticized view of Ireland.

Even though no hibernicon paintings remain, descriptions in newspapers, broadsides, and songsters as well as some of the original source sketches and prints suggest that the shows took an approach to Irish scenery similar to that in travel literature, Currier and Ives prints, and Irish melodramas. Although the travelers also visited cities and towns, advertisements, broadsides, and programs heralded the beautiful western landscapes as the highlight of the show. Broadsides and songsters list the Giant's Causeway, Meeting of the Waters, Loch Foyle, Glen of the Downs, and Rock of Cashel among the local sites displayed. The program for *McGill and Strong's Mirror of Ireland* promises spectators that they will see "a perfect realization of these beautiful and picturesque Lakes [of Killarney], with their sheets of transparent water, glassing the sunniest skies, dotted with innumerable islands while around stand the grim masses of the McGillicuddy Reeks, frowning, like stern sentinels, over so much beauty."[58] These types of descriptions directly echoed the romantic depictions of landscape and held the potential to similarly reinforce a narrative of a premodern, mostly empty, idyllic Ireland ideal for tourism, colonial settlers, and industry. For a "visitor" without any connection to Ireland, it provides an opportunity to experience "timeless" scenery, dehistoricizing the continuing struggles of the Irish.

Appealing to the desire for travel culture and an increasing number of Irish migrants and their descendants, the MacEvoys' show became a hit with audiences, and the family confirmed its success with a long New York City run in the spring and summer of 1863. By 1864, hibernicon companies began to form across the country and by the end of the decade, they toured in the Mid-Atlantic, New England, the Midwest, San Francisco, Southern California, and Virginia City, Nevada.[59] Although the hibernicon business took off in the 1860s, it was not until the 1870s that dozens of companies toured the country. The height of the hibernicon's popularity coincided with moving panoramas' second period of widespread popularity. Some companies simply called themselves the *Hibernicon* or *MacEvoy's Hibernicon*, but troupe names also played on words and phrases such as *Hibernia, Erin,* and *Mirror of Ireland.*[60]

By the 1870s, the hibernicon became so profitable in the United States that occasionally two companies performed in town at the same time.[61] Documenting the arrival of one "everlasting" hibernicon after another in his *Annals of the New York Stage*, George Odell complained that "I am inured to visits of *MacEvoy's Hibernicon*" and "I cannot wax enthusiastic about this apparent rivalry" between touring companies.[62] Comparing the hibernicon phenomenon to what scholars have referred to as the most popular moving panorama in the United States highlights the extent of the hibernicon's popularity. John Banvard's Mississippi River panorama had seven companies depicting the Mississippi running at the same time between 1846 and 1849. Between 1873 and 1876, however, a conservative estimate suggests six hibernicon companies consistently ran without major interruption, and any single year in that three-year period saw a minimum of nine different companies simultaneously touring.[63] This level of popularity placed the hibernicon

FIGURE 13. *MacEvoy's Original Hibernicon,* ticket, author's collection.

in the position to propagate its implicit and explicit politics across the nation. From the fragments that remain, it is possible to see how many Irish migrant and Irish-American theatre artists and the hibernicon's dramaturgies of mobility reworked print culture's lexicon of Ireland to suit their own political purposes.

Dramaturgies in Practice:
Mobility, Ideology, and Moving Panoramas

The hibernicon's dramaturgy developed through its imagined Irish journey. As with any dramaturgy of mobility, if the evidence exists, it is important to investigate the ways the performance context and audience reception impacted how it might be understood and experienced. Complicating theories that position moving panoramas as technologies of colonial ideology, this section argues for the disruptive potential of the hibernicon's practical operations, its audiences, and its nationalist context and demonstrates their importance in understanding how its performances created meaning through their imagined travel.

As scholars have argued, moving panorama conventions had the potential to naturalize the shows' colonial ideologies for a passive, accepting audience. According to scholars like Miller, the moving panoramas' success as communicators of dominant histories depends, in part, on the progressive, fluid construction of images and a clear beginning, middle, and end that places the audience in the position of mastering unfamiliar scenes. It is the "illusion of continuity" that created the potential to function as Miller's type of historical devices.[64]

In nineteenth-century theatrical practice, creating a fluid, coherent entertainment presented challenges. Many panoramas, such as the Mississippi panoramas, attempted to present a continuous view of the river and its shore. Yet, this narrative goal became a challenge as panorama painters expanded the distances covered by the performance and types of views it depicted, such as small cities and local life onshore. Many panoramas featured scenes that could not logically follow from a continuous journey on a riverboat. The hibernicon made no attempt to depict a continuous view and jumped between geographical wonders and historical and local scenes across time and space without pretending that the audience could view all the images from a cart or boat over several hours. As a result, the visuals did not implicitly unify the entertainment. Rather, the shows' potential for a fluid narrative and visual experience rested not only on the painters' talent, but also on the skills of the mechanist and the lecturer. The mechanist held the responsibility of smoothly unrolling the panorama with consistent speed at the right moments in the performance. This was tricky to maintain throughout a two-hour performance, and newspaper accounts record many mechanists' uneven efforts. Lecturers could provide continuity through their performances, but inexperienced lecturers could lead a production to fall into "catastrophic atomism."[65]

In practice, who viewed the hibernicon performances contributed to whether the audience passively accepted the narratives and ideologies presented. Although we cannot know for sure how many Irish attended the hibernicon, reviews and letters recognized their large presence in hibernicon audiences, especially in major cities. Scattered audience accounts recognize the Irish's presence. Aside from brief references in newspapers, some anecdotal evidence supports Irish attendance. Sarah

Davis, wife of Supreme Court justice, U.S. senator, and former Abraham Lincoln campaign manager David Davis, remarked on the hibernicon's draw for her Irish servants on two occasions in Bloomington, Illinois. In 1872, Davis recorded that "A show in town called the 'Hybernnean' a sort of panorama of Irish life as near as I can find from Willie [her servant], has been attracting the Irish."[66] In November 1874, she commented on her servants' attendance again and wrote, "The servants in town are being entertained at Durley Hall with the Hibernicon in a new dress — Willie and Julia went last night."[67]

Advertisements suggest that hibernicon companies targeted the Irish. The hibernicon's advertisements played off Irish migrants' longings to return home in the *Irish American,* a New York–based newspaper in the 1860s and 1870s. During the MacEvoys' first major tour in New York, an advertisement explained that the performance "comprises all the most agreeable features of a glimpse at the old scenes of our childhood."[68] In April, the MacEvoys stated that their show "cannot fail to excite the enthusiastic love of our people for the spot which they hail as that of their birth."[69] Soon after, the MacEvoys started framing the entertainment as a vehicle for reinforcing Irish racial identity and pride. When attending a performance, Irish migrants, the advertisement claimed, "will with pleasure recognize the dear old scenes of their youth; and the little ones will feel a renewed pride in being descended from the people of fair Ireland."[70] This tactic was later used in performances throughout the United States. For example, a New Orleans advertisement noted, "all Irishmen who have not the time nor the money to return to the old country but who, nevertheless, would like to get a glance at her green fields, will find it the last chance they will probably get."[71]

Brief notes in newspapers that read like puff pieces are even more direct in targeting an Irish audience. One note bragged that the hibernicon "during the past week attracted immense crowds of our Irish citizens, to whom it is peculiarly adapted to entertain and amuse."[72] Toward the end of the same run, a short paragraph explained how the show "remains very attractive to our Hibernian fellow citizens, who nightly fill the little theatre."[73] Attempting to target the increasing number of Irish Americans, a hibernicon company in Cincinnati reminded its audience members, "The Irishmen of the city, and their descendants to the remotest degree will find a fitting place to spend an evening during the stay of the *Hibernicon*."[74]

In addition to newspaper advertisements, songs also provide hints about the hibernicon audiences. *McGill and Strong's Mirror of Ireland* claims that it created its show "[i]n the desire of presenting to the Irish people of America an entertainment of unexceptional merit."[75] *Charles MacEvoy's Original Hibernicon* and *Howorth's Grand Hibernica* took a broader approach that singled out the Irish, while arguing that a broad American audience also could enjoy the show. The song "Invitation to the Hibernicon" provides a plot summary for the audience through its lyrics. Aside from highlighting the exciting historical sites and scenery, the lyrics begin by stating, "Hibernians! Haste to make the Tour of Ireland!"[76] A few verses later, the song splits their audience into two groups. In one verse, it proclaims, "Come on then Irishmen, come ye Mac Connells, Mac Ginns, Mac Graths, Mac Cartheys, and Mac Faddens."[77] The next stanza declares, "Come on Americans, ye generous true boys."[78] The song then unites them through their common presence in the theatre.

If Irish and Irish Americans attended in the numbers suggested by many newspaper reports, hibernicon audiences included people who did not have an outsider relationship to Ireland. Although some Irish Americans may have felt little connection to their ancestors' home, many in the audience may have heard about Ireland's struggles from family or the typically nationalist Irish-American community. The presence of knowledgeable audience members held the potential to destabilize the Anglo-Saxon colonial histories adapted from the British travel literature as well as scholars' assumptions about passive moving panorama audiences. For audience members with a connection, real or imagined, to Ireland, the experience of hibernicon performances involved active recognition, witnessing, and engaging with scenes from home. This level of engagement was established with the panoramas of Ireland in the 1850s. One panorama of Ireland "pictured [Thomas Meagher's] sufferings in the penal colony of Van Diemen's Land."[79] It is not surprising that the panorama chose to represent Meagher because "The iconic 'Meagher of the Sword' was the most celebrated of all the Young Ireland rebels in America."[80] The performance seemed to celebrate Meagher and hold him up as a martyr for the Irish cause, depicting his sufferings as a result of his rebellion against the British. On this evening, however, the *Panorama of Ireland* became not only an event for remembering and celebrating, but also for keeping abreast of contemporary developments. After presenting the painting, "W. E. Robinson, of this City happening to be present, rose and stated that he had just come from New York, and that Mr. Meagher was safe in that City."[81] Along with other Young Irelanders over the past year, Meagher had managed to escape to America. According to the *Irish-American*, "The scene that followed showed in what estimation Mr. Meagher is held by the people in this country."[82]

One reviewer commented on the key role of the visual and the joy of "seeing" Ireland again for Irish audience members at hibernicon performances as well. He wrote, "All that skillful painting and fair sing-ing can do toward bringing the Green Isle home to its children in this country, is done. . . . [T]he greatest bursts of applause seem to follow the recognition of familiar views in the panorama."[83] Another remarked that the hibernicon's success relied on how quickly Irish migrants rec-ognized the scenes.[84] In these instances, the show did not create a sense of ownership; the Irish and Irish-American audience members *came in* to the theatre with a sense of belonging as Irish people, either based on experience, an imagined family past, or nationalist sentiment. For these audience members, the productions engaged with already established sentiments and politics that typically favored the Irish Celts over their Anglo-Saxon colonizers. If audience members recognize the visuals' accuracies, they also have the opportunity to recognize the disjunc-tions between idealized landscape and Ireland's current struggles. The images of the lakes, green hills, and majestic castles do not betray the famines that continued to plague the country or the English military presence in Dublin, where the tour often begins. A thriving, lush coun-tryside that seems to promise health and bountifulness appears instead. Instead of desensitizing Irish migrants to the struggle, the moving pan-orama may have reinforced their sense of Ireland's oppression and need for help from Irish migrants to fight British colonizers. Seeing what Ireland could be, but clearly was not, may have spurred some audience members to renew their commitment to help Ireland move closer to freedom and the ideal depicted on stage.

Extending beyond the politics brought into the theatre, the images' ideological flexibility also opened up the show's nationalist potential. Depending on the company and audience, some companies may have unintentionally mobilized the panorama paintings in the same fashion as many British travel narratives. Around the time MacEvoy first started his Irish moving panorama, however, the Young Ireland nationalist movement solidified landscape, historical, and Celtic racial associations with Irish nationalism. As a result, even without explicit nationalist commentary, the hibernicon gained the potential to signify a nationalist message supporting the triumph of the Celts over the Anglo-Saxons.

Emerging in the 1840s, Young Ireland, a group started by young Irish, mostly Protestant, intellectuals, advocated a romantic view of Irish nationalism that "was concerned with the claims of a proud nation to its own identity."[85] Young Ireland initially supported Catholic nationalist leader Daniel O'Connell and the Repealer movement, which advocated repeal of the Act of Union. However, the groups broke over Young Ireland's commitment to using violence to achieve independence. The Young Irelanders' romantic vision influenced the rhetoric of Irish nationalism for the rest of the century and made nationalism a fitting complement to the hibernicon.

Although not the first to make the connection between Irish landscape and nationality, the Young Irelanders supported the notion that the land belonged to the Celts and that this historical belonging constituted a central piece of their collective identity. Through their publications and speeches, the Young Ireland rebels linked traveling through the landscape with the Celtic past and emphasized the importance of a historical consciousness in Irish nationalism. Highlighting the importance of knowing local Celtic names for places, as opposed to the Anglo-Saxon ones, Young Irelander Thomas Davis remarked on the importance of the Celtic poor's history filled with "those names and stories which people the hills and tombs and ruins of his neighborhood with heroes, victims, fairies, kings, and ghosts."[86] Young Irelanders encouraged people to connect with their past and showed preference for walking tours over books. Like O'Connell and the Repealers, they framed the battle between the Celts and the Anglo-Saxons as timeless.[87]

Repeatedly invoked by many nationalist leaders for the rest of the century, "[t]he invented, manipulated geography of the West portrayed the
unspoilt beauty of landscapes, where the influences of modernity were
at their weakest and which evoked the mystic unity of Ireland prior to
the chaos of conquest."[88] In these ways, the same visual imagery that
in some contexts supported colonial ideologies became resituated in
support of Irish nationalism. The use of historical images, landscape
scenes, the evocation of timelessness, and even the choice of the journey
itself tied to Young Ireland's sense of national identity. As discussed
before, the first Irish moving panoramas established a close connection with Young Ireland nationalism through their inclusion of Young
Ireland rebel imagery and the exchanges about Young Ireland rebel
escapes during performances.

Irish-American nationalism remained a vital context for the hibernicon as other segments of the movement appropriated Young Ireland's
rhetoric. After the Young Irelanders' failed uprising, many Irish Americans continued to back the revolutionary arm of the movement, which
led to the 1858 establishment of the Fenians in New York. Intended
as the U.S. wing of the new Irish Republican Brotherhood, the organization quickly became popular in Irish-American communities and
among Irish soldiers during the U.S. Civil War. It also organized groups
in Ireland. The Catholic Church opposed the Fenians for most of their
existence, which placed many religious Irish-American nationalists in
a difficult position. Founded in 1867 as a secret society by disenchanted
New York Fenians after a series of embarrassing Fenian failures, the
Clan na Gael pledged to fight for "the complete and absolute independence of Ireland by the overthrow of English domination by means of
physical force."[89] For the Irish-American community, nationalism remained a lingering concern, especially for the working class. The working class comprised the membership of the Clan na Gael, which saw its
numbers grow throughout the 1870s.[90]

At the end of the 1870s, however, the Catholic Church and middle-
and upper-class Irish Americans found a more respectable segment of
the Irish-American nationalist movement that did not conflict with
their morals. In 1879, a series of crop harvests failed, and western Irish
tenants organized to protest landlords' rents. Nationalist Michael Davitt

organized this protest into the Land League, which raised money for Irish relief, demanded an end to evictions, and called for widespread land reform that would redistribute land from landowners to tenants. The League elected Charles Stewart Parnell its leader. The U.S. affiliate, the Irish National Land League of America, became the first mass Irish-American nationalist movement with over fifteen hundred local branches and two hundred thousand members. During the Land War (1879–1882), the Irish tried to convince the British government to end the landlord system through primarily nonviolent forms of resistance. With the passage of the Land Act (1882), the British addressed the Irish peasantry's major grievances and the concerns of many Irish-American nationalists shifted toward Home Rule, which helped revive the parliamentary nationalist tradition. The Catholic Church supported its Irish worshippers by backing this nonviolent movement attempting to work with the British. Led by Parnell, the Home Rule movement focused on establishing an independent government for Ireland within the British Empire instead of an independent Irish republic. This focus exacerbated divisions within the Irish-American nationalist movement. Some Irish-American nationalists wanted to continue to prioritize further land and social reforms. Whether through politics or violence, other nationalists wanted the establishment of an Irish republic.[91]

Hibernicon companies played a tricky balancing act with their audiences. Regardless of its appeal for many Irish Americans, the Irish-American nationalism could alienate native Americans, aspiring middle-class Irish Americans, and the Irish who were indifferent to Ireland's plight, complicating any inclusion of nationalism in the show. The continuing tension between the Catholic Church and the Irish-American nationalist movement also created a potential problem for hibernicon companies who courted Catholic support.[92]

However, the Irish-American working class's enthusiasm for the nationalist movement provided hibernicon companies with a strong financial incentive to include nationalist ideology. Support for Irish-American nationalism remained strong throughout the century among the Irish-born working class, who became the main financial contributors to Irish-American nationalist causes. A nationalist leader once remarked that "the dollars of those who though they can least afford it are ever

the readiest to give support and sustenance to the Irish Cause."[93] One
newspaper commented that the Fenian Sisterhood brought "$4,000 into
the treasury," which caused "lamentations over the robbery of the poor
Irish servant girls."[94] A *New York Times* writer explained, "The money
that has kept the Land League together has come mostly from the day
laborers and servant maids of America."[95]

   The importance of Irish-American nationalism in working-class life
helps explain the hibernicon's continued popularity and the national
resonance of its imagery. Feelings of exile and nationalist memories
remained present within the Irish-American community, even as emigrants aged and had American children. New immigrants continually
brought reminders of the wrongs still committed at home, but experiences in Irish-American culture also helped perpetuate these feelings
for years. According to Kerby Miller, "many of the letters written in the
1870s and 1880s expressed burning hatreds of landlordism and English
rule directly traceable" to the Great Famine.[96] Irish Americans' mental
picture also relied on the turbulent decades of the late nineteenth century. As Miller discusses, post-Famine Irish Americans "were the most
effectively politicized, Catholicized, and nationalized in history: heirs
not only transmitted Famine memories but also of Fenianism, of the
Land War, of the mass mobilizations of the Irish National and United
Irish leagues, and of the pervasive, multifaceted Irish-Ireland movement."[97] Miller quotes one emigrant who observed that "those enthusiastic Irish youths . . . seem to live, move, and have their being in the
memories of Sarsfield, Emmet, Fitzgerald, [and] Tone.'"[98] Memories of
home contributed greatly to sustaining this nationalist consciousness,
but the hibernicon also played a role in keeping nationalism and its
symbols present in Irish-American lives.

   The hibernicon was not the only popular entertainment to examine
nationalist themes. In his study of nineteenth-century New York Irish
performance, Rohs writes that "the national culture of Ireland was musical, and that performances of Irish culture furnished a link to the
past—a crucial element of nationalist thought."[99] He discusses songs
like "Bold Soldier Boy" and performances of Dion Boucicault's *Colleen
Bawn* and Edward Harrigan's *Mulligan Guard Ball.* In William H. A.
Williams's analysis of sheet music, he finds only 16 percent of songs

spoke to Irish nationalism during the 1860s and 1870s, and he specu-
lates that publishers were wary of narrowing their audience through
such a targeted product. The songs published tended toward "vague,
overblown romanticism."[100] The hibernicon reflected both of the core
elements highlighted by Rohs and Williams. It traded on romantic and
historical themes, especially in its music. However, the hibernicon was
distinct in *how* it used mobility in support of nationalism.

Performing Nationalist Historiography Through Mobility

As a performance that transformed the popular fascination with travel,
the hibernicon had the potential to support various ideological stand-
points. However, the imagined and frequently unpredictable movement between the hibernicon's geographical sites, historical scenes,
and contemporary moments created the show's dramaturgy of mobility. In contesting the panorama's narrative borders, the dramaturgy
functioned as an unpredictable historiography suggesting a multiplicity
of Irish histories, especially in the shows produced and performed by
Irish migrants and Irish Americans. The performances' use of Irish
nationalism destabilized colonial narratives, but their incorporation
of violent and nonviolent nationalist traditions refused to suggest only
one way forward toward Irish independence. Through the lecturer,
songs, and sketches, the performers' bodies in action created abrupt
moments of disjunction from the visual narratives. These embodied
moments propose Irish histories in conflict and a continuing struggle for
Ireland.

In her discussion of Henry Box Brown's *Mirror of Slavery*, Brooks analyzes the potential of the moving panorama form to resist dominant histories. She explains, "The form of the panorama alone then manifests
an unbridled spirit that provides for the possibility of transgressing fixed
and constrictive representational boundaries. . . . [T]he panorama contests narrative borders."[101] If, as Brooks argues, it is possible for performers to trouble the moving panorama's conventions, participating in a
"radical unframing of the genre," then each hibernicon moment with
a jarring juxtaposition of images or in which lecturers and comedians
discuss events, conflicts, and realities beyond the standard framing of

the landscape painting and British travel literature "offer[s] a critical point of possibility."[102] This critical point of possibility depends on how the hibernicon's mobility engages with print culture, the lexicon surrounding Ireland, and embodied histories. Scholar Della Pollock theorizes anthropologist Allen Feldman's conceptualization of historicity for performance. Pollock writes:

> Allen Feldman characterizes the difference between history and historicity as a tension between two temporal planes: the atemporal plane of legitimation and domination or "myth," and the more ephemeral plane of agency and action. For Feldman, "sites of legitimation and authorization suppress historicity through linear, teleological, eschatological, or progressive temporalities. Action, however, unfolds time as difference and radical heterogeneity." In historicity, the body practices history. It incarnates, mediates, and resists the metahistories with which it is impressed. It wrestles with the totalizing and legitimizing power of such historical tropes as *telos* and progress. The body in action makes history answer to the contingencies and particularities, or what Feldman calls the "radical heterogeneity," of everyday life. It performs its difference *in* and *from* history and so articulates history *as* difference.[103]

In its transformation of travel narratives into action, into performance, the hibernicon provided an opportunity to generate "history *as* difference" through its mobility.[104] In the process, the hibernicon had the potential to undercut dominant histories through its historicity.

Irish migrant and Irish-American producers, managers, and performers ask audiences to imagine traveling with the performers through Ireland. The bodies of the performers *and* audiences hold the potential to mediate and resist the histories perpetuated by the adapted elements of print culture and stereotyped stage conventions. As Pollock notes, "Historicity is, in effect, where history works itself out, in and through and sometimes against its material subjects. It is where concrete practices not only 'embody and perform differences' but also contest claims for material agency. From the perspective of historicity, history is never total: it produces contradictions and tensions that it must, in turn, continually work to overcome."[105] Through practices of difference performed through the hibernicon, the performances continue to work out historical and contemporary notions of Ireland onstage. This does not mean that the shows do not potentially reinforce stereotyped, clichéd, and romanticized images, but it does mean that these moments are performed alongside others that call into question their dominance as "the" history of Ireland.

The hibernicon's structure and fractured narrative is predicated on its mobility and action, literal and imagined. Describing how one production moved across space and time demonstrates the ways the hibernicon's imaginary journey destabilized any continuous and consistently logical travel narrative. In *MacEvoy's New Hibernicon*, after arriving in Dublin from New York, the tourists and the audience move through a sequence of contemporary views of Dublin architecture. Next, the scene jumps to images tied to "Grattan, Flood, and Plunkett," which implies a jump back through time to the turn of the nineteenth century. The show returns to the present for an "Illuminated View of St. Patrick's Cathedral" before traveling over a thousand years in the past to portray "Illuminated Scenes in the Life of St. Patrick." Then, back in the present, the Tourist hires Barney, who introduces himself.[106] Each segment progresses similarly, moving through a specific geographical region and exploring a range of events, figures, and political positions from Irish history. Reinforcing the unpredictability of the show's imagined travel, companies changed songs and sketches frequently, and others even altered how they featured the panorama. For example, companies in town for several days or weeks often did nights focusing specifically on one area of the country to encourage audiences to attend more than one performance. Unlike travel literature, this tendency meant each hibernicon performance could provide audiences with a distinct imagined trip.

Hibernicon companies run by and featuring Irish immigrants and Irish Americans, such as John and Charles MacEvoy, Gavin and Ryan, and McGill and Strong, utilized their shows' dramaturgies toward more radical, nationalist ends.[107] An independent Ireland is not presented as a predictable, definitive end but as a goal in need of continued struggle to achieve. This openness creates a narrative messiness, even as the characters' journey ends with the show's conclusion. It is not surprising that managers and performers with more recent ties to

Ireland offered a more critical perspective on Anglo-Saxon colonial narratives. The companies' and lecturers' connections to Ireland transformed the lecturer from the supposedly objective counterpart of the British traveler to a witness of Ireland and its struggles. In *Performing History*, Freddie Rokem theorizes that the performer has the capacity "to be transformed into . . . a hyper-historian, functioning as a witness of the events vis-a-vis the spectators."[108] These performers broke the panorama's narrative framing and pointed to struggles outside the performance's picturesque framing. In the process, through their witnessing, they legitimized alternate histories of Ireland that contrasted with the picturesque imagery onstage.

In his lectures, John MacEvoy, an Irish migrant, described the struggles he witnessed in Ireland as well as passed on stories supposedly from family or friends. The *New York Evening Post* observed:

> MacEvoy *pere* explains those paintings in an intensely Hibernian lecture, much of which is intelligible only to recent [unclear] from "County Tip" or other portions of the downtrodden isle. MacEvoy *pere* is so thoroughly permeated with the wrongs of his country, that his patriotism is constantly exuding, as it were, from him, and finding expression in belligerent phrases or in disquisitions on Ireland's past and future glory. [The] reminiscences of "me residence in Dublin" add a unique charm to the professor's extremely national remarks.[109]

In his lecture, MacEvoy incorporated his own personal experiences of Ireland's struggles not depicted in the picturesque paintings. The writer's perception of MacEvoy's details as only being perceptible by Irish migrants or Irish Americans suggests MacEvoy went beyond general nationalist platitudes of injustice. With the lecturer shaping the narrative and interpreting the moving panorama images scrolling by, his position of authority as a witness validates the alternate histories that he points toward beyond the frame of the panorama paintings. The writer also suggests that Irish and Irish-American audience members had a different experience than did Anglo Protestants and other groups. Even the acknowledgement of not knowing for Anglo Protestants — the creation of a space in which there is an absence of information about

Ireland as opposed to a master narrative—starts to break down any totalizing technologies inherent in moving panorama performances. The contrast drawn as the productions move between the mostly picturesque paintings and the stories about the real Ireland as remembered by the lecturers undermines the creation of a progressive, cohesive Irish history. It raises the question of whether the show is illustrating the full story.

Listening to the lecture also allowed audience members to witness the lecturer's testimony, transforming the performances from a passive experience into an experience of active verification. One audience member observed how the lecturer's testimony held the potential to inspire more active audience participation: "MacEvoy was an Irishman, and he was talking about Ireland. He spoke with lively disrespect of her oppressors; said that justice had not been done to her; and intimated a hope for better days; whereupon a loud-voiced Irishman in the pit vociferated 'Amen.'"[110] Reports of the family's performances as late as 1879 suggest that other members of the family often expressed patriotic sentiments on stage as well. During one Long Island performance, "The exercises opened with an article upon the warm affection and true patriotism of the Irish race read by Miss MacEvoy in a clear voice and an expressive style."[111] Summing up his experience at the *MacEvoy's Hibernicon*, another reviewer commented that the performance "is calculated to arouse the admiration and secure the attendance of every wearer of the green and hater of the red in New-York. N.B.—No English need apply."[112]

As the originating company, *MacEvoy's Hibernicon* set the standard for how hibernicon companies used the lecturer's comments as part of the shows' structure. Their performances brushed up against the imagined journey through picturesque Ireland and highlighted histories of difference. James A. Gavin and J. H. Ryan, Irish migrants from Dublin, made explicit how they viewed their panorama and its connection to Irish nationalism. In comments published in the production's songster, they claim that they run their hibernicon to help stir up support for Irish rebellion, which contrasts with the relatively standard landscape and historical scenes depicted in their panorama:

We place Ireland on the stage in its true colors and really characteristi-
cally, viz:—pure, simple, moral, social, combined with sorrow, misfortune, trouble, and down-trodden, as she is by an alien government. We
exhibit her as though the last chord of her harp had been torn from its
place; and again we place her, if so, before the world as a nation though
down-trodden, glorious; though in sorrow, proud, as it were, looking towards the utmost ends of the earth to see her bereaved children in exile
come to her aid. . . . They hear and rise! And to promote their rising in
her holy cause, we have, though in a very limited manner, sought to put
her present blighted condition, condensed within the space of a few yards
of canvass, and only indeed pictured before the public.[113]

From the program and lecture included in their production's songster,
it is unclear how the company's paintings significantly departed from
other hibernicon productions. Yet, this framing of British oppression
and Irish hardship draws the audience's attention to Ireland's colonial
situation and highlights how the picturesque images do not tell the full
story.

Aside from breaking the unified frame by pointing to Irish struggles,
the content of the lectures and scenes further supported nationalist lean-
ings and undercut Anglo-Saxon colonial overtones. The productions
journeyed between histories of more current events and struggles as
well as mythical romantic Irish visuals and sentiments. The shows work
against direct cause and effect and progressive storytelling as well as
disrupt the standard "beaten path" from British travel literature about
Ireland. At the same time, the dramaturgy of mobility unites these
disparate moments into a common Celtic history. While in Dublin,
MacEvoy's lecturer tells anecdotes about Saint Oliver Plunkett, who
was tried for treason and executed by the English for promoting Catholicism. He also speaks of nationalist leaders Daniel O'Connell, who
led the Catholic Emancipation movement during the first half of the
nineteenth century, and Henry Grattan and Henry Flood, who led
the push for Irish legislative independence in the eighteenth century.
Gavin and Ryan's Emerald Isle and *McGill and Strong's Mirror of Ireland* also
celebrated Daniel O'Connell.[114] One of the most contemporary references to the fight for Irish independence occurred right after *McGill*

and *Strong's Mirror of Ireland* combined with *Howarth's Hibernica*. Their production included a painting of "Parnell, making his famous speech in favor of the land league, and boycotting, etc."[115] It is not surprising that for their contemporary depiction, the company chose to illustrate Parnell, who received widespread acceptance by Irish Americans and Anglo Americans as a result of his preference for a parliamentary as opposed to a violent resolution to Irish independence.

The performances situated the nonviolent Plunkett, O'Connell, Flood, and Parnell alongside violent revolutionaries like Robert Emmet. *MacEvoy's New Hibernicon* paid special attention to Robert Emmet and visualized "his Love and Death."[116] According to scholar Charles Fanning, "No other Irish historical figure had so powerful and lasting an effect on the consciousness of Irish America in the nineteenth century as Robert Emmet," who was executed by the English after he led a failed rebellion in 1803.[117] Emmet's "Speech from the Dock" appeared in American performance only three years after his death. Along with figures like O'Connell, Grattan, and Flood, Emmet became one way to evoke "the importance of oratory in the struggle for Irish freedom," which "was a constant theme at nationalist gatherings in the United States."[118] The hibernicon recalled Emmet's symbolic use in songs, plays, and contemporary nationalist movements. Even though these figures technically remained in the past, they also had a life of their own in the present, which made references potentially seem more personally relevant to audience members.[119]

Shows often framed this nationalist struggle as a battle between the Celts and Anglo-Saxons. In an 1868 recitation written specifically for *McGill and Strong's Mirror of Ireland* and performed in Scranton, Pennsylvania, John M. Burke, who played Barney, exclaimed, "And I long to meet those tyrant bands, Who would make the brave Celt kneel . . . To strike one blow at the Saxon foe, Which would make poor Erin free."[120] The song "The Brigade at Fontenoy" appeared in the songsters for multiple MacEvoy companies. Aside from speaking to a sense of global nationalism, it also aspired "To smite to-day the Saxons' might, to conquer or to die!"[121] The singer wished Anglo-Saxons "to flee, From the chivalry of Erin."[122] Other songs advocated for the more peaceful Home Rule movement, similarly framed within Irish racial language.

In the aptly titled "I Hope They Will Win," the singer describes how "The Irish race fought nobly for our dear country's sake. . . . Here's success to Home Rule, and since tyranny's a sin, May the noble sons of Erin their liberty soon win."[123] Framing the performance through a timeless Celtic battle against the Anglo-Saxons enabled the show's dramaturgy to construct Celtic racial identities as opposed to erasing them.

Hibernicon companies also performed songs alongside the panorama that may or may not have supported the displayed painting. All hibernicon companies performed generic Irish nationalist songs and songs from Thomas More celebrating Ireland. Most productions performed songs that championed Ireland's natural beauty and rooted the land in a Celtic past. "Dear Land" in *Frank MacEvoy's New Hibernicon* songster exemplifies this type of romantic nationalism and demonstrates how productions' music reinforced its visual imagery. For the song's narrator, gazing on the Irish landscape reminds him of Ireland's political struggles. He recounts how "When I behold your mountains bold, / Your noble lakes and streams, / A mingled tide of grief and pride / Within my bosom teems. / I think of all, your long dark thrall / Your martyrs brave and true."[124] Later in the song, the strongest evocation of hatred for Britain still is minor and cloaked in romantic and vague language. The narrator remembers, "Ere Norman foot had dare pollute / Her independent shore. / Of chief's [*sic*], long dead, who rose to head / Some gallant patriots few, / Till my aim on earth became / To strike one blow for you."[125] Songs like these reinforced romantic, Celtic nationalism as the lens through which to view the journey throughout Ireland.

The companies led by Irish migrants also performed more pointed nationalist songs that center the Irish's fight against the Anglo-Saxons. Multiple songs discuss and champion nationalist leaders, including "A Toast to the Sons of Ireland." "A Toast" not only recalls Emmet and O'Connell, it also celebrates the more recent, violent nationalist heroes of Young Ireland and the Fenians. Discussing "our own day," the song praises "Jim Stephens, our patriot so great, / Who baffled England's devils, boys, in dreary Forty-Eight. . . . Hurrah for gallant Stephens, and the Fenians of the day."[126] In "Invitation to the Hibernicon," John MacEvoy asks his Irish audience members to remember heroic Irishmen and reminds them of Ireland's continued oppression:

Come, soldiers of Sarsfield, and see it portrayed — / No country for valor and beauty surpasses. . . . Men of Wexford, your sires won honor and glory; / Still stained with their blood are Bullring and Gorey; / Sons of Redmond, Walsh, Sinnot, Roche, Grogan and Power, / Your fathers fell fighting by Fitzstephen's Tower, / That stands a proud records by Slaney's soft waves, / To mark where they sleep in their patriot graves. / Come, look on these scenes, their sad history scan, / Scenes dear to the heart of the true Irishman. . . . / There's the house where the thunder of Grattan was heard. . . . / Your generous hearts will be moved when you see / The land of the brave, but, oh, not of the free.[127]

Through the song, MacEvoy creates a genealogy of oppression and valiant Irish fighters, a history that jars in its contrast to the mostly peaceful images. The song also aligns this narrative with the imagined journey on which the audience is about to embark, emphasizing the lack of freedom and sense of Celtic ownership for the Irish people living in the country represented in the paintings.

Erin and the Brennans, starring Miles Morris, closely copied the MacEvoys' and Gavin and Ryan's approach to breaking the frame of the landscape panorama to reference Ireland's oppression. Morris performed songs like "Terrible Times," which described the current events in Ireland. The song outlines how "Oh these are the Terrible Times, If one's single why so you must tarry, For except a few fools that are mad, There's no one would venture to marry, For bacon is nine pence a pound, And sorrow much cheaper the meat is."[128] Later verses reference the unrest and fighting in Ireland, which the song ties to the failed potato crops and the conflicts between landlords and tenants over "Tenant Right."[129] "Paddy Burke" evokes the Fenians and characterizes America as "the land where Erin's Harp is free from British tread, Where every noble Fenian can go forth with warlike tread, And raise the noble banner, the Green above the Red, And freedom on Old Ireland will be dawning."[130] These speeches and songs all rupture the potential for a linear narrative by presenting the possibility that the peaceful Irish landscape represented by the panorama might burst into violence at any moment. They demonstrate through their embodiment in front of the paintings a stark contrast that opens up multiple Irish histories.

In their variety sketches, Barney the Guide and his love Nora demonstrate the ways that the depictions of the Irish people embodied on stage
informed the performances' dramaturgy. The hibernicon shifted the
conventions of British travel literature by providing the audience with
an "inside view" of Barney and Nora's life, when the Tourist is not present. In these instances, Barney and Nora perform scenes on their own
or with friends and family only witnessed by the audience. By including
some "backstage" moments, in which the audience sees Barney and
Nora not performing for the Tourist, it gives the illusion that the audience, not the Tourist, is positioned for the truest view. These moments
provided a double-edged sword for the Irish in America.

In most cases, the access given to audience members simply reinforced stage Irish stereotypes and standard racial humor. Jerry Cohan
managed hibernicon companies and performed as Barney on and off
for the first few decades of his career. His repertoire book contains the
only remaining hibernicon sketches. They depict fairly standard Irish
racial variety comedy misunderstandings and conventions. Comic business and one-liners between the Tourist and Barney ensue over issues of
his employment, including exchanges over whether Barney drinks and
how much he should be paid. At the beginning of one scene, Barney
asks the Tourist's permission to say goodbye to his love Nora before
they leave to see Ireland's sights. When he goes to Nora's home, he faces
the opposition of Nora's mother, who wants Nora to marry a rich man
instead of Barney. Barney convinces the mother to give her consent
by complimenting her, but after a series of comic mishaps, the mother
once again refuses to let Barney marry her daughter. The sequence ends
with Barney and Nora declaring that they will find a way to marry. The
comedic scene would not be out of the ordinary in any variety house
in America.[131]

However, companies run by Irish emigrants and Irish Americans
took advantage of these brief moments on stage to complicate these
stereotypes. Showing the private struggles of many Irish and offering an
alternative narrative for Irish men like Barney, hibernicon companies
commonly performed a sketch between Barney and the recruiting of-
ficer for the Eighty-Eighth, an Irish regiment in the British army. Like
other variety performers, hibernicon companies shared, sold, or stole

sketches and multiple companies performed this sketch. For *MacEvoy's New Hibernicon*, the sketch depicted "Barney at the Races, meet[ing] a Recruiting Sergeant, who persuades him to enlist in the 88th or Connaught Rangers." In a following scene, the audience sees Barney go to war for the British and his parting from Nora.[132] In Jerry Cohan's sketches, after embarking on their journey around Ireland, in scene 3, the Tourist explains to the audience, "Barney our car driver fell in with a country sergeant who got him tipsy and induced him to enlist as a soldier. Nora who by the way has been engaged as waiting maid to the ladies is nearly heart broken."[133] Although Cohan notes the Tourist's comment is followed by a "soldier song," the exact song performed in Cohan's performances remains unclear.

Charles MacEvoy's Hibernicon provides some insight into how this common hibernicon sketch may have been performed. Its heroine, spelled Norah, sang a song entitled, "Barney I Hardly Knew Ye," slightly adapted from the famous Irish antiwar song, "Johnny I Hardly Knew Ye," first published in 1867. The humorous song mocks sentimental ballads, with soldiers happily returning home from war. Although humorous, the scene conveys the personal heartbreak caused by Barney's recruitment, the gruesome horrors of war, and how it impacts the Irish. The song is a lament by Norah about how war has changed Barney. The consequences that she lists are devastating. Norah sings, "Where is your nose, ye pitiful crow, ahoo! / Ye had it when going to scatter the foe; / The loss of it has disfigured ye so." She then talks about how he lost his legs: "Where are the legs wid which ye run, ahoo! / When first ye went to shoulder a gun; / I fear your dancing days are done." She describes how Barney has lost the twinkle in his eye and how "Wid drums and guns, and guns and drums, The enemy fairly slew ye; My darling dear, ye look so queer — Och! Barney I hardly knew ye." Even though she declares him an "object of woe," Norah still pledges to stand by Barney's side. This moment connects the wrongs caused by British colonization presented as part of Ireland's past with Ireland's present.[134]

Although how Barney and Nora's mobility constructs their race and gender is not the focus of this chapter, the song illustrates how "the gendered and racialized body is marked by a lessened ability to move and by its belonging to particular spaces."[135] Barney has the privilege of movement, which in part defines his masculinity. He travels around Ireland with the Tourist. In this song, he goes abroad for military service. No evidence shows that Barney appeared permanently injured on the stage, but the song states a violent consequence to his mobility when tied to British colonialism. In contrast, Nora remains mostly tied to her cottage and Ireland. Although mobility and immobility, like gender, is on a spectrum as opposed to a binary, her immobility often defines her as she is repeatedly left behind. In some productions, Nora joins Barney on his travels, but in the bulk of my research, her scenes occur at home and nothing suggests she ever leaves the country. The association between Nora and immobility may result in part from conceptualizations of Ireland and its landscape as feminine, which in colonial discourse seemingly justified its domination. Irish nationalists appropriated this language, and it later became ingrained in nationalist symbolism and cultural movements. A comic character, Nora remains marked by poor Irish racial comedy conventions, but the connection opens the possibility that Nora remains tied to Ireland, in part, because her femininity is rooted in an essentialized idea of the Irish nation.[136] By illustrating the material consequences of Britain's presence on the mobile bodies of Irish men and lives of the women they left behind, the song contrasts with the colonial narratives of Ireland as a land of opportunity for British expansion.

The importance of Irish migrant and Irish Americans' presence in these performances should not be underestimated. Companies without close Irish ties, such as later iterations of *Howarth's Hibernica*, tended to present more straightforward narratives, even though their productions' dramaturgy remained fragmented. The disruption created through the hibernicon's dramaturgies did not obliterate British colonial narratives; instead, in Irish migrant and Irish-American performances it demonstrated a multitude of histories that held radical potential. It encouraged questioning, highlighted gaps in romanticized histories, and presented multiple Irish narratives through how it moved through its scenes, songs, and sketches. At the same time, it reinforced associations with Irish-American nationalism rooted in landscape, Irish history, and the Celtic race. In the process, the performance created the potential to construct Irish belonging for Irish and Irish Americans, even if the audience never saw the real Ireland in person.

The Legacy of the Hibernicon

This chapter has argued for the ways the hibernicon complicates theories of moving panoramas as technologies of ideology through how its mobility operated onstage. Pushing against rhetoric framing popular Irish representation as inherently damaging to the Irish-American community, the hibernicon illustrates how Irish migrant managers and performers mobilized entertainment for nationalist purposes. The hibernicon's impact went beyond the content of its productions. Hibernicon comics are a generation of forgotten Irish and Irish-American performers that gained fame and success, at least on a local level. The companies provided an important training ground for turn-of-the-century vaudeville and musical comedy stars. They supported and sustained many Irish male comics, such as Bryan O'Lynn, J. H. Ryan, and John Burke, many who were Irish immigrants or their descendants. For decades, performers moved from company to company or started their own. They bragged about their connection to multiple hibernicon companies in their advertisements, demonstrating how performers built entire careers through hibernicon entertainments.[137]

Even after Jerry and Nellie Cohan, George M. Cohan's parents, achieved national stardom with their family in vaudeville, audiences still remembered their time performing with the hibernicon. They performed on and off with hibernicon companies for twenty years "in almost every city, town and village in the United States."[138] Some scholars even claim George first appeared on stage during *The Two Dans,* a hibernicon sketch.[139] Regardless of whether the anecdote is true, much of Cohan's introduction to popular performance occurred through the hibernicon. Robert Grau, theatre impresario and manager, remembers, "George M. Cohan was a violin prodigy at the age of five, and his nimble feet first availed him a few years later in a hibernicon entertainment which his father, Jerry Cohan, toured with in the early 1880s."[140]

The Cohan family's hibernicon performances inspired other important twentieth-century theatrical figures to join the theatre. Before relating anecdotes about his time working with James O'Neill, George Bernard Shaw, the Irish Players, and a wide range of American and European stage stars, prolific American theatre producer and manager George C. Tyler reminisced about how he fell in love with the theatre:

> My first theatrical entertainment—witnessed when I was a good deal less than knee-high was Jerry and Helen Cohan . . . in Haworth's [*sic*] Hibernica—a program that consisted largely of the Cohans and a panorama background on hand-cranked rollers. A few seconds earnest twisting of the crank brought about a miraculously quick change of scene from the Giant's Causeway to the Streets of Dublin to Lakes of Killarney and so forth through the whole gamut of Irish scenery—and the Cohans did something gloriously exciting in front of each scene: a song and dance, or a jig, or a reel, or a sentimental ballad perhaps . . . and their show was out and away the most magnificent thing I'd ever seen.[141]

In addition to the next generation of artists and producers, the hibernicon also influenced how prominent aspects of the Irish-American community viewed theatrical performance. The next chapter considers the meanings generated by the hibernicon's mobility offstage. Focusing on partnerships with the Catholic Church, the subsequent discussion moves the analysis from representational to the interactive practices that linked the hibernicon's mobility to Irish-American Catholic belonging.

CHAPTER FOUR

Networking Community

Variety Touring and
the Irish Catholic Church

I N 1884, Father Larkin from New York's Catholic Church of Holy Innocents spoke against Dion Boucicault's *The Shaughraun* for its depiction of priests, wakes, and the Irish. In a speech reprinted by newspapers around the country, Larkin denounced *The Shaughraun* as "a disgrace to the Irish race. It pretends that the Irish priests are so depraved that they don't know the difference between whisky and the milk in their tea. In the wake he presents the Irish dancing."[1] Condemning popular Irish and Irish-American performers and writers across the board, he declared, "The anathemas of the church should fall upon Boucicault and his place. No church member in good standing will go to see it; and those men, Harrigan and Hart, are of the same sort, and all of their plays tend to degrade the Irish. Don't go near them. All they care about the Irish is for the Irishman's dollar."[2] In the eyes of Larkin and like-minded Catholic priests, the theatre went against the sober morals upheld by the church and painted Catholicism as uncivilized and irreligious. They viewed many Irish and Irish-American performers as willing to abandon their communities' interests in the pursuit of profit. In spite of Larkin's failure to impact *The Shaughraun*'s success, attacks on the theatre profited churches financially as they rallied Catholic congregations around their leaders in defense of religion and nation. As Father John Talbot Smith noted, in the late nineteenth century, "if one wished to arouse vivacity in the Catholic turtle asleep on the American beach, one poked him with a long stick called theatre. . . . [T]he theatre was the ante-room of Hades."[3]

In spite of the outspoken, anti-theatrical Catholic Church leadership, in the 1860s and 1870s, popular performance started to make inroads into the Catholic Church. As a result of the expansion of variety touring, the hibernicon started to break down the Catholic Church's staunch opposition to the professional theatre on a local level. This chapter examines in depth the hibernicon's relationship to the Church. On rare occasions, companies raised money for organizations such as the Ancient Order of Hibernians, but as a result of their unusualness, these interactions fall outside the parameters of this study. This chapter expands the concept of dramaturgies of mobility to performances offstage. It investigates how the repeated performative practice of visits to Catholic parishes during the hibernicon tours generated meanings tied to Irish-American community and belonging. Drawing on actor-network theory and its critiques, I argue that these dramaturgies became one way in which popular entertainment constructed and perpetuated a sense of Irish-American Catholic community.

Performance scholar Christopher Balme claims, "the itinerant theatre is by definition primarily commercial in orientation, and not motivated by the imperatives of art, community or nation."[4] Hibernicon companies' touring strategies complicate this frequently repeated assertion about popular entertainment and extend previous studies of theatrical networks in the nineteenth century. Tracing the hibernicon companies' tours illustrates how commercial itinerant theatre held the potential to function in commercial *and* community interests. Hibernicon companies established temporary partnerships with local Catholic parishes as part of new strategies for marketing and survival as well as, in some cases, dedication to the Irish Catholic community. Directly rejecting Church policies and, in some cases, formal rebukes, parish priests searched for new methods of fundraising and saw an opportunity to address their parishes' challenges through the touring hibernicon companies. The existence of these interactions along hibernicon touring networks revises the historiography of antitheatricalism, Catholicism, and the professional theatre at the end of the nineteenth century.

The hibernicon's interactions with the Catholic Church also represented an experimental approach to expanding the variety audience. Catholicism played a fundamental role in Celtic racial identity, and this intersection contributed to the intensity of anti-Irish sentiment in the nineteenth century. Middle-class Irish Americans, however, viewed the church as one respectable expression of their racial identity. In addition, the Church existed as one of the few spaces outside the home that welcomed Irish and Irish-American women. Through their fundraising, the companies entered a Church space often led and organized by women. The hibernicon not only created a more respectable entertainment to draw more middle-class and female audiences to the theatre, but they also directly went to the spaces occupied by the new markets targeted by first-class variety companies. Through the dramaturgies that established their association with the Catholic Church, the hibernicon also attempted to appropriate the Church's respectability by association.

Variety Touring After the Civil War

Although companies benefited from transportation improvements before the Civil War, the railroad's rapid expansion in the 1860s increasingly eased touring companies' travel and made it more cost effective. The first transatlantic railroad line's 1869 opening finally made it practical for companies to travel from coast to coast by land instead of by ship. Although variety started expanding beyond New York and Philadelphia before, after the war, variety appeared along the transportation lines, especially in commercial centers with large laborer populations, and started to expand into the South and Midwest. When touring, variety companies had to create shows that appealed to communities across the country and could not necessarily depend on acts or sketches reliant on local references or audience familiarity with the performers. Depending on the town, companies had to be prepared to appeal to male working-class audiences as well as audiences across class and gender lines. The increasing number of companies performing more respectable variety opened the door to these audiences.[5]

By the 1870s, circuits developed across the country, offering opportunities for companies to stay several weeks in different regions. These circuits did not resemble the later vaudeville circuits and took several forms. As Gillian M. Rodger discusses, "In some cases, these circuits represented a number of managers working cooperatively in order to attract the best possible entertainments to their region or state, but in other cases one or two powerful managers with interests in several theatres were instrumental in forming the circuit."[6] These small circuits included one run in the South by Spalding and Bidwell and another by variety manager William E. Sinn in Baltimore and Brooklyn.[7] These circuits provided opportunities, but they did not dominate variety touring or restrict where a company could perform. For example, some poor variety companies moved from town to town performing in whatever open venues they could find, including town halls, schoolhouses, and courthouses.[8] The emergence of theatrical agents further enabled a more organized and efficient touring system. In the absence of dominant major circuits, agents became critical components in how touring worked after the Civil War.

By the 1870s, theatrical agents became the touring system's essential middlemen. The growth of combination and touring companies and the rising number of theatres created an increasing need for managers to book talent and for companies to find venues. Theatrical agents stepped in to book and advertise companies' tours, "thus controlling the heart of the dramatic enterprise."[9] In his anecdotal travel guide of the St. Lawrence River, E. F. Babbage, Charles MacEvoy's agent in the 1870s, described the range of his duties. He "secure[d] all dates, la[id] out the routes, order[ed] all printing, and d[id] all of the business connected with the success of the entertainment. . . . [MacEvoy] follow[ed] in my track, pa[id] all bills contracted by me. . . . I didn't see them sometimes for six weeks."[10] The expanded role of theatrical agents made hibernicon companies' national touring networks possible.

The economic depression starting in 1873 decreased variety's momentum, especially in terms of variety stock companies' establishment and sustainment. Until the Panic, the largest number of touring variety companies tended to travel during the summer, when many closed their stock company theatres. The depression created a demand for touring variety as many regional managers in towns and smaller cities moved from stock variety companies to filling their bill with touring companies in order to survive the downturn. Touring companies increasingly bore the theatres' operating costs, further stressing their economic situation. The growth in hibernicon companies reflected the general increase in touring companies caused by these advances and shifts.[11]

The letters between Edward Harrigan and his wife Annie from the 1875–1876 theatre season provide a rare, personal view into variety touring's successes and challenges. After breaking from Josh Hart's Theatre Comique in 1875, Harrigan and Tony Hart started their own touring variety company. The depression's impact on audiences in factory and mining towns forms a narrative thread throughout the letters. Harrigan believed their appeal to Irish audiences helped them make a profit or at least break even in tough markers. In Scranton, Harrigan happily reported, "we pleased the natives very much. The citizens of the latter place are all Irish."[12] Yet, the economic devastation of the town struck Harrigan, who described how the "town here looks deserted all the workshops closed, over 500 dwelling houses unoccupied. If we get out of this place with expenses we are very lucky."[13] The company especially faced issues in towns with fewer male workers. He complained that Lawrence, Massachusetts, was "a bad one for Harrigan and Hart. It seems to me there are no men in this place. I have saw [sic] an army of girls coming from the mills where they work 10 hours a day. Oh they look wore out."[14] Even with rough business in New England, Harrigan reported that there still were "about 6 different [variety] shows traveling."[15]

In other instances, Harrigan and Hart's company emerged victorious over other variety companies, making a substantial profit that helped them survive their less successful stops. In December 1875, three variety touring troupes crossed paths in Columbus, Ohio: Harrigan and Hart's, James S. Maffitt's, and Charles Ravel's. Harrigan explained how the other shows "are not doing very well . . . they all look rather blue. . . . We done immense business in that town — You wouldn't believe the reputation we are making."[16] In one instance, Harrigan even comments on his company manager, Martin Hanley, taking members of the company to church. "Martin has just gone to church with the boys," he reports to Annie. "How is that for an advertisement. The Gallan[t] 69th singing Hymns, imagine that."[17] Harrigan, a Catholic, avoided references to Catholicism in his shows and does not seem to have cultivated any long-term relationship with parishes. In this instance, however, his letter recognizes the potential value in appealing to Catholic audiences. In the midst of audience challenges, Harrigan reports on rowdy teenage company members, performers accidently leaving costumes behind in New Jersey, and a lucky break when they escaped a fire with their lives and their property.[18] Workers' expendable income, town demographics, theatrical competition, and company dynamics all contributed to a company's success or failure. By partnering with the Catholic Church, hibernicon companies sought to temper the unpredictability of the road by building a lingering relationship with one segment of its audience, Irish-American Catholics.

Conceptualizing Theatrical Networks

Aside from a general understanding of its operations and discussions in Rodger's two studies on variety theatre, variety touring has received minimal scholarly attention. This chapter expands on Rodger's work by investigating how variety touring extended outside of theatre spaces and developed long-term relationships with a specific migrant, religious, and racial community. To examine the hibernicon's touring, I draw on actor-network theory (ANT) as theorized by Bruno Latour and its critiques. These ideas develop how mobility shapes ideas of community and becoming.

By its nature, ANT is "less a matter of precise definitions than one of an (allegedly) shared sense."[19] As a result, scholars have debated its meaning and utility. Incorporating human and nonhuman actors, its importance for this study rests on its insistence on the performance of networks and how they "become" through their interactions along the way. As performance studies scholar Leo Cabranes-Grant explains, "[f]or Latour, performance is not something that reflects or illustrates a social network—performance *is* the armature of the network itself. In his view, what we call 'the social' is never a given, but is constantly being worked out, remade. 'Society' is our shorthand for a performative *becoming* that accelerates, proliferates, or slows down according to how its actors realign their connections."[20] ANT prioritizes the interactions that bring the network into being. Along the network, anthropologist Christian Vium argues, "One cannot . . . pass through these intersections without becoming somehow transformed."[21] In these networks, as anthropologist Ilana Gershon states, "durability only exists because something is repeatedly performed in familiar patterned ways."[22]

Drawing on these theories centers the interactions between the hibernicon and the Catholic Church and questions how they brought a network into being. As opposed to assuming a connection, this chapter emphasizes the importance of these touring interactions in generating belonging and community. How might the notion of dramaturgies of mobility be extended beyond the stage to consider these repeated interactions along the hibernicon's touring routes and the meanings they generate for the Irish-American Catholic community? How did these interactions become spaces of transformation for parishes?

Critiques of ANT highlight its innovations in describing networks and introducing nonhuman actors as equal and viable agents, but they point to drawbacks as well, such as the theories' failure to prompt concrete explanations. For some ANT theorists, pushing beyond previous approaches to circulation involves avoiding these types of conclusions. One main critique provides a critical supplement to my analysis, however. Sociologist Tim Dant cautions against how ANT "downplay[s] . . . the particular capacities that the human component brings to the mobile-assemblage [created through interactions on the network]. This has two key dimensions: the intentionality that motivates the mobility and intentionality that directs it."[23] Sociocultural anthropologist Noel B. Salazar draws attention to similar missing factors that would provide a deeper understanding of how the networks function. He explains, "In order to understand how circulation works, we not only need to study what is circulating but also the socio-cultural structures and mechanisms that make that circulation possible or impossible."[24] As a result, this chapter not only explores how the network is formed by the interactions between the hibernicon and the Catholic Church, but also what motivated the network and made it possible. This approach reflects the analysis of dramaturgies of mobility in other chapters. Why the dramaturgies are produced, how, and for what audience shape their existence and meaning.

In its consideration of touring interactions in relation to a specific migrant, racial, and religious community, the chapter expands on performance scholar Christopher Balme's analysis of touring and of theatre entrepreneur Daniel E. Bandmann at the end of the century. Partnerships, as conceived by Balme, act as actor-network theory mediators that "transform, translate, distort, and modify the meaning or elements they are supposed to carry" within the network.[25] These partnerships "cast light on the social dynamics of touring theatre" and "were perhaps the most important mediators, connecting the peripatetic entrepreneur with the culture of the locale."[26] In Balme's analysis of Bandmann's international tours, business partnerships refer to how Bandmann leased and built new theatres along his tour route. Unlike "normal touring, where an artist or company would pass through a city with little long-term impact," Balme argues Bandmann's theatre partnerships were an attempt to develop more permanent connections.[27]

The hibernicon's partnerships with Catholic parishes functioned similarly. I argue, however, that hibernicon touring networks illustrate the necessity of expanding Balme's notion of partnerships beyond strictly business and theatre relationships and the establishment of theatre buildings. Revealing the way symbiotic relationships impacted the dynamics of touring, the hibernicon's interactions contributed to the Church's infrastructure and played a vital role in breaking down Catholic prejudices against the theatre, at least on a local level. Unlike Balme's conception of partnerships, for the hibernicon, they were not solely rooted in the business of theatre but also in loyalty to the Irish Catholic community and, for some, in a sense of religious duty. The history of the Catholic Church in relation to the theatre is critical to understanding why and how the hibernicon succeeded in creating these partnerships.

Theatre Historiography and the Catholic Church

The Catholic Church's denunciations of theatre, such as Larkin's, have long shaped the Catholic Church's historiography and nineteenth-century U.S. popular theatre. Most studies of the nineteenth-century stage and Christianity focus on the relationship between Protestants and theatre, especially the lingering impact of Puritan antitheatrical prejudices from the seventeenth century. When discussion of nineteenth-century theatre is not entirely omitted, scholars analyze the popularity of amateur performances within the Catholic Church, especially among the Jesuits, and some briefly address the amateur parish theatres that emerged at the turn of the twentieth century. The prevailing narrative is one of Catholic antitheatrical prejudice toward the professional theatre.[28]

The absence of scholarship and the prevalence of antitheatrical narratives reinforce an oppositional binary between Catholics and the nineteenth-century professional theatre. It places church and theatre in a narrative of conflict, one that, as theatre historian Odai Johnson analyzes, acts as a common trope in theatre history scholarship. As Johnson argues in his study of colonial American theatre, "the trouble with telling such tales of cannons and contests is exactly the fine tales they make. What they do not account for is the evidence of the support for the theatre."[29] The antitheatrical narrative's dominance leads to overlooking the nuanced perspectives and interactions of many Catholics and parishes.

Historians base antitheatrical narratives on the actions of the Catholic Church leadership. After the Civil War, national and local American Catholic councils repeatedly banned priests from attending the theatre and discouraged the laity's theatre attendance. Historians speculate that there existed several causes for the Church's antitheatrical position. Historian Frances Panchok suggests that American Catholic antitheatricalism may have resulted from the "vestigial remains of heretical Jansenism" that "influenced the spirituality of the American Church."[30] Catholic leaders worried about the direct moral impact of the theatrical experience on their parishioners, especially when theatres encouraged drinking and permitted prostitution. The Church also vocally opposed the rise of naturalism, a rising visual and performance aesthetic in the nineteenth century, with Pope Pius IX denouncing naturalism in 1864 and Pope Leo XIII reinforcing the Church's rejection in 1885. Catholic leaders feared that naturalism placed nature over the law of God or morals.[31]

As demonstrated by *The Shaughraun* denouncement, the Church also opposed the representation and caricaturing of Catholic figures, which reinforced the worst of anti-Catholic prejudices. Traveling with British settlers across the Atlantic, a long tradition of anti-Catholicism existed in the United States. Many colonies passed laws discriminating against Catholics before the Revolution, after which most anti-Catholic statutes were eliminated from state and federal law. Beginning in the antebellum period and continuing after the Civil War, the large Irish Catholic and German Catholic migrations heightened Catholicism's threat for many Anglo Protestants, and anti-Catholicism increasingly played a fundamental role in local and national politics. In the 1830s and 1840s, public anti-Catholicism violently emerged again, including the 1834 burning of an Ursuline convent in Massachusetts and riots in Philadelphia. Resulting in the Know-Nothing Party in the 1850s and the proliferation of anti-Catholic societies, anti-Catholic sentiment raised fears about how Catholics' loyalty to the pope and their "superstitious" religious traditions would subvert American democracy. Know-Nothingism linked nationalism with Anglo-Saxon supremacy and argued that the Republic depended on rational Anglo-Saxon Protestantism for success. These anti-Catholic arguments advocated preventing Catholics from attaining elected office to execute what the Know-Nothings viewed as the pope's plot to take over the United States. Through this rhetoric, anti-Catholicism became closely linked to anti-immigrant politics that argued for the migrants' inability to assimilate into U.S. culture. Although anti-Catholicism subsided to an extent in the 1860s and 1870s, it never disappeared: it became incorporated into the philosophy of the Ku Klux Klan founded in 1865. Tensions flared again in the 1880s over increased concerns about new Catholic migrants, who some Americans thought would bring social unrest from Europe.[32]

Within the Catholic community, anti-Catholic sentiment led to concerns about efforts to take away Catholic rights and about Catholics' physical safety. Irish communities viewed anti-Catholicism as a primary foundation for anti-Irish discrimination. With Celt often viewed as synonymous with Catholic, Irish-American newspapers did not reflect a "fear of their 'unwhiteness,'" but, as McMahon notes, "Irish editors felt challenged by the belief that the United States' laws, customs, and manners were the inheritance of a transnational Anglo-Saxon race."[33] As a result, anti-Catholic discrimination led to Catholic attempts to demonstrate migrants' dedication to America and their suitability for American democracy. It also reinforced a sense of solidarity within the U.S. Catholic community. As historian Jay Dolan discusses, "Bishop Hughes believed that the anti-Catholic and anti-Irish attitudes 'tended powerfully to unite Catholics.'"[34] This unity in the face of Anglo-Protestant prejudice further supported the central role played by the Church for many Irish migrants.

The life of theatrical entertainments beyond the stage threatened to keep anti-Catholic images circulating in the culture for years after the initial performance. Boucicault adamantly denied any anti-Catholicism within *The Shaughraun,* and its continued popularity encouraged managers to produce it through the end of the century. Songsters provided another way anti-Catholic images lingered. As a result, songs like "Who Would be a Nun?" (1870) could reach Catholic parishioners under the guise of entertainment. Comically sending up the restrictions placed on nuns, the lyrics complain about how "They musn't speak without consent, too early musn't rise. . . . Should one omit to clean her boots, Or trifles slight as these, She'll have to clean and scrub the floor, all day upon her knees."[35] The song then uses its critique to undercut the Catholic Church's theology and tradition in its last verse, which states that Catholic "customs are so strange, They take you by surprise, This may be called religion, But I can't see where it lies."[36] Considering the sexist depictions of women in other variety songs, the critique is less a defense of women than an effort to denigrate Catholic figures and mock Catholic religious beliefs.

For these reasons, American bishops began prohibiting theatre in 1866, even though the Vatican did not pass a canon law pertaining to theatre until the early twentieth century. In the autumn of that year, the Second Plenary Council of Baltimore banned priests from attending plays, shows, and dances. It also asked parishes to "prudently turn the faithful away from theatres, and plays, especially those which are known to be evil and full of danger."[37] Not wanting to violate Catholics' "evangelical liberty," the Council stated that churches should not completely forbid attending morally acceptable performances, but they did not indicate that much theatrical entertainment was worthy of Catholic patronage.[38] In 1882, the Fourth Synod of the Diocese of New York repeated the ban on priests' attendance at "public theatres, profane shows, horse races and other diversions of this kind even outside the boundaries of the diocese."[39] It emphasized the negative ramifications of the laity seeing priests at these events. "Indeed," the Synod decreed, "it offends the very eyes and soul of secular people to catch sight of Clerics at theatres . . . since indeed even the most degraded men consider priests as raised above the things of the world in a higher place and others look at them as if looking in a mirror to take from them what they should imitate."[40] By explaining that priests should model ideal behavior, which did not involve viewing theatre at all, the Synod implied that attending "moral" plays also was not proper for parishioners.

Subsequent councils and synods repeated these decrees' essence, but emphasized the seriousness of the prohibition, even though there is no evidence of enforcement. The Fourth Provincial Council of New York (1883) "most severely forbid clerics under penalties to be established by the bishop from attending theatrical spectacles."[41] The nature of the penalties remained unclear. In 1885, the Plenary of Bishops "commanded" priests to stop attending theatre, horse races, and other entertainments.[42] The following year, the Fifth Synod "decree under the most grave penalties that our clerics shall never attend horseraces, public theatres, those shows which are called operas and other spectacles of this kind even outside the limits of the diocese."[43] Through the twentieth century's second decade, all Church decrees on theatre repeated almost verbatim the 1886 statement. These repeated bans arguably resulted from priests as well as the laity continuing to publicly support the theatre.

The diary of Father Richard Burtsell suggests why the bishops felt compelled to reissue their anti-theatrical decrees. Not only did priests openly attend the theatre, they attended with little fear of consequence. From 1865 until 1912, Burtsell, a New York priest, wrote one of the few personal accounts to detail the inner workings of the nineteenth-century Catholic Church. The diary reveals how Burtsell and his clergy friends attended professional entertainments as part of their daily lives. It is not possible to generalize about priests' personal lives based on this one account. However, Burtsell's diary provides a narrative that challenges previous historiography and offers a window into the relationship between nineteenth-century Catholicism and the theatre on the local level.[44]

Burtsell's diary indicates he was a life-long theatregoer. Attending the shows with his mother or clergy friends, Burtsell saw everything from Shakespeare and musical concerts to minstrelsy, circuses, illusionists, comedies, operas, melodramas, jugglers at horse races, ballet dances, and acrobatics. He made sure to see his favorite performers when they visited town and enthusiastically watched new acts passing through the city. Fond of Edwin Booth and Edwin Forrest, Burtsell often saw multiple productions a week when they performed in town. Burtsell favored Booth, as he explained in 1865: "In the evening I went to see Edwin Forrest play Hamlet: Here I could make a fair comparison between him and Edwin Booth: the latter is far more refined, more intelligent, and interesting actor. Forrest is too uproarious and not sufficiently deliberate."[45] The same year, he criticized British actor Charles Kean because "[h]e does not enter into the character fully."[46] Burtsell also recorded his amazement at popular entertainers who performed awe-inspiring feats. He found the Hanlon Brothers "truly astonishing: the brothers rolled over, as if a barrel [sic], at full length. . . . Two dogs were trained to jump the rope: one walked on his fore-legs: the other on his side legs alone."[47] In 1874, he saw Boucicault's *The Shaughraun*, but expressed none of the concern Larkin did ten years later. Even when he traveled to Washington, D.C., or Rome, Burtsell took time to attend the theatre.[48]

Throughout the diary entries from the 1860s to the 1880s, Burtsell never expresses concern about his theatrical attendance in light of the Synod's decrees. In February 1867, he notes becoming aware of the new documents produced by the Baltimore Synod, but he does not mention the theatre.[49] Burtsell worries about Church leadership possibly disagreeing with his position on amusements in March 1867: "I preached on 'lawful and unlawful amusements' in our church in such a way, I am afeared, as to warrant [unintelligible] severe judgment of me. The boys of the exhibition were disappointed because I did not enter into great detail about theatrical representations."[50] He does not record any negative ramifications. At the very least, Burtsell's diary demonstrates the

Church leadership's lack of enforcement of its antitheatre decrees. The support for, or at least lack of strong opposition to, the theatre among some clergy also begins to explain how hibernicon companies managed to establish partnerships with Catholic churches across the country.

In the 1860s, hibernicon companies frequently visited Father John Talbot Smith's hometown in upstate New York. As a child, Smith "trembl[ed] with delight" as he "drank in the jokes of Pat and his colleen, laughed to the point of exhaustion, envied their nimble and exquisite dancing and marveled at the real moonlight on the pictured lakes of Killarney."[51] Even though the church "taught [its parishioners] to hold the theatre in the same horror as sin itself," Smith watched the hibernicon alongside clergy in local theatres and parish buildings.[52] Years later, Smith remembered how the hibernicon "was an exception" among the various popular entertainments of the late nineteenth century.[53] In an article for *Donahoe's Magazine*, Smith recalled how the hibernicon did "[a]cute work . . . [on] behalf of the stage. While the clergy denounced the theatre from the pulpit, at intervals, and the parents daily at home, and its visitation became a matter for woful [sic] and trembling confession, the sinful institution was actually getting inside the Church itself through the Hibernicon and the other charming panoramas of Ireland."[54] For Smith, the hibernicon's visits and interactions with his Catholic community transformed the fundamental relationship between popular entertainment and the church.

Burtsell and Smith highlight the absence of consistent, direct influence on Catholic parishes by the institutional Catholic leadership. This division is not surprising considering, as historians have discussed, conflict defined much of the nineteenth-century Catholic Church, especially between the church hierarchy and parish priests.[55] Tracing the networks created by hibernicon companies tells a story of professional managers and performers viewing the Catholic Church as a potential partner and (for some) remaining obligated to spiritual expectations. It offers a view of parish priests as leaders looking for inventive approaches to funding and uniting their religious institutions. In the process, hibernicon companies generated a nationwide network of touring partnerships that helped them attract audiences as well as constituted a sense of American Catholic Irishness.

"The Acting and Songs Take with the Irish People":
The Hibernicon and Parish Partnerships

The partnerships formed between hibernicon companies and local Catholic parishes transformed how popular entertainment interacted with the Church and, more enduringly, how the Catholic Church interacted with the theatre. Although "Catholic" had long been synonymous with "Celt," the church hierarchy in Ireland and the United States worried about the Irish's relationship to their faith. Before the Great Famine, many Irish identified as Catholic, but Irish Catholic practice often was informal and incorporated pagan traditions. In the following decades, the devotional revolution in Ireland aimed to change these practices and bring Irish Catholic practice more formally in line with Vatican policies. These efforts extended across the Atlantic and resulted in Catholicism becoming "the central institution of Irish life and the primary source and expression of Irish identity."[56]

During this period, Catholic parishioners were "disproportionately" working class and "largely of foreign birth or parentage."[57] As historian Sheridan Gilley discusses, "the Irish-American parish was the most important social centre, meeting place and focus for the expression of a common identity for large numbers of casual Catholics."[58] The parish also became viewed as one method of attaining respectability for the Irish. The Irish-American community maintained mostly gender-segregated spaces, a way of life they brought with them from Ireland. However, as historian Hasia Diner notes, "The Church provided the only formal institution in which women participated on any regular basis."[59] Significant numbers of Irish women became nuns and others assumed leadership roles in church fundraising.[60] This meant that the Church became one Irish-American space in which the hibernicon had the potential to reach Irish-American women. By aligning itself with the Catholic Church, the companies created the possibility that parish priests might *encourage* a cross-gender and cross-class audience to attend their fundraising performances, either in a theatre or in a church building. This possibility marked a radically different position compared to other variety touring companies during these years.

The hibernicon walked a delicate line between appealing to working-class audiences and still maintaining the standards of respectability expected by aspiring Irish Catholics and women. Compared to other forms of popular entertainment, the hibernicon started at an advantage because of common associations with moving panoramas. As Mimi Colligan discusses, moving panoramas emerged as "part of an answer to a perceived need for 'acceptable' popular entertainments."[61] As "rational amusements" or "entertainment that carried elements of instruction under the sugar coating of aesthetic or sensational diversion," panoramas, the upper and middle classes presumed, allowed for the improvement of the lower classes through educational scenes and lecture material. Moving panorama's origins in lower-class popular entertainment forms, such as peep shows, the lecturer's transformation into more of a comic entertainer than an authority figure, and the inclusion of variety entertainment problematized this moral agenda.[62] The potential educational value of the moving panoramas' images, however, imparted to the hibernicon an air of middle-class respectability that other popular entertainments and variety shows lacked. When the hibernicon first started touring in the 1860s, many Catholics had already accepted the idea of performance for educational purposes, albeit on an amateur level. Father Smith's writings also suggest an additional reason for the hibernicon companies' escape from condemnation. Smith notes that minstrel shows often were "judged moral by the local theologians, as not being a play."[63] With the hibernicon similarly avoiding the formal designation of "play," its structure may have helped the show avoid rejection by priests and parishes. The hibernicon's celebration of homeland also worked in dialogue with other social structures within the church, such as parish societies, that similarly created a space for remembering and celebrating the culture left behind in Ireland.[64]

Through its fundraising efforts for the Church, the hibernicon also took on a role frequently fulfilled by Irish-American women. A brief glimpse into church fairs reveals a parallel system of circulation of goods tied to Irish culture as well as an Irish-American community constructed in part through charitable efforts benefiting the church. Sometimes referred to as "ladies' fairs," Catholic women of all ages and classes took a leading role in organizing church fair booths and entertainments, which played a major economic and social role in the development of the nineteenth-century Catholic Church. A rare opportunity for women's leadership and agency outside the home, church fairs also created one space in which women determined how people moved and how goods circulated. This was a temporary, radical switch, compared to women's movement and agency in the broader Irish-American community.

The fairs ranged from small events lasting only a few weeks to large affairs held for a month or more. Historian Colleen McDannell has traced Catholic fairs back to at least 1834. After the Civil War, the demographics of the Catholic Church shifted to include a higher percentage of women, which contributed to an explosion of church fairs around the country.[65] Through the fairs, women "raised money for communal needs" and created a social event that reinforced community and religious identity.[66] By 1882, a *Chicago Daily Tribune* writer observed that the church fair "has become almost as regular a feature of the church machinery as the prayer-meeting."[67] Church fairs peaked in the 1870s and 1880s, and McDannell observes that parishes of Irish heritage held all the major fairs between 1870 and 1900.[68]

Building churches and schools and operating social welfare organizations and charities created a large financial need within the expanding Church. By 1878, the New York archdiocese owed $3.04 million. As McDannell notes, this was three times more than any other New York religious organization.[69] Other causes, such as the Catholic New York Foundling Asylum and new church buildings and cathedrals, also benefited from the fairs. From the figures collected from newspapers, histories, and diaries, late nineteenth-century Catholic Church fairs contributed anywhere from a few hundred dollars to $172,625 for St. Patrick's Cathedral. The amount raised frequently rivaled the funds earned from pew rentals, the other major contributor to church income.[70] Burtsell frequently comments on attending and organizing church fairs in his diary entries for 1865 to 1867, and these comments reflect the financial challenges of running a parish. In spite of Burtsell's financial victories, it is not long before he is involved in organizing another fair.[71]

These fundraising events became incorporated into the social lives of Irish-American women and the working class. In 1879, the *New York Times* reported that "The effect of raffles at church fairs, particularly in entertainments of this kind gotten up by Roman Catholics, has been to make this species of alms-giving exceedingly popular among the lower classes in our large cities. Those who will take the trouble to question their servants . . . will learn that they have almost daily calls made upon them to take a chance in this or that raffle."[72] A few years earlier, the *New York Times* explained, "The most profitable patrons of Catholic Fairs are servant girls, who are very profuse, and often spend a month's wages in an evening."[73] This behavior reflects the broader general pattern of servant girl donations to the church. In Hartford, Connecticut, Judge Thomas McManus described servant girls as "the best of Catholics, and the most liberal supporters of the church."[74]

Part of the appeal of Catholic Church fairs depended on its variety of amusements, which had the potential to appeal to a wide audience. A series of booths selling donated or homemade goods comprised the fair's main event. Yet, unlike Protestant fairs, instead of buying the goods, Catholics purchased raffle tickets for an item. This allowed participants an opportunity to win a wide range of prizes, including flour, furniture, pianos, clocks, china tea sets, silver pitchers, dolls, paintings, embroidery, food, religious paraphernalia, and occasionally livestock.[75] The parishioners won the goods through luck instead of purchasing power. This method allowed Catholics from all classes to participate and reflected the church's recognition that their parishioners had limited funds to spend on leisure activities.[76] The types of goods varied, but they usually included some items with Irish connections, such as portraits of Irish nationalist leaders or pictures of Ireland.[77]

Through their efforts, the hibernicon tapped into a habit of fundraising events attended by men and women, a rare exception to Irish Catholic gender segregation, and a dedication to community rooted in social gatherings and charitable contributions. The companies also entered a fundraising tradition that frequently used Irish goods to appeal to parishioners. On a commercial level, partnering with the Catholic Church to raise funds for their various causes appeared strategic for a performance form attempting to move beyond variety's standard male working-class audience.

Looking across national and Irish-American newspapers provides a general, if still incomplete, picture of how hibernicon companies engaged with Catholic communities. Starting with his first hibernicon tours, John MacEvoy established partnerships with parish priests along his tour route by holding benefits for local Catholic Churches in theatres and church buildings. Evidence suggests many hibernicon companies copied MacEvoy's interactions, which I consider as nodes on a broader Irish-American Catholic network. *MacEvoy's Hibernicon, Morrissey's Grand Hibernicon, Dan Morris Sullivan's Hibernicon, McGill's Mirror of Ireland, John Burke's Tableaux of Erin, Gavin and Ryan's Emerald Isle,* and *Dan MacEvoy's Hibernicon Irish Comedy Company,* among others, all performed benefits for the Catholic Church and its organizations. Sometimes these events were one-time occurrences, and in other instances, companies returned to host benefits for the parishes in subsequent years. Across the country, these companies held benefits for parishes, new church buildings, Catholic schools, orphan asylums, and Catholic social organizations. Some buildings supported by these performances continued to be used by Catholic parishes for decades. The expansion of touring networks allowed more Catholic communities to see theatre and, in this case, witness and experience more positive Catholic and Irish representations and charitable companies. Through these interactions, the hibernicon seems to have established closer, more consistent relationships with parishes across the country than any other group of performers.[78]

Expressions of thanks occasionally appeared in newspapers and provide clues about these relationships beyond solely commercial links. After an 1864 benefit performance for the Boys Orphan Asylum associated with St. John's Conferences of the Society of St. Vincent de Paul, MacEvoy and a committee from the Society exchanged a series of letters in the *Utica Daily Observer.* The committee issued a series of resolutions in honor of Professor MacEvoy, his company, and his service to the Irish Catholic community. "We cannot permit the present occasion to pass," the committee explained, "without some expression of our admiration for the truly Christian charity of Prof. MacEvoy."[79] Subsequent resolutions commended MacEvoy "as a Christian gentleman and one who, not alone by his ardent devotion to the social and political elevation of his native land, but to the cause of charity deserves the favor and best wishes of every patriot and philanthropist."[80] Three months later, a Syracuse paper also described MacEvoy's charity and aligned him with the Church in its fight against immorality, praising MacEvoy for proving "his innate charitable disposition and goodness of heart, which has characterized him in every place that he has visited, where an institution of this kind has been found established."[81] For parishioners and other community members who did not attend the benefit performances, these notices publicly declared the partnerships between MacEvoy's company and the local parishes, the moral and charitable nature of the variety company, and the benefits received by the community through their alliance.

MacEvoy responded to the Utica parish's praise a few days later. He starts his letter by "begging to assure you that I did not expect and do not require such manifestations of gratitude. . . . I felt happy that an opportunity had been offered to show my humble gratitude to the Almighty for many blessing bestowed on me and my family, by assisting his 'little ones,' and also of making some return, however small, to the good citizens of Utica for their very liberal patronage given to the Hibernicon."[82] MacEvoy asserts his Catholic belief that his actions will be rewarded in the afterlife and constructs a romantic image of his mourning family, torn by his passing, but comforted by memories of his past good deeds and future rewards.[83] His comments point to how commercial goals did not override his loyalty to his faith, even if the commercial viability of his company also was a crucial consideration in the formation of these partnerships. He closes his letter by evoking camaraderie with the Utica community and the Catholic Church.[84] MacEvoy's letter helps solidify his image as a good Catholic role model, which served both as a good advertisement for his shows and as a useful propaganda piece for the Catholic Church.

The extent of the Irish Catholic network developed through these partnerships, and their importance to the success of the hibernicon's touring is illustrated through efforts to maintain trust as well as in the advertisements bragging about their association. These notices suggest that the partnerships lent the companies respectability. In 1872, John MacEvoy published a letter addressed "[t]o the Reverend Catholic Bishops, Clergy and Laity of the United States" that informed them he sold his hibernicon to Mr. W.S. Humphreys. MacEvoy "recommend[s] [Humphreys] to the Reverend Catholic Clergy and citizens, wherever he may exhibit, as a liberal and patriotic Irish gentleman in every respect worthy of their patronage."[85] It is possible that MacEvoy wrote the letter, as the signature claims, but it is also possible that a new hibernicon owner wanted to use the Catholic network established by MacEvoy and his family to attract an audience. Either way, it highlights the belief that many in the Catholic Church viewed hibernicon companies as acceptable popular entertainments. MacEvoy's son Charles started his own hibernicon company, which toured fairly consistently in the 1860s and 1870s. Charles saw his family's long-term relationship with the clergy as a selling point for his company and bragged in one advertisement how "for the last ten years [the hibernicon] has received the sanction of the clergy, the press, and the public wherever it has been exhibited."[86] Advertisements for *McGill and Strong's Mirror of Ireland* even state that the clergy encourages parishioners to attend performances, describing how "the clergy have not only honored it with their presence, but endorsed this entertainment, their pulpits cordially inviting their congregations to bestow upon it their patronage."[87] In spite of anti-Catholic sentiment, no evidence suggests these associations hurt the companies in any way.

Burtsell's diary and papers provide the most intimate view into these partnerships and how they functioned to sustain a network. In 1862, the New York archdiocese assigned the young Irish-American priest Burtsell to assist the pastor at the Church of St. Ann's in Greenwich Village, New York. In 1865, the first year in his diary, Burtsell expressed his growing desire to start his own parish in Gramercy. Archbishop McCloskey repeatedly rejected his requests to start a new parish. Burtsell searched for a suitable location, negotiated with its owners, and developed an economic proposal before he approached the archbishop again. His determination and planning finally paid off in late 1867, when the archdiocese approved his plan for the Church of the Epiphany on Twenty-Second and Second Avenue. Through his efforts, Burtsell typified the "brick and mortar priest" of the nineteenth century. Raising enough money to buy the land and pay for the new church remained the final obstacle to Burtsell's ambitions.[88]

A year after receiving approval for his church, Burtsell celebrated its first anniversary at the Cooper Institute. He spoke to his future parishioners about his fundraising activities for their church building. Several Catholic parishes donated about $14,200, and individual donors raised about $5,600. Burtsell credits funds raised by "picnics, hibernicons and fairs" with bringing their grand total to $44,500.[89] According to the Church of the Epiphany's account records, the hibernicon earned the church $1,959.55.[90] Once his church building opened, hibernicon companies returned in April 1872, September 1875, and December 1876 to raise money for his parish, with *Gavin and Ryan's Emerald Isle* visiting two years in a row. It is not entirely clear, but it seems these companies performed in church and commercial theatre spaces.[91]

For Burtsell, the hibernicon allowed him to tap into what he viewed as one of the church's strongest funding bases. In his diary entry for February 6, 1866, Burtsell explains that "[t]he Irish are a grand exception for they still give their money with generosity to build churches to God's honor."[92] If Burtsell wanted to appeal to this group, the hibernicon seemed ideal. When *MacEvoy's Hibernicon* gave a series of performances for Burtsell's church in September 1868, a *New York Tribune* reviewer remarked, "[w]ith the Irish population [the hibernicon] is already very popular."[93] On the first night, he described how "[t]here must have been three thousand persons in the house. Most of them were Irishmen."[94] The reviewer admitted, "If each [performance] is as profitable as that of last evening, we fancy that the cost of the new church will soon be paid."[95] For these benefits, audience members and parishioners were encouraged to attend Pike's Music Hall, a new New York popular entertainment venue, to help improve their community.

Even with their good intentions and charitable pursuits, hibernicon companies still confronted resistance from some Catholics. During the April 1872 run for his church, Burtsell remarked how the "acting and songs take with the Irish people."[96] News of the performance spread throughout New York's Catholic community, and two days later Burtsell received a letter from the archbishop, including a clipping from *Freeman's Journal*. The clipping, a letter from John James O'Reilly to the editor, denounces the show because the "acting and songs" are "low" and the posters "indecent." The archbishop details his agreement with O'Reilly and explains, "he does not consider the strictures unwarranted, and warns me not to have such unseemly exhibitions in the future."[97] In particular, the archbishop is scandalized by a description of a group gathered around a "picture of Nora in her red flannell [sic] petticoat" on Holy Thursday.[98] The archbishop's concern reflects general antitheatrical sentiments about the damage of sexualized images perpetuated by the theatre. Although the diary gives no other details, variety entertainment still had a reputation for sketches with bad language and acts sexualizing women through revealing costumes and suggestive songs. Catholic gender ideology expected Catholic women to "be pure and pious, domestic and submissive, celebrating the harmony of domestic life and endorsing motherhood as women's natural destiny."[99] The public display of a woman, let alone one that seemed to violate Catholic notions of purity, undermined the gender ideals they hoped to instill and held the potential to "corrupt" female and male minds with its subversion. The archbishop seems to have feared that the placard and entertainment offered women a dangerous alternative to the ideals taught by the church as well as tempted men to lust after a woman who was not their wife. There is no evidence suggesting that the hibernicon ever offered a more sexualized or "low" variety show, but the incident demonstrates the difficulties variety companies faced in their attempts to provide more respectable entertainment and how religious and gender expectations presented a continuing obstacle. Five days later, Burtsell recorded his defiant response, "denying the possibility of the scene described . . . as no placard with figures was exposed on that day or any day of Holy Week."[100]

The performances continued, and Burtsell invited hibernicon companies back multiple times after his disagreement with the archbishop. The hibernicon performances' value for his parish superseded any concerns about breaking Church policy. It is unclear how many other priests faced resistance for hosting and working with the hibernicon. However, the seeming absence of any public rebukes of hibernicon companies by priests or Church leadership and the continued partnerships across the country reinforce the value of these arrangements for parishes and theatre companies.

The increasing role played by Catholic parishes in the daily lives of Irish Catholics may have motivated priests to seek out nontraditional methods of generating income and instilling a sense of Catholic community. Anti-Irish and anti-Catholic sentiment thrived among Protestant moral reformers, and the Church stepped in when government-supported services were denied to Catholics. Protestants made a concerted effort to "save" Catholics through conversion. Outdoor public welfare was increasingly eliminated, which impacted many of the Irish Catholic working class and poor, who did not want to commit themselves to the poorhouse. Organizations such as the Children's Aid Society sent poor Catholic children out west to Protestant families, often without their parents' consent.[101] Theatrical benefits helped popular entertainment to become a sanctioned, integrated part of Catholic economic and social life by demonstrating its potential for social good. By contributing to the construction of churches and schools, theatrical benefits for the Catholic Church helped provide essential services and safe spaces for migrants and the poor.

The dramaturgies created by hibernicon companies through their tours also may have helped generate a sense of Irish-American Catholic community. As reminders of national and transnational community, Gilley notes that Irish newspapers and fraternal groups were "elements which held the expatriate Irish Catholic communities together."[102] I argue that the hibernicon had the potential to function in a similar way. With migration, global nationalism, and the mobility inherent in the working-class labor market, it was not unusual for Irish Americans to imagine their community on the move. Operating as a rallying point for Irish Catholics, the hibernicons' benefits for the Catholic Church allowed audiences to temporarily consider hibernicon performers, many of whom were Irish migrants or descendants, to be part of their community. The knowledge that the companies would travel to other Catholic parishes across the country held the potential to instill a sense of unity among the dispersed Irish Catholics across the continent. Although theorizations of community are often tied to notions of dwelling and settlement, it is important to consider how hibernicons' transience might not destabilize the community but simply provide another way for it to be constituted. Each repeated interaction renewed the commitment of the hibernicon to Catholic communities and performed the partnership within the network. Considering how ANT views the constitution of relationships through action, at least for their moments of interaction, these community nodes came into being.

Facilitating Parish Partnerships:
Imagining Catholic Ireland through the Hibernicon

The partnerships between hibernicon companies and parishes across the country support Father Smith's assertions about the hibernicon "getting inside" the Catholic Church after the Civil War. The content of the hibernicon shows helped facilitate these networks and interactions. During these years when priests denounced Catholic imagery as obscene and derogatory, the hibernicon companies structured their Irish and Catholic imagery in a way that would not inspire charges of malicious caricature or concerns about moral corruption through sexualized performance. The hibernicon avoided major controversy by omitting the embodied representation of priests or other religious figures and by limiting the depiction and discussion of the Church in songs, sketches, and panorama paintings to certain acceptable themes and conventions. Through their shows, the companies demonstrated how performance might serve the goals of the struggling late nineteenth-century Catholic Church.[103]

Within the fragmented archival record of the hibernicon, songsters provide the most evidence of what companies may have performed for audiences and how companies aligned their public image with Catholicism to different degrees. Depicting priests and the Church as a common part of everyday life became the most popular form of Catholic representation in variety song.[104] The songs illustrate how the Church plays a social, everyday role in addition to its religious function. The tangential nature of the songs' references also reflects the position of the Church for many Irish-American Catholics in post–Civil War life. It was an important institution but not necessarily the focal point of their lives.[105]

Comic representations of priests and St. Patrick appeared rarely, but the songs typically avoid the worst stage Irish characteristics. In "The Birth of Saint Patrick," Father Mulcahy provides the solution to the song's comic debate over the birthdate of St. Patrick. The group then "all got blind drunk."[106] The priest is not directly implicated in the celebration, which is tied more to a joke about the typical St. Patrick's Day celebration than any actual religious person or practice. Except for "The Birth of Saint Patrick," most St. Patrick and St. Patrick's Day songs in hibernicon shows romanticize him and place him within an Irish nationalist heritage. For example, J. H. Ryan's "St. Patrick's Day" is more about the Irish-American experience and the symbolism of the St. Patrick's Day parade for the Irish-American community than it is about religious spirituality. Ryan's marchers walk "down through the Bowery, our banners we display . . . Glory of old Ireland on St. Patrick's Day."[107] He writes, "There's Emmet and Moore, and O'Connell sure, Were they here to-day, They would be proud of our glorious turn out, Upon St. Patrick's Day."[108] These lines place his marchers on the side of Irish nationalist heroes. Similar themes commonly appeared through-out Irish-American popular entertainment and circulated through American culture by word of mouth and songsters.

Few songs directly defended the Church, but these songs tend to ap-pear in songsters for companies with the closest relationships to the Catholic Church. In one songster, Charles MacEvoy included "Fa-ther Tom O'Neil." The song tells the story of how Father O'Neil sur-vived a challenge to his faith soon after his ordination. In Ireland, a young widow lives with her three sons. Her youngest son, Tom, tells his mother, "Your land is too small to support us all, and if you would agree, I am fully bent and well content a clergyman to be."[109] O'Neil's experience would not be unusual to audience members familiar with the Irish economic situation. Since the end of partible inheritance after the Great Famine, the eldest son typically inherited the parents' land and the other children often emigrated or joined the Church. The song not only depicts this reality, it also portrays O'Neil's choice to join the church as necessary and noble. O'Neil receives acclaim for his clever-ness at college, and when he returns to his hometown after his ordina-tion, "you never saw such welcome."[110] During the celebration, he is tempted by a wealthy young woman who lives nearby. She asks him to resign his priesthood and marry her. She offers him her fortune. Yet, O'Neil resists her and pledges "if you offer ten times more, I would not resign."[111] As a result, the woman arranges a pregnancy and charges O'Neil with fathering her child. He is brought to court where he refuses to bow to the court's pressure to marry her. When the court sentences him to seven years in Australia, he retorts, "Our Savior suffered more than that."[112] Then the true father of her baby rides in on a horse and explains the woman's plot to force O'Neil into marriage. O'Neil is freed, and he thanks God for his goodness.

Through its series of events, the song emphasizes priests' good character and the importance of truth and self-sacrifice. The ending implies that God will protect those who serve him. The song not only portrays the Church in a good light and presents an idealized version of a priest, but it also encourages the faithful to continue to serve the Church. The portrayal of the woman as a temptress also reflects nineteenth-century Catholic representations of dangerous female sexuality.

By denigrating sexualized women, the song ultimately supports the gender ideology of the Church along with the rest of the production. Regardless of the archbishop's concern, the depictions of Barney and Nora also seem to have provided an appropriate model of gender and sexual behavior for their audiences. With the amount of improvisation in performance and gaps in the hibernicon's archival record, it is impossible to say that every production always upheld Catholic gender and sexual norms. The fragmentary evidence suggests the narrative framework kept the characters within acceptable boundaries, however, with both genders on the path to heterosexual, monogamous marriage. Although Barney flirts with multiple women in the remaining Cohan sketches, a typical stage Irish tendency, in the end, Barney and Nora always marry or become engaged. Other than the archbishop's complaint to Burtsell, I have found no evidence of any controversy caused by Nora's portrayal. She seems to be performed as a dutiful daughter to her mother and a loyal love for Barney.

Some companies avoided referring to religion altogether in their songs, but all companies told stories about Catholicism through the panoramas. In 1865, Burtsell complained, "half of our Irish population is Catholic merely because Catholicity was the religion of the land of their birth. This is owing to the neglect in which their instruction is left."[113] Gilley finds a similar conflation of Catholicism, Irishness,

and nationhood explaining, "to be Catholic in Ireland was to be a nationalist, and to be an Irishman was to be a Catholic."[114] For parishes
that were predominantly Irish, this association made reinforcing the
connection between Ireland and Catholicism a way to highlight the
importance of church membership. As Miller discusses, "Convinced
that 'Irishness' (as clerically defined) was an essential bulwark of religious faith, the Irish-American clergy homogenized and reinforced
immigrant group identity and integrity, for instance through ethnic
parishes and clerically controlled St. Patrick Day celebrations, by dis-
owning religiously 'mixed' marriages, and by teaching pride in a sani-
tized, Church-centered version of Irish history in parochial schools,
which were themselves designed to insulate Irish American and other
Catholic children from pernicious 'Anglo-Saxon' (that is, Protestant)
influences."[115] The hibernicon provided an entertaining way to view
Ireland's Catholic past and present and to reinforce the connection between Irishness and the Catholic faith.

The hibernicon characters visit a religious historical moment or
landmark in each new region on the journey. Examples include "Illuminated scenes in the life of St. Patrick," "Caithleen, the Chieftain's
daughter, on her journey to Luggela to hear St. Kevin preach," and
"The history of Holy Cross Abbey and the Seven Churches; or, the
Cross of Clonmacnoise during the characters' visit to County Tipper-
ary."[116] At the benefit for Burtsell's church building, a review in the
Irish Citizen critiques the performance and singles out a religious scene
as particularly worthy of appreciation. Although the reviewer remarks
that the "historical and allegorical pictures might have been omitted
with advantage, especially if replaced by a few more of Irish scenery,"
he states, "that scene in which the monks and priests are shown as pro-
ceeding in the Cathedral of St. Patrick's, was perfect in artistic and me-
chanical arrangement."[117] The focus on events hundreds or thousands
of years in the past allowed hibernicon companies and parishes to latch
onto a common mythic history with the potential to unite their Irish
audience or parishioners.

Even though the hibernicon's visual components erase any contemporary Irish violence, they depict the long history of conflict between
Anglo-Saxon Protestants and Catholic Celts. Typically, the events de-

picted are moments of Irish Catholic pride. For example, *Gavin and Ryan's Emerald Isle* depicts the Siege of Limerick during the war between King William of Orange and King James II. Outnumbered and outmaneuvered, the Irish in Limerick believe they have lost the battle. Yet, after an explosion startled King William's troops, "with a wild cheer the Irish rushed on the panic-stricken foe. The women, with disheveled hair streaming behind them, flew to the front, calling on the men to follow them. One last desperate charge, and the enemy were hurled back through the breach in confusion and dismay, and chased into their camp by the victorious Irish."[118] The description ends by highlighting the event's and participants' eternal significance. It explains that the "deeds on that eventful day will be remembered while the blue waters of the Shannon flows beneath the city walls, in defending which, they so nobly died."[119] The event illustrates the importance of defending faith and country, which would have resonated with Catholic authorities and audiences.

When the panorama depicts present views, the audience sees, rather than current events, images of magnificent *permanent* structures, such as St. Mary's and St. Patrick's Cathedrals and holy ruins, that mark the landscape as Catholic. These physical markers tie Ireland's past to its present and emphasize the lasting presence of Catholicism, not only for its current people, but also for the generations of unborn Irish. This choice also signals the importance of these structures, an importance that the audience may have extended to the many churches supported by hibernicon performances. Any implied parallel between the painted structures and contemporary American church buildings holds the potential to transform church buildings into spaces also tied to the Irish's religious and ethnic past.

In a few instances, the panoramas depicted Irish people interacting with these sites. One hibernicon lecturer described a "Blind Girl at the Holy Well": "Many a weary mile have these poor pilgrims traversed, and now they have reached the longed for Holy Well. An aged man is leaning reverently on his staff, besides the stone cross, contemplating the well of holy water. On the one side a youthful mother is instilling into the mind of her child a lesson in connexion [*sic*] with her peculiar creed; while on the other a young girl, all simplicity and prettiness, is

drinking water from her hallowed hand. In the distance are seen the
ruins of an ancient abbey."[120] Aside from depicting a romanticized view
of the Irish peasantry, these images indicate not only the resilience of
Ireland's poor, but also their need for help and sustenance through religion. Introducing the Seven Churches, the lecturer of *Gavin and Ryan's
Emerald Isle* explained how "on a wild and dreary piece of grass land
on the borders of the Shannon . . . stand the time-worn relics of primitive Christianity in Ireland."[121] He continued to detail how St. Kiernan
founded them as a "seat of learning" in the medieval period and how
"the place was in good condition up to the year 1201 when the work of
dilapidation commenced by a sack of it under the English soldier named
Fitz-Henry."[122] Through the lecturer's narrative, the ruins signify the
history of Anglo-Saxon oppression as well as Catholic tradition.[123]

Old religious sites appeared in all hibernicon company productions
in different variations. They helped contribute to the sense of an ancient
Irish race rooted in Catholicism, even for productions that downplayed
the Irish-American nationalist strains that the MacEvoys and Gavin
and Ryan's hibernicons emphasized. The performances suggested that
supporting the Church also served the Irish's racial and national community, which extended well beyond their town and city lines.

When Partnerships Fail: Continuing Tensions

Established through the exchange of funds, favorable representations,
and repeated visits, the success of the partnerships between hibernicon
companies and the Catholic Church helped sustain hibernicon national
touring networks. In her indispensable study of transatlantic Broadway networks, Schweitzer examines how "all networks are contingent,
vulnerable, and subject to failure."[124] She points out the importance of
studying these failures within actor-networks to understand how the
networks function as well as how "new networks form."[125] If the partnerships between hibernicon companies and parishes were based on
a symbiotic relationship that benefited both, with parishes receiving
benefit funds in exchange for the clergy's blessing for Catholic audiences
to attend performances, the moments when these partnerships failed
reveal crucial details about variety touring. The failed partnerships

illustrate how companies negotiated the financial challenges associated with itinerant performance and varying local laws. The repeated performative practice and what it meant for Irish communities created an opportunity for scammers to take advantage of parish hospitality.

In 1884, a *New York Clipper* writer exposed a widespread "playing-for-the-church benefit scheme" that he accuses hibernicon companies of perpetuating. After the church publicly endorsed the performance form, certain companies benefited from large audiences wanting to support their local parish but conveniently forgot to donate any proceeds to the church in question. Although evidence indicates that many hibernicon companies, including the ones owned by the MacEvoys, cultivated a strong relationship with Catholic parishes, the writer claims priests "throughout the country complain[ed] bitterly of the treatment received from certain 'will-o'-the-wisp' Hibernicon managers" who "defraud[ed]" priests and churches.[126] Communities believed that "[c]harity and pleasure combined should suffice to fill the hall, floor and gallery" and indeed, many charity performances were well attended.[127]

With only the *Clipper* article outlining this scam, it is unclear whether the issue was as common as the writer states. Although not the same scam outlined in the *Clipper*, Burtsell bitterly complained about the difficulty of obtaining funds promised to him by *Gavin and Ryan's Emerald Isle*, a company who had performed successfully for his parish the year before. On multiple nights in December 1876, Burtsell bemoans, "Mr. Gavin did not give what he promised."[128] One night, Gavin gave Burtsell $125 and then "asked $25 for costumes."[129] Burtsell records the audience attendance and implies he was due substantially more. The companies became successful enough and built up enough trust with local parishes that they created a situation profitable to scammers. In cases like these, church leaders' fears about theatre professionals' morals were not unwarranted.

Other than scamming the parishioners looking to support their local parish, the companies benefited from pretending to give to charity because it enabled them to avoid many state and local licensing fees. These laws operated differently across the country, but with theatre managers passing on more costs to touring companies, they presented an additional expense during tough economic times. In some towns, companies may have helped cover the license cost through the share of profits given to the theatre. Although some towns only charged between one and ten dollars for a performance license, some cities, including New York City, Springfield, Illinois, and Wilmington, Delaware, required payment of the yearly fee, even if the troupe planned on performing for only a few nights.[130] In New York City, if the troupe wanted the license for less than three months, the law allowed the mayor to decrease the fee from $500 to between $150 and $250.[131] For a touring company, especially one in dire financial straits, these laws could prevent a company from continuing to operate if it could not pay for a license. By using the provision that allowed performances "for charitable and religious purposes" without a license, troupes could save significantly, especially since most laws did not specify how much of the profits had to be donated to charity.[132]

A lawsuit in 1879 illustrates how charitable as well as dishonest touring hibernicon companies took advantage of the charitable and religious purposes exemption made possible by their parish partnerships. The village of Sag Harbor filed a complaint against *MacEvoy's Hibernicon* for not obtaining a license, and "[t]heir defense was that they were performing for a charitable object."[133] The trustees claimed that the state exemption conflicted with the village charter, and the troupe "paid $3 thro' Rev. JJ Heffernan."[134] It seems that at least for the MacEvoy family, their friendship with local Catholic leadership helped them settle legal matters, even if it did not help them avoid the licensing fee. In this case, consistent with MacEvoy's dedication to clergy, the local church seems to have received the promised funds. For companies unwilling to fulfill their promises to parishes, a successful run could mean substantial profits with little, if any, pay out.

Despite the *Clipper*'s warnings, parishes continued to partner with the hibernicon for decades. Even when the form practically had disappeared, the partnerships remained a crucial piece of their tours. In 1910, *Dan Morris Sullivan's Hibernicon* performed in a church in Brooklyn. The *Brooklyn Daily Eagle* stated that "Those who remember MacEvoy's 'Hibernicon,' with its quaint panorama, will be delighted to learn that that pleasing form of entertainment has not been entirely squelched by the advent of moving pictures."[135] Although hibernicon companies may have almost disappeared by 1910, arguably, its impact continued to have ramifications for the relationships between the theatre and the Church.

The partnerships may have helped convince church leaders to seek out more formal partnerships with other performers in support of the Church. In 1886, Archbishop Corrigan in New York asked Augustin Daly to take charge of the Roman Catholic Orphan Asylum benefits, which he would then organize for several years.[136] As mentioned earlier, the hibernicon helped convince Father John Talbot Smith about the importance and power of theatre in Catholic spiritual life, and he became one of the most vocal Catholic advocates for theatre through the early twentieth century. He claims that companies like the hibernicon inspired churches to "train amateur companies for social aim as well as for profit."[137] Smith struggled for decades to weaken the Church leadership's staunch position on entertainment and encouraged Catholics to attend professional theatre as well as to participate in parish theatres. Starting in the 1880s, Smith published theatre articles in various Catholic and Irish-American publications, including the first theatre reviews in an American Catholic publication after he became the *Catholic Review*'s editor in 1889, a position he held until 1892. In 1914, Smith finally convinced the archbishop to approve the creation of the Catholic Actors Guild in 1914 to serve Catholic actors' spiritual needs.[138]

Although the evidence of these partnerships remains fragmentary, it is important to consider how they may shift historiographical questions pertaining to the theatre and the Church. The hibernicon provides an early glimpse into the tensions that later came to a head with the Irish and Catholic protests against the Russell Brothers and John Millington Synge's *Playboy of the Western World* at the turn of the century.[139] Scholars claim that before 1920, the Catholic Actors Guild (CAG) and Catholic Theatre Movement (CTM) comprised "the total organizational response of the New York Archdiocese towards the theatre."[140] Yet, focusing on these two institutionally sanctioned organizations emphasizes the Catholic leadership's consent and the attempt to create a national movement as necessary conditions for lasting relationships between the Catholic Church and the theatre. As demonstrated through Burtsell's experiences and the hibernicon partnerships, many late nineteenth-century Catholics did not view these two conditions as pre-requisites. As opposed to beginning a more formal relationship between the theatre and church, the CTM and CAG attempted to centralize and regulate the dispersed, diverse, and local interactions between the theatre community and Catholic parishes, which had developed over the preceding decades.

CHAPTER FIVE

Those *"Plucky Pedestrians"*

Irish Pedestrianism and
Disciplined Mobility

AFTER THE CIVIL WAR, newspapers vacillated between celebrating and denouncing "The Walking Mania" and "Pedestrian Fever," as professional and amateur men and women
participated in walking matches ranging anywhere from
half a mile to several hundred miles.[1] The *New York Clipper* described
how the competitive walking craze swept the nation, with matches "an-
nounced in pretty nearly every town in the country . . . challenges are
flying about in such numbers that it is out of the question to keep track of
them all."[2] In New York, the sport enthralled the city's working classes.
According to the *New York Times*, "The fever has broken out worse in the
Bowery [the city's working-class amusement district] than in any other
district of the City."[3] The only solution, the paper claimed, was "for
them all to walk themselves to death, but some of them hold out well."[4]
Ever attuned to novelty, variety managers attempted to entice these
pedestrian-crazed people into their theatres by featuring pedestrian
matches as part of their performances. In both variety and the sporting
arena, Irish and Irish-American pedestrians played a starring role.

Two recent studies have addressed the pedestrian phenomenon. Historian Matthew Algeo's comprehensive book provides the first in-depth
history of pedestrianism. He examines the rise and fall of its popularity,
the major stars, and pivotal events. Rohs also considers pedestrianism in
his broader study of Irish performance in New York. In part of his final

chapter, Rohs argues that "sport, like Irish performance culture, found itself in between the vulgar and the genteel, a popular meeting point for mass culture."[5] This intersection reveals, he claims, how "sporting men and performers took advantage of its ascendancy to advocate for Irish interests. But in doing so, they also affirmed already-manifested stereotypes and celebrated them as markers of Irish identity."[6] He juxtaposes Harrigan's *Mulligan Guard Ball*, Irish-American pedestrian Daniel O'Leary's final 1879 match at New York's Gilmore's Garden, and nationalist readings of Robert Emmet's "Speech at the Dock." He argues that through their stage readings, nationalists attempted to portray a more inclusive Irishness than the stereotypes reinforced on stage and through sports.[7]

This chapter argues for the connection between pedestrianism, variety, and aspiring Irish and differs from these two pivotal studies in critical ways. It is the first to explore how low- and first-class variety managers incorporated pedestrian matches into variety performance. Even with the many holes in the archival record, newspapers and memoirs illustrate how variety theatre benefited from the craze by creatively incorporating it within and alongside their entertainments. Second, it approaches pedestrian performances through the lens of mobility. This focus enables an examination of pedestrians' bodily movement in relation to race, class, and gender. Although pedestrians did not erase Irish-American stereotypes, the performances suggest that Irish-American pedestrians transformed the Irish-American male image through their mobility. Both Algeo and Rohs discuss how Irish pedestrians gained fame and social mobility through their pedestrian successes. This chapter offers one argument for *how* their performances of mobility contributed to their respectability and social mobility.

Complementing the discussion of the tramp in chapter 1, the chapter suggests how performances of walking played a role in the national dialogue about who belonged in the United States. Examining pedestrian performances within the culture of gentility reveals how they reshaped pedestrianism's potential to embody middle-class, gendered ideologies of respectability. Class, race, and gender, however, complicated and restricted for whom and in what performance context pedestrianism offered a path to respectability and social mobility.

Drawing on Cresswell's concept of "correct mobility," the chapter investigates how "forms of 'correct' and 'appropriate' movement are produced in relation to 'inappropriate' forms of movement through a complicated representational process."[8] Exploring pedestrianism across variety theatre and the sports arena, I examine what I refer to as disciplined bodily mobility, an embodiment of middle-class ideals of posture, movement, and physical form that became a method of social and cultural access as much as an indicator of athletic success. Although the Anglo-Protestant middle class ultimately viewed female pedestrians as transgressing gender expectations, male pedestrian performances reflected a taming of rough, working-class masculinity encouraged by genteel culture. As a result, the dramaturgy of disciplined mobility earned them a constructive currency within middle-class culture.

From the 1860s to the 1870s, the public perception of disciplined mobility and Irishness's incompatibility weakened. Newspapers viewed the failures of Irish-American pedestrian Young Miles on the variety stage as reflective of his Celtic background. A decade later, however, Irish immigrant Daniel O'Leary's successful performances of disciplined mobility on the international pedestrian stage demonstrated the equality, or even superiority, of Celtic men compared to their Anglo-Saxon competitors. Although scholars have examined the international competitions and the significance of races pitting Anglo-Saxon and Celtic pedestrians against each other, I argue for how O'Leary's performances of disciplined mobility participated in the dialogue surrounding the races and broke down Irish-American stereotypes, even if it did not erase them. His performances opened up conversations about the Irish's suitability for American citizenship and right to freedom from British oppression.

Respectability, Gender, and Culture in the United States

At the intersection of class, race, and gender, the culture of gentility shaped nineteenth-century notions of respectability. Inherently gendered female, the culture of gentility emerged alongside an Anglo-Saxon Protestant bourgeois culture during the antebellum period. Historian John F. Kasson analyzes the ways genteel culture attempted to "establish order and authority in a restless, highly mobile, rapidly urbanizing and industrializing democracy.'"[9] Framing it as an issue of individual responsibility, the Anglo-Protestant middle class advocated for "personal governance, social propriety, and 'good taste.'"[10] The culture centered on middle-class white women as carriers of respectability. Rooted in restraint and self-control, genteel culture determined how women acted, how they related to others, and how men treated them.[11] As moral, domestic mothers and wives, women were expected to teach men proper behavior and control. This involved eliminating the aggression, bravado, and physically rough characteristics that defined masculine culture at the start of the century and continued to develop through the century's end.[12]

Advocates of genteel values believed people in various social positions could access respectability. Since etiquette advisors assumed servants, leisure time, and independence to an extent, realistic class obstacles remained.[13] Irish-American community leaders and clergy assigned Irish and Irish-American women a similar role to that of their Anglo-Protestant middle-class female counterparts, however. These leaders warned of men's tendency to cause family disorder and championed women's stabilizing and moral influence. According to Diner, they believed Irish women "propelled the family out of poverty and into the respectability of the middle class" by acting as "civilizers" who tamed male aggression and advocated temperance.[14] This view was not limited to the Irish alone: Anglo-American Protestants also viewed Irish women as a possible positive influence on family life through their behavior.[15]

Respectability extended beyond the home in its influence and reshaped theatre in the years before the Civil War. As legitimate theatre managers attempted to expand their market, they started to court women as possible audience members. This resulted in a years-long domestication of theatre into moral, family entertainment safe for women and children. The transformation involved eliminating the pit, installing parquet seating, rejecting any plays deemed lewd, and introducing matinees for women. Managers attempting to lure women who were out shopping into the matinees relied for success on the increasingly pervasive culture of consumption that encouraged women to define their identities through what they purchased. After the Civil War, managers also insisted on more restrained audience behavior, which had previously included feet stamping, shouting, and calls for encores.

Alongside these changes, managers prohibited drinking.[16] Referring to the change in audience behavior, actor Joseph Jefferson characterized the audience as "imprisoned" by the new restrictions.[17] Through the demasculinization of the theatre space, theatre managers succeeded in attracting women, but at the same time many men felt pushed out by these new passive behavioral requirements. As they attended drama less frequently, more men began to patronize sports and popular entertainments that retained a masculine culture.[18]

As previously discussed, first-class variety theatres similarly attempted to lure women and the middle-class to their performances. Through women's presence, managers hoped to lend their enterprises a legitimizing respectability. In addition to managers' economic aspirations, middle-class reformers urged the domestication of variety through legal means. In New York, during and after the Civil War, middle-class reformers and legitimate theatre managers collaborated to pass the Concert Bills in 1862 and 1872. Aside from requiring that places of amusement pay a license fee to operate, the bills denied licenses to establishments selling alcohol or featuring waiter girls. Reformers believed that mixing women, men, and alcohol in concert saloons and variety theatres encouraged immoral behavior. Although sexualized variety continued to prosper during these years, the legal restrictions in combination with managers' efforts ultimately transformed variety into the family-friendly vaudeville, roughly by the mid-1880s. Scholars have extensively examined vaudeville in relation to this culture of respectability, and it remains outside the parameters of my study.[19]

It is impossible to know the extent to which first-class variety theatre succeeded in diversifying their audiences, but evidence suggests that men continued to dominate variety audiences throughout the 1860s and 1870s. During the years covered by this study, variety theatre remained a space rooted in male working-class values, even as some houses gained more respectable reputations than others. Sexualized variety continued to portray controversial representations of women. Variety in theatres and saloons also remained potential sites of solicitation for prostitutes, whose public display and unrestrained sexuality embodied the polar opposite of the respectable middle-class woman. Examining pedestrianism and its intersections with variety illuminates only one avenue through which respectability reshaped male working-class behavior within this broader cultural process. The close focus on pedestrianism enables an analysis of *how* these ideas were formed, perpetuated, and validated. It investigates how pedestrians performed, where, and for whom and how these elements together generated mobility's meanings.

Transformations in Walking

How pedestrians performed mobility was closely tied to the transformation of walking's social role. Until the late eighteenth century, in Europe and the United States, walking served a necessary, utilitarian purpose as a means of transport, whether locally or as part of forced migration. Roaming people signified poverty and, to some observers, possible criminality. The upper classes traveled by carriage and horseback, which separated them from the tedious lower-class walking experience, kept their shoes clean of dust and mud, and prevented walking's physical toll. During the century's last few decades, cultural understandings of walking began to change as the upper classes started to connect walking to leisure and the thinking process as well as in response to improved transportation, such as better roads and the emergence of public transport, which increasingly separated walking from its utilitarian function.[20] Continuing through the nineteenth century, this shift altered not only the perceived purpose walking, but also the notion of how one should walk. In the United States, walking transformed alongside the emergence of the middle class, respectability, and its urban reform movements.

In the eighteenth century's last two decades, the European pedestrian tour and rise of Romanticism helped redefine walking as a cultural practice. During pedestrian tours, the upper and professional classes chose to walk as a means of exploration. Linked to the rise of picturesque tourism, these tours involved rambling through rural landscapes to examine the scenery and encounter local people. Hiking and wandering became viewed as desirable, healthy leisure activities. Alongside these changing attitudes, the idea of walking as a form of knowing developed.[21] According to scholar Joseph Amato, Romanticism modified the "intrinsic worth" of walking "as a unique way of experiencing and knowing the world."[22] Improved transportation also made travel less expensive, more convenient, and increasingly accessible to the lower classes, further detaching walking's connections to the poor. By the first decades of the nineteenth century, these new associations, scholar Robin Jarvis claims, "hardened into an ideology which to all appearances has wide social acceptance."[23]

The experiences of the urban working and middle classes provided a stark contrast to the bucolic landscape imagery and leisurely wandering experiences of pedestrian tourism and Romantic excursions, however. In the nineteenth-century city, walking remained the primary everyday mode of transportation for the population's majority. Until the mid-nineteenth century, where sidewalks existed at all, boundaries between them and the road were ambiguous, blurring the distinction between space for pedestrians, peddlers, horses, and carts.[24] As a result of crowded tenement housing, the social and economic lives of the working class and poor filled city streets. Children played, women socialized, and people carried out their work as peddlers, street cleaners, rag pickers, and prostitutes. Uneven roads, crowds, the lack of sanitation and sewer systems, inadequate street drainage, and animals made moving through the city a challenging, often perilous experience. Through their interactions, streets and sidewalks existed as multipurpose, contested sites in the nineteenth-century city.[25]

In New York, where and how a person walked down a city street had class, gender, and racial connotations. As scholar David Scobey examines, male and female bourgeois New Yorkers promenaded down fashionable city streets in "a performative utterance of gentility."[26] Scobey describes the scripted body in the drama of promenading, in which "[n]ot only were functions like spitting and belching to be suppressed, but also any mode of corporeal or sensory contact which breached the physical frontiers between persons. Jostling, staring, loudness and most hand-shaking were impolite. . . . Tipping a hat rather than shaking a hand, passing by rather than conversing: the socializing effect of the promenade came precisely in its curtailment of contact, its staging of bodies in the act of 'daring not venture too near.' "[27] Scobey's work illustrates how the middle classes already conceptualized walking through the city as a method of performing and maintaining respectability.

They were not alone, however, in using how they walked for social purposes. Scholar Christine Stansell analyzes how working-class men and women participated in their own promenade practices on the Bowery. In contrast to the restrained behavior of the middle classes uptown, the white working classes marked their class, racial, and gender identities through their boisterous demeanor and colorful clothing, which drew attention to working-class women in particular as they moved down the street.[28] Encoded with its own notion of working-class civility and contrasting with upper- and middle-class restraint, these promenades, Stansell claims, remade class as "heterosexual association, one that granted women the ability to claim something of the republican pride that had been the workingmen's heritage for some fifty years."[29] At the start of the nineteenth century, how black Americans walked down New York sidewalks also breached social and racial boundaries. Although social convention insisted black Americans make way for white Americans and walk closer to the gutter, on Sundays, some black "promenaders moved in lines of four or five and dominated the entire sidewalk to establish, literally, their unequivocal command of this weekly ritual and the entire public transcript."[30] These social meanings associated with urban walking continued to shift throughout the century.

In New York after the Civil War, increasing anxiety about the poor and migrant populations magnified concerns about how the city's streets and sidewalks functioned. These concerns played a prominent role in conversations about city life and urban planning among vocal citizens, newspapers, and middle-class reformers. The middle class increasingly characterized multipurpose crowded public spaces as chaotic, inefficient, and dangerous. Letters to the Mayor illustrate the heated debate over the use of the city's sidewalks. One resident complained, "During the years of misrule in New York, the taking possession by certain dealers of our sidewalks is one of the most outrageous."[31] He explained that along Greenwich and Washington streets, "our Irish citizens have taken whole possession of the side walk. . . . They actually put all their store goods on" it.[32] Aside from the writer's view that this behavior broke laws, he also singled out the plight of "ladies obliged to go off the walks," implying the slight to their social status, and bemoaned how "[i]t's almost impossible to get along there."[33] Some expressed distress over oversized store signs and stands obstructing sidewalks, which they argued took business from the stores paying rent. When threatened by eviction, others pled with the mayor to permit their sidewalk stands, which supported their families.[34] In addition to obstructions, residents complained about the filth and condition of the streets, which made them difficult to use and a health hazard.[35]

Urban reformers had their own beliefs about how public space should be used and ideas for how public spaces should be regulated and restructured. From their efforts emerged new notions of how to walk in urban spaces during the decades following the Civil War. Middle-class reformers advocated for reformed urban planning on several grounds. First, they feared the ramifications of industrialization on the working class and poor and the resulting potential for riots, protests, and violence. Second, a long-held, fervent belief suggested that crowded, "unnatural" urban environments contaminated inhabitants and led to immoral behavior. These beliefs reflected anti-immigrant and anti-black prejudices that asserted cities failed to Americanize their diverse populations and attributed city's moral and economic decline to minority populations.[36] Fear of mobs and immigrants intersected in cultural commentary and reform writings about the city's streets. "Walk down [Broadway] on a holiday, when the Irish crowd the sidewalks," an *Atlantic Monthly* writer commented, "and all you have . . . dreamed of savagery will gleam . . . from those . . . daredevil eyes. The materials of riot in the heart of the vast and populous city then strike one with terror."[37] The middle class viewed working-class use of the street for leisure, socialization, and work as signs of parental neglect, poor family home lives, criminality, and immorality.[38]

Reformers believed that reshaping the urban environment and increasing municipal and police regulation of city streets offered one possible solution to the perceived urban crisis. This disciplinary control rested on separating and legitimizing public space for functions relating to home life, commerce, travel, and play.[39] Through spatial reorganization, reformers wanted to eliminate social and sexual chaos to create a stable, harmonious civil realm that embodied bourgeois culture and norms. These thoughts reflected the restrained culture of gentility and other middle-class efforts to domesticize space.[40]

Urban reformers moved toward a philosophy of circulatory efficiency. For sidewalks, reformers aimed to ensure pedestrians smoothly traveled from their starting point to their destination. Any obstacle that impeded this journey—beggars, strolling musicians, pushcarts, stands, store signs, unsanitary and damaged sidewalks, prostitutes, playing children, and protests, among others—came to be viewed as opposed to the public good and the ideal pedestrian flow required for orderly and efficient city life. Expansion of police power to remove these obstacles assisted this transition. In the 1860s and 1870s, the city government started requiring licenses for peddlers. Police arrested and dispersed large gatherings in streets and public parks without permits, even when they were nonviolent, as in the case of the 1874 workers' demonstration in Tompkins Square. Cities also began to build extensive sewer and drainage systems to guide the muck out of the streets. The separation of urban space reflected the growing differentiation of city geography by class and race as well as by commercial, industrial, and residential uses.[41] These changes built on legal rulings, such as *People v. Cunningham* from 1845, which found against a Brooklyn distillery for prioritizing individual over community need by blocking roads with its slop wagons.[42] In 1879, Judge Van Vorst of the New York Supreme Court asserted, "the streets and sidewalks of the City are for the public at large, and for their travel and passage to and fro."[43] Enforcing the prioritization of pedestrian circulation took decades, as the city faced pushback and questions about liberty and discrimination.[44] In the interest of civic responsibility and reform, however, walking became the city sidewalks' primary sanctioned use, even if on a daily basis the spaces remained contested.

This shift contributed to transforming notions of how to walk. At the beginning of the century, Romanticism's reconsideration of walking started a cultural conversation about the connections between walking, physiology, and health. The emergence of evolutionary science and eugenics extended this train of thought and linked bipedalism and erect posture to the emergence of humanity and physical, moral, and racial superiority.[45] These developing theories connected physical form with mental health, intelligence, and character.

Books detailing the connection between posture, walking, and character became widely popular after the Civil War. Joseph Simms's *Nature's Revelation of Character*, for example, later retitled *Physiognomy Illustrated*, went through nine U.S. editions between the early 1870s and 1889.[46] Simms explains, "the plain, easy walk is indicative of an unassuming mind; the plunging or stamping step, an unvarnished mentality. The unsteady gait results from unreliability of character.... [T]he close observer can detect at a glance each person's idiosyncrasy, and thus can tell, almost certainly, the physical, mental, and moral qualities and tendencies of the individual."[47] When describing the different types of lurching gait, he singles out people from the midlands in England and Scotland, the Irish, and Africans. As Cresswell discusses, "degenerate" mobility is often "coded as being from elsewhere and not British."[48] As a result, "correct" mobility becomes wed to Anglo-Saxonism. Simms ties their walk and posture to physical facial characteristics and violent behavior:

> They are always ready with the word of defiance, the fist, the shillelagh, the revolver, the bowie-knife, or the stiletto, according to the nation of which they belong.... [S]ee his squat snout, compressed, puckered lips, broad underface, square, broad chin, bull-neck, and short, broad hands.... When he stands, he naturally poises himself in an attitude of defiance, with his feet well apart ... as much as to say, "I'm ready, come on."[49]

This description contrasts with the depictions of moral and upstanding characters' walk. The "Firm Gait ... [is] found only in strong characters, whether physical, moral, or religious ... ," Simms notes. "The whole structure of the person whose walk is firm, manifests compactness, solidity, and stability."[50] One article entitled, "How to Walk Well," recommended "drawing in the chin" so "the shoulders are naturally thrown back, the lungs given full opportunity to expand, and the head carried erect."[51] These writings held implications not only for migrants and the poor, but also the disabled.

These conversations and debates led to a scripting of how walking should be performed. The script for walking involved consistent flow and walking smoothly from the origin to the destination, whether for travel or leisure. Middle-class reformers suggested a proper, disciplined way for people to walk on this journey that enforced "appropriate" behaviors in public spaces, such as avoiding fighting, spitting, urinating, or blocking the flow of walkers. They encouraged people to walk on the sidewalk, not the streets or gutter, to walk on one side, and not to push through people to make one's way. During these years, cities started to make the transition from wooden to cement sidewalks, which, along with efforts to improve sanitation, impacted how a person could walk down the sidewalk.[52] The smoother surface with fewer obstacles allowed "walkers to wear lighter shoes and glide on their speeding feet rather than stomp and clomp along as their ancestors had done since time immemorial."[53] By changing the environment cities "paved the way for the boot-clad pedestrian to exercise his feet as a stepping machine. No longer did he have to pick his way, with care and dexterity."[54]

Although in reality, urban planners and middle-class reformers did not substantially eliminate differing behavior through their legal reforms until the first decades of the twentieth century, they succeeded in creating an *idea* of what was proper, civic behavior, whether it was regularly followed or not. Imagining the pedestrian as a "stepping machine" presented the walker as controlled, regulated, and restrained, a perfect embodiment of a respectable, genteel American. An 1879 lithograph published in *Puck* illustrates the contrast between classes, nationalities, and proper movement. Showing a male and female churchgoer trying to move along the sidewalk, the image depicts the human obstacles that stand in their way, begging for money. The middle-class churchgoers stand erect and tower over the poor, hunched people, many displaying signs of disability that would prevent them from moving smoothly down the sidewalk. Several figures reflect stereotypically Irish simian characteristics. Entitled "The Streets of New York—Running the Gauntlet of Horrors," the image reinforces notions of who moves appropriately and who is a "horror" to be removed and overcome. Through how they move down the sidewalk, the sketch distinguishes who belongs in the United States from who does not (see figure 14).

After the Civil War, the rise of pedestrianism as a popular sport intersected with these emerging ideals for walking. Although competitive

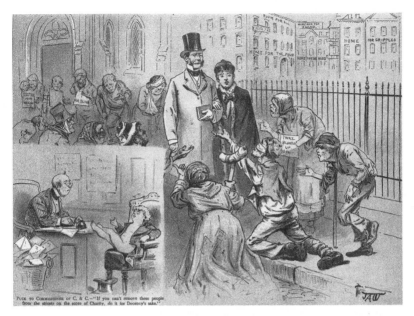

FIGURE 14. A couple tries to walk down the sidewalk, but the poor obstruct their path. In the image's lower left corner, Puck comments, "If you can't remove these people from the streets on the score of Charity, do it for Decency's sake." "The Streets of New York—Running the Gauntlet of Horrors." *Puck,* November 26, 1879. Library of Congress Prints and Photographs Division Washington, D.C.

walking existed in North America and Great Britain throughout the nineteenth century, the emergence of modern sports culture launched pedestrianism into a national cross-class phenomenon. Before the Civil War, working-class male athletes dominated pedestrianism and its audiences. Pedestrianism, like many sports in antebellum America, remained intricately tied to notions of manliness that reflected courage, aggression, and physical prowess. During these years, mass spectatorship for sports developed with thoroughbred racing and pedestrianism drawing large audiences. In addition to amusement, athletes and audiences viewed popular sports as opportunities for camaraderie and profit through gambling. During the late 1860s and 1870s, the audience and culture of pedestrianism shifted as urban middle-class attitudes toward sports changed. Emerging from middle-class reform movements geared toward improving the lives of the poor and offering moral amusement outlets for the middle class, the middle class's now positive attitude toward sports focused on athletics' transformative effects.[55] Sports, the middle class believed, "could be uplifting and promote public health, improve morality, and build character."[56] These beliefs aligned with long-held middle-class expectations that amusements serve a virtuous purpose. Pedestrianism combined notions of walking and leisure with ideologies that characterized disciplined, smooth walking as physically and morally superior. At a time when modern sport was still developing, pedestrianism offered opportunities to propel Irish Americans beyond anti-Irish stereotypes and into a respectable middle-class position.

Pedestrianism, Women, and Low-Class Variety Theatre

Even though antebellum pedestrianism existed as a working-class sport, the pedestrian feats of Rhode Islander Edward Payson Weston helped transform it into a national craze. After losing an election bet to a friend, Weston became a minor celebrity when he walked the 476 miles from Boston to Washington, D.C., in ten days for Lincoln's 1861 inauguration. Over the next decade, Weston worked to build pedestrianism into a national phenomenon. Attempting to take advantage of roller-skating's growing appeal, he started walking around skating rinks to beat pedestrian records, such as walking five hundred miles in six days. His physical feats and the vast amounts of money attached to his victories attracted widespread attention and mass crowds. In an attempt to find similar fame and fortune, pedestrian matches and individuals trying to beat Weston's records popped up across the country.[57]

Between the 1860s and 1870s, the pedestrian craze spread to a range of entertainment venues in urban areas. In addition to the auditoriums, roller rinks, and theatres that hosted exclusive walking matches, theatre managers incorporated pedestrians into their entertainments throughout the Northeast and Midwest. "Walking is the great amusement in the music halls," the *New York Times* reported in 1879, "and nearly every one of the museums, where giants and dwarfs hold court, has its pedestrian match. In beer saloons, distinguished pedestrians walk for schooners, while countless thousands mourn because they cannot walk 5,000 miles in 5,000 half hours, and become great and glorious in a week."[58] Aspiring pedestrians came from all over the country and represented the United States' diverse population, with native-born white and black Americans as well as Irish, German, English, and Scottish male and female migrants walking for fortune and fame.

As variety theatre frequently incorporated new popular trends, it unsurprisingly started to feature pedestrians during their shows in the late 1860s. Walking around a temporary track constructed on stage, male and female pedestrians appeared in low-class and first-class variety. Pedestrianism's appearance in both types of variety illustrated how it continued its struggle toward respectability. Evidence for pedestrians in variety is scarce, especially since it seems to have had a larger presence in low-class and sexualized variety, which newspapers rarely covered in any depth. This section looks across accounts in newspapers to piece together a rough picture of how pedestrianism operated in these spaces and how the disreputable associations with low-class variety followed female pedestrians into the sports arena.

As part of low-class variety, pedestrianism took on a salacious connotation that reinforced the sport's working-class, less-respectable origins. Within these venues, worn, pained female or nonnormative male pedestrian bodies that failed to perform the expected restraint tied to respectable notions of walking received the most criticism. Scholars such as Algeo and Dahn Shaulis have written cultural histories about the rise and decline of female pedestrianism in sporting arenas and halls and its stars, such as the German Bertha Von Hillern and the English Ada Anderson.[59] Focusing on how female pedestrians' performed walking on and off variety stages illustrates how these performances contributed to the moral and legal backlash against female pedestrianism. The display of female working-class pedestrian bodies came to be considered a violation of genteel and gender norms, even when they performed mobility successfully. Their experiences demonstrated how only certain male pedestrians, including the Irish, had access to the respectable potential of disciplined mobility championed by the middle class.

By the 1870s, standards had developed for pedestrian matches. Depending on the context, pedestrianism as an umbrella term covered other track and field sports, including running. Contemporaries also frequently used it as a synonym for competitive walking, however, defined by the heel-toe rule. Englishman John Goulding, a competitive walker and author of a pedestrianism-training guide, explained the heel-toe rule for novices:

> In WALKING, the body should be kept perfectly upright, the shoulders back, the arms drawn well across the chest, at the same time keeping the chest out; the loins should be slack, as this gives freedom to the hips, the leg thrown out from the hip, well in front of the body, the heel being first to reach the ground, the body being brought forward over the heel almost before the toe touches the ground, the ball of the foot and the toe should hardly remain on the ground for a perceptible time. . . . [O]ne foot should always be on the ground in fair walking, which consists of a succession of steps, not of leaps.[60]

Lifting the feet and moving into a trot disqualified a walker. As demonstrated by Goulding, upright posture, not dissimilar to how middle-class reformers discussed walking and health, defined the expert pedestrian. Female pedestrians entered a sport upholding these physical standards of posture and movement that, in most cases, were originally written by male pedestrians.

The mid-1870s saw the rise of the nation's first female pedestrian stars. In spite of mostly positive coverage for the 1875 matches between the German Bertha Von Hillern and the American Mary Marshall that attracted thousands, some newspapers, such as the *Chicago Daily Tribune*, remained hesitant and championed "good, honest contest[s]" between men.[61] In 1877, Madame Ada Anderson emerged as the decade's major female pedestrian star. As an actress, singer, and circus performer, the middle-aged, part-Jewish Anderson embraced the spotlight, rejected Victorian standards of modesty, and confidently stated her plans to win wealth and international renown through her victories.[62] The forwardness and aggressiveness of her personality put her at odds with middle-class female standards of gentility.

When she started her long-distance walks, she received mostly positive press, even with Sunday matches, and inspired other women to take up competitive walking.[63] The positive reviews remarked at her ease and smoothness of walking. "Madame Anderson's walking is the poetry of motion," the *Brooklyn Daily Eagle* noted, going on to praise "[h]er graceful, swaying movements and even, steady tread awaken the admiration of every beholder. . . . Her form is beautiful because it is so healthy, and her being responds to the harmony of her physical being."[64] The *Spirit of the Times* reported, "Imitators of Mme. Anderson are becoming so numerous that we have hardly room to catalogue them."[65] Dahn Shaulis claims she helped inspire more than a hundred women to compete throughout the country by 1879. For a short period of time in the 1870s, the suffragette movement embraced female pedestrians as examples of female strength. Shaulis then documents how press coverage shifted and began to echo concerns by temperance and religious reformers.[66] Although support for female pedestrians was never unanimous, this public shift began around the same time that coverage expanded detailing the increasing appearance of female pedestrians in sexualized, low-class variety and saloons.

In Chicago, New York, and Philadelphia, among other northern cities, pedestrianism moved into low-class variety and saloons and drew public rebukes, even as male pedestrians in more respectable venues continued to gain national and international renown. Echoing middle-class critiques of concert saloons and variety, newspapers critiqued the immoral behavior encouraged by pedestrianism and the mixed-sex, working-class audiences. The articles emphasized the irregularity of the pedestrians' bodies, which failed to perform the restraint expected for respectable pedestrians. The *Chicago Daily Tribune* complained:

A Splay-footed female or half-grown lad is engaged to a tramp around upon a sawdust track, a broken-down musician gets a dollar a night and all he can drink to torture the keys of a dilapidated piano, a few tables and chairs are put in, and lo! the two-for-five-cent beer-hall blossoms out into a place where Mme. Brown or Patrick Maloney is engaged to walk so many thousand miles in so many hundred minutes, or vice versa . . . [they] are simply places of assignation and gathering-grounds for prostitutes, thieves, pimps, and loafers. The pedestrianism and the alleged music are features of these places, and they have become within the past few weeks entirely too plentiful.[67]

The female pedestrian's feet are characterized as abnormal. When describing the men, they typically tarnish their image as able-bodied men, as in the description of the male competitor as "half-grown," implying his youth and lack of physical stature. In other instances, disability or a nonwhite racial category marks the walking men, such as the "one-legged man" who walked "against a woman carrying a twelve-pound musket" and the two "war-painted moccasin Indians."[68] As the *Philadelphia Inquirer* remarked, most of the pedestrians in these venues were "random specimens of the demoralizing side of the pedestrian question. The mania does not stop with them by any means. It is said that in a down-town saloon a match is in progress between a cripple and a blind man."[69] Newspapers mocked how managers and saloon owners easily replaced these flawed pedestrians with walking animals, such as "Jackass Rowell" an old mule who took to the track at a Chicago saloon.[70] The *Chicago Daily Tribune* stated, "it really begins to look as if it was a misfortune that we ever encouraged Dan O'Leary," the Irish immigrant champion pedestrian who started his career in Chicago.[71] These descriptions looked to how these pedestrians performed their walking in combination with their gender and race to not only mark them as others, but also to mark them as not quite human.

In particular, anxiety surrounded the increasing number of female pedestrians, especially those performing at lower-class venues.[72] Concern about women in public, as possibly sexually available and targets of sexual advances, filled critiques of female pedestrians. As Kasson discusses, "[t]o preserve a woman's privacy in public," when walking down the street, etiquette writers advised women to diminish "her own expressivity in dress and deportment. She minimized bodily contact, keeping herself to herself and remaining alert to other pedestrians' movements. She minimized eye contact with all but her acquaintances."[73] Most importantly, women were not supposed to court and enjoy attention. If they did, "they were not respectable—according to the dictates of middle-class gentility."[74]

Along these lines, newspaper reports highlight the failed public bodily management of female pedestrians. The *New York Times* explained that audiences sexualized even the women walking in more respectable venues, such as the arena matches: "The women are subject to all manner of jesting and insulting remarks from the crowds of men, who hang over the rail surrounding the track, and pass comment on each as she passes."[75] Others discussed how female pedestrians attracted local and tourist audiences who clamored to see women on display in seedier venues. Continuing its crusade against female pedestrians, the *Chicago Daily Tribune* bemoaned, "Almost every beer-saloon that can boast of a few rickety tables and chairs and plenty of spare room has had an attraction in the shape of a 'Madame,' somebody who is 'the champion pedestrienne of the world,' and who is doing 'a feat never accomplished by any other lady in the world.'"[76] One letter writer declared that the monetary, competitive, and public aspects of the matches conflicted with women's nature and degraded them: "When a women will so far forget her sex and condescend to place herself on a level with animals in the race-course, what may we not expect from man? Our modern female pedestrians are a disgrace to themselves and dishonor to society, and an outrageous insult to every virtue which adorns true womanhood. Preaching and exhorting can have little effect in its attempts at moral reformation so long as such sinful spectacles are witnessed and patronized by our respectable citizens."[77] Similar stories circulated in papers across the country that linked female pedestrianism with moral degradation.[78]

Newspapers, doctors, and reformers used the appearance and movement of female pedestrians to justify why governments should suppress the sport. Her gaudy, short, and often inappropriate costume and footwear prevent smooth, consistently flowing walking. A gradual increase of exhaustion and pain reaches the scale of torture as husbands, managers, and hall owners force the women to continue walking in spite of their physical limitations. This repeated narrative of mobility became a tool for oppressing and limiting female athletes. It appeared across pedestrian spaces, in arenas, theatres, variety halls, and saloons and especially in relation to endurance walking, in which women walked over multiple days to reach a certain mile goal. The association with working-class entertainment layered further sexual connotations into the narrative, making the walk a sign of physical and moral inferiority.

Reformers and doctors argued that women's fragility and lack of innate physical and mental strength prevented them from successfully competing in walking matches. Women's biological flaws, they argued, also made them further susceptible to moral corruption in lower class venues.[79] In its report on "Broken Down Female Pedestrians," the *New York Clipper* painted a tragic picture of helpless, physically broken, and mentally deranged women, unlikely to recover from their pedestrian feats. The writer describes Eva Sinclair "lying helpless . . . suffering intensely from pains in her limbs and body. She says she does not expect to recover from the effects of the struggle. . . . Mrs. Farrand is at the Bellevue hospital. . . . She is broken down in body, mind and spirits. . . . It is very doubtful whether she will ever recover fully from the effects of her late disastrous walk. All that could be learned of Miss Rich was that she was roaming about in a deranged condition of mind."[80] The article also emphasizes how some of the women only competed out of necessity—poverty—as opposed to any joy or skill at the sport. As a result, the article erases or denies any female agency, training, or skill involved in the pedestrian competitions, and the women's achievements and ailments become indicative of a cruel society and poor female judgment.

Female pedestrians' physical pain also represented a substantial part of the performances' spectacle. As Carol Martin discusses in her research on twentieth-century dance marathons, the theatre of the long, arduous physical competitions made the often-boring viewing experience palatable and entertaining. "Spectators came to see the contestants hurt," she explains, "and the competitions tried to make the audience's pleasure at seeing the physical strain and pain acceptable by emphasizing the competitors' enjoyment and voluntary participation."[81] Pedestrian competition similarly operated with pain, and the pedestrian's failure or endurance engaged audiences for walking matches that often lasted days. For the female pedestrians, their experience of pain on the track and how it impeded their smooth, regular walking became part of their mobile performances' patterns.

A reporter for the *New York Times* visited Brewster Hall, which became a central venue for female pedestrianism in 1879. His description of pedestrian Annie Bartell upon his morning visit, especially in contrast to John Hughes, an Irish pedestrian, brings together all the elements of the costumed, tortured spectacle of female pedestrians and illustrates the contrast with male pedestrians:

> [Bartell] was accompanied by a man, who was at once recognized as Hughes, the walker, clad in civilized garments. The woman pedestrian at his side looked the picture of misery. She was clad in a short walking suit of black velvet; with gilt ornament which fell to her knees only. . . . She walked with a sleepy, listless air, dragging a whip in her hand, and her features bore evidence of great fatigue, while the calves of her legs and her feet were swollen, her shoes being burst in several places. . . . [S]he was really an object for pity, rather than congratulation, and for tender nursing, rather than constant goading to a physical exertion, which if appearance were any criterion, could only result in serious and permanent injury to her system.[82]

Remarking that Bartell's morning audience was comprised of the "sporting" type, the writer reports that as she walked in front of a mixed-sex audience that evening, "she looked haggard still, her eyes drooped heavily, her limbs were more swollen, and her left foot was lame."[83] This contrasts with the controlled and "civilized" description of the Irish Hughes alongside her. Unlike male pedestrians, reporters, reformers, and police disrupted the potentially pleasurable spectacle of the female pedestrian's theatricalized pain by insisting they performed because her husband and managers forced her. In one famous instance, the police and doctors interrupted a walk by Madame Anderson to ensure she walked voluntarily.[84]

Police and government officials tried to shut down venues hosting female pedestrians and eventually some passed prohibitions on female walking. One entrepreneurial police captain in New York used an old law to close halls featuring pedestrianism on Sundays. The Philadelphia County Medical Society sent resolutions to the mayor asking him to prohibit female pedestrianism, which they described as cruel. In Chicago, police cracked down on entertainments featuring pedestrians, and the trend died out. The papers also called for further regulation of waiter-girl saloons, where female pedestrians found success.[85] New York's Board of Aldermen called for the suppression of all female

pedestrianism and supported a resolution "reciting that public exhibitions of female pedestrians are offensive to the sense of propriety and
decency, demoralizing in their influence on the community, and cruel
and inhuman to the participants without affording any redeeming feature in their favor."[86] Incorporating active women into these entertainments did not bring them respectability. Instead, the women's public
display of their bodies and the ways their walking often failed to uphold
genteel culture's gendered ideologies led to their denigration and dis-
missal, even when they were successful outside of low-class variety and
saloons.[87] In stark contrast, disciplined mobility's public performance in
first-class variety houses and arenas opened up the possibility of breaking down long held associations between Irishness and chaotic, undis-
ciplined/degenerate mobility.

Performing Disciplined Mobility

In 1876, Daniel O'Leary, pedestrian champion, crossed the Atlantic
to compete against Edward Peyton Weston. This Atlantic journey
differed significantly from his last. Born during the Great Famine in
Clonakilty, a village in the south of Ireland, the poor twenty-year-old
O'Leary emigrated to the United States by himself in 1866 and settled
in Chicago. Now, he returned to Britain as the United States' reigning
pedestrian champion to compete in a rematch receiving international
attention. O'Leary beat Weston, the previous American pedestrian
champion, in an 1875 race in Chicago. Weston later cried foul play and
complained that O'Leary won because he had hometown advantage.
Embarrassed, Weston went to England to compete and won a series of
victories. O'Leary traveled to England to face Weston again on neutral
ground before Weston's new supporters.[88]

The April 1877 competition drew crowds of fifteen to twenty thousand people to London's Agricultural Hall, who watched as O'Leary
and Weston circled the track for six days. After Weston's British successes, many in the English aristocracy, including Sir John Astley, bet
on Weston, only to be quickly disappointed. O'Leary not only took
an early lead, he also completed five hundred miles in record time.
The accomplishment caused the "wildest excitement" and "the crowd

could scarcely be restrained from rushing the track."[89] The next day, O'Leary clinched his victory as the "champion walker of the old and new worlds."[90] In addition to his victory, O'Leary's enthusiastic international reception arguably also resulted from his success at performing disciplined mobility. O'Leary demonstrated that codes of respectability and discipline were not inherently Anglo-Saxon but were accessible and possibly even natural to Irish men. Through his disciplined mobility, O'Leary illustrated his equality and even Celtic superiority to the Anglo-Saxon Weston supported by the British.

This chapter's final section selectively focuses on arguably the most successful and well-known Irish-American pedestrians on the variety and sports stages, Young Miles and Daniel O'Leary. It does not attempt a survey of Irish pedestrians, nor does it claim that performing disciplined mobility was exclusively Irish. However, this concentrated approach allows for a detailed analysis, in light of available evidence, of how the most successful Irish-American pedestrians utilized disciplined mobility with varying levels of success, the impact of performance context on its meanings, and the responses in the auditorium and Irish international community. Comparing these two examples illuminates the relational meaning of mobility and the significance of setting and of the pedestrian's behavior outside the competitions on how their mobility related to respectability.

Rohs discusses how first-class variety theatre and pedestrianism shared a common tenuous position in American culture as they struggled toward respectability. Even as they started to become more respectable through the taming of working-class masculine culture, including rough, lewd language and drinking, pedestrianism and variety also maintained a "stylish unseemliness" that attracted the slumming elites. As Rohs examines, in these venues, Irish stereotypes remained a substantial part of Irish representation.[91] This examination points to the potential of disciplined mobility to destabilize these stereotypes. Leaders within the Irish and Irish-American communities recognized these performances as a tactic for disproving anti-Irish prejudices and demonstrating the Irish's right to equal treatment and freedom in the United States and Ireland.

In pedestrianism, training guides and newspaper columns reinforced beliefs that working-class men were physically flawed and therefore less likely to be able to execute the disciplined mobility necessary for long walking matches. These guides and columns reinforced urban reformers' cultural perceptions about how working-class people moved and walked. The *New York Clipper*'s pedestrian training column describes how a working-class man lacks discipline in all areas of his life. Therefore his mind as well as his body, it argues, is less predisposed to the training and rigor required for pedestrian success: "[S]uppose the case of a young man in a lower rank, who has been brought up on a spare and rigidly abstemious fare, and who from circumstances is sufficiently allowed to indulge in all the temptations of the public-house; he has no other resource — no hunting or cricket to take up his attention . . . and the consequence is that beer and tobacco commence the day, and tobacco and spirits wind it up. Such a man suddenly finds all his energies going, his mind dull and . . . his body weak, flabby, and bloated."[92] The ideal, disciplined body of the pedestrian represented in training columns tied to middle-class notions of hard work. Rooted in ideas of discipline and organization that emerged during industrialization, these notions resulted in the increasing regimentation and mechanization of time, space, and workers. The heel-toe-rule descriptions in guidebooks reflected these ideas of precise, repeatable, and regimented movement.[93] The class, race, and gender-based notions of disciplined walking infiltrated discussions of pedestrianism on and off the variety stage.

Irish migrants had long competed in sports in attempts to achieve social acceptance and wealth.[94] The emergence of modern sport and the developing connotations of disciplined mobility offered new opportunities for social advancement and respectability. Pedestrianism's position at the intersection of working-class and middle-class culture post–Civil War tempered its potential as a route for social advancement, however. In spite of its middle-class aspirations, pedestrianism remained tied to working-class culture, as illustrated by its relationship to variety.[95] First-class variety theatres incorporated pedestrianism during their attempts to expand their audience to women and the middle class while maintaining their working-class appeal. Although pedestrianism and variety reinforced negative Irish images, they held transformative potential for Irish pedestrians through their performances of disciplined mobility.

With pedestrian matches lasting anywhere from a few minutes to a several days, variety managers creatively incorporated pedestrianism into their entertainments. Often, managers included pedestrians in the variety olio, the range of acts preceding the afterpiece. A typical act involved pedestrians trying to beat the record for walking a mile or half a mile around a track constructed onstage. A timekeeper stood nearby and often a judge or two watched to ensure the pedestrians walked heel-to-toe.[96] Other pedestrians attempted longer walks tied to variety entertainment. In New York, for example, pedestrian James Kannaven pledged to walk for seventy-five hours with only a ten-minute break every twenty-four hours. Throughout his attempt, "[t]he performance of variety artists . . . will relieve the monotony of the entertainment."[97] In other instances, variety managers staged the longer walks in the theatre's attached saloon, so that patrons could enjoy the entertainment and then check in on the pedestrian from time to time.[98] Pedestrians also held benefits for themselves that they tended to stage as a variety entertainment. These benefits demonstrated their connections to the variety industry, even if the pedestrians did not regularly appear on variety stages.[99] These events allowed amateurs and rising professionals to practice their skills and pedestrian stars to stay in shape in between major arena competitions. Sometimes pedestrians, such as Weston, Edward Mullen, and William E. Harding, performed a pedestrian feat and then made a celebrity turn in a comic act, similar to the celebrity roles played by boxers and baseball players.[100]

Variety managers also played an active role in organizing pedestrian matches outside the variety halls. Harry Hill's Dance House, for example, featured variety shows and was best described as a cross between a dance house and a concert saloon. Known for his strong religious beliefs, Hill advertised his venue as a more respectable establishment for variety, dancing, and sports. Frequently hosting boxing matches and other sporting events, Hill attempted to profit from the attention and gambling surrounding Irish pedestrian Daniel O'Leary's victories. He organized an opportunity for another Irish immigrant pedestrian, John Hughes, whom he sponsored, to challenge O'Leary's six-day walking record. Hill, among other managers, remained involved in the sport throughout its popularity.[101]

Variety sketches also burlesqued the pedestrian craze. Tony Pastor staged a burlesque, *The Fawn*, that briefly mocked Weston's early exploits.[102] At the Theatre Comique, Edward Harrigan staged a burlesque of the widely publicized pedestrian competition at Gilmore's Garden entitled the *Great In-Toe-Natural Walking Match.* Although the variety schedule often changed each week, the sketch proved so popular with audiences that it ran for two months through the end of the theatre season, and Harrigan revived it the following fall for at least four weeks.[103] Throughout the country, other sketches, such as *The Arrival of O'Leary: The Pedestrian* and *Weston the Walkist* appeared as managers took advantage of the national craze.[104] Popular songs also mocked the pedestrian fever, such as "Walk, Walk, Walk," demonstrating how walking captivated the imagination of many Americans.[105]

As variety juggled ways of incorporating pedestrianism, Young Miles entered the national news as a champion pedestrian in the late 1860s. Born in England to Irish parents, Miles won races in Australia and California before competing in East Coast matches.[106] Tony Pastor arranged for Miles and William E. Harding to participate in a series of matches around St. Patrick's Day during matinee and evening performances. Walking half a mile around a roped ring constructed on stage, the pedestrians had to complete forty-seven turns around the track to win the gold medal offered by Pastor. According to William Ellis Horton, "A time-keeper was selected from the audience, the stage manager would tell how many laps there were to the mile."[107] Having previously walked an eight-minute mile on stage, Miles quickly emerged as the favorite. The papers reported, Miles's admirers offering "30 to 20 that he walks the half mile inside of 3 minutes and 30 seconds."[108]

Leading up to the match, advertisements defined Miles by his victories' location and compared him favorably to Harding. Advertisements bragged about Miles as "the champion walker of Australia" and "Champion Pedestrian of England, Australia, and California."[109] Although it is not clear how much Miles identified with or claimed his Irish background, by identifying him with these locations, newspapers assigned him a generic whiteness, especially through the ambiguity of the language used to describe him. Although both Harding and Miles fell at one point while walking around the ring, writers characterized

Miles as having the more ideal walking form, and one writer critiqued Harding's failure to conform to proper heel-to-toe walking standards.[110] Ultimately, Miles emerged victorious, walking the half a mile in four minutes and two seconds. Describing the first night of performances, the *New York Clipper* claimed the evening's amusements "attracted one of the largest audiences every seen in the establishment . . . and Mill [*sic*] was called before the curtain."[111] The weekend seemingly proved successful for Pastor, who continued to balance serving his downtown working-class audience with his aspirations to attract middle-class men and women.

The press recognized Miles's Irishness when he attempted a more challenging feat of pedestrian endurance about a month later: walking a thousand miles in a thousand hours against English pedestrian John Goulding. Taking around six weeks, Miles and Goulding planned on walking around a billiard room with forty circuits around the billiard tables comprising a mile. Papers continued to identify Miles as "the champion of California and Australia."[112] In an article that first appeared in the *New York Herald* promoting the event and reprinted from coast to coast, the writer labels Miles as of "Irish extraction" and offers one of the first critiques of his pedestrian form. The writer explains, Miles "swings his arms very much; his motion is a kind of gliding stride."[113] In comparison, Goulding "looks more of a pedestrian than Miles does. . . . Goulding's motion is more upright, and he is a handsomer heel and toe walker than his opponent."[114]

After being widely marked as Irish, descriptions of Miles's actions descended into stereotypes of a weaker body and a violent nature. After walking 628 miles, Miles injured his ankle and was exhausted. When someone awoke him from a nap, he refused to stand up without assistance from his trainer. Seeing his trainer sleeping, Miles pulled a gun out of his pocket and shot at the trainer, supposedly to wake him up. He hit the trainer in the neck. While others rushed the trainer to a doctor, Miles continued to walk, and no one notified the police until later that night. Miles's attempt to beat Goulding ended with his arrest. The papers attributed the violence to Miles's inability to deal with the walk's physical strain: "No cause can therefore be assigned for the shooting except that it resulted in a derangement of Miles's nervous

system, consequent upon the undue exertion and loss of proper refresh-
ment and sleep."[115] Although both pedestrians suffered from pain and
exhaustion, only the Irish pedestrian almost killed someone in his distress. In Miles's case, his excellent performances of disciplined mobility
were not considered reflective of his race, but his failure to perform
disciplined mobility properly was explained by his supposedly innate
Irish characteristics.

The frequently repeated "origin story" for O'Leary's career illustrates the prevalence of these negative images as well as O'Leary's
desire to combat anti-Irish prejudices. Before discovering his pedestrian talents, O'Leary worked in a lumberyard and as a door-to-door
bookseller in Chicago and spent another winter in Mississippi picking
cotton. According to anecdotes, he entered his first pedestrian match
after overhearing men discussing Weston in a dry-goods store. After
one man stated, "None but a Yankee can place on record such a giant
performance," O'Leary suggested, "perhaps a foreigner could do it."
The men laughed at him. "Ireland has sent forth good men," he insisted
to their anti-Irish protests. A man sarcastically responded, "they can
accomplish almost anything with their tongues."[116] Even if the anecdote was apocryphal, it linked O'Leary's goals for his pedestrianism
to disproving anti-Irish prejudices and demonstrating Irish equality or
even superiority. O'Leary's quest to transform the popular Irish image
related directly to how he performed his mobility.

For example, Irish pedestrians who failed to carry their bodies in
a disciplined manner are derided for their poor form and compared
to a variety Irishman. During a pedestrian competition between professional and amateur pedestrians, one *New York Clipper* reporter held
particular disdain for an Irish pedestrian, James Mahony, from County
Kerry, explaining, "Much of the merriment in which the spectators so
loudly indulged was due to the presence on the track of the member . . .
whose carriage and general appearance bore so striking a resemblance
to the representatives of the North of Ireland, so popular in our variety
theatres, that he was at once christened 'Pat Rooney,' and by that name
will he be known during the week. He is a good, if not a graceful walker,
and strides steadily along, looking perfectly unconcerned."[117] The crowd
fails to take Mahony seriously. The reporter and the crowd saw what

they expected of an Irishman: the caricatures they witnessed on the variety stage. Another Irish pedestrian adopted the alias "Johnny Wild," seemingly after the popular variety comedian who performed the tramp comic. Variety performers also competed as pedestrians. For example, James Maas, "well known on the stage of our variety theatres as a musical-sketch performer," came in third place during an 1878 race.[118]

O'Leary shattered stereotypical expectations with his performances of mobility during his pedestrian match-ups. In contrast to Miles, he portrayed an Irishman with restrained, controlled masculinity. Unlike female pedestrians, this performance imparted respectability to him. It is likely that O'Leary's performances had the capacity to signify in this way in part because he chose to perform primarily in organized sporting events rather than variety. Newspapers on both sides of the Atlantic commented on his disciplined, subdued walking style. He had success before the 1877 match, but this victory earned him an international reputation. Detailing O'Leary's superior form over Weston's became a theme in the coverage of the 1877 Islington match, especially in the Irish press. This commentary reflected what scholars have discussed as the battle between Anglo-Saxons and Celts inherent in their match-ups.[119] The *Cork Examiner* compared Weston's and O'Leary's walking styles: "One is not favorably impressed with Weston's style of walking, it looked sluggish, dragging, not at all like O'Leary's style. He walks erect, steady, and carries himself, if I might so express it, handsomely."[120] The *Liverpool United Irishman* explained, "The wonderful thing about O'Leary's walking is that while he appears to be going at an exceedingly easy pace, he covers the ground very rapidly. He has a beautiful style of walking; he is one of the most modest and undemonstrative pedestrians we have seen; and there is none of that bounce and dash and tossing of the head about him which unfortunately is the characteristic of Weston."[121] This description drew on the language of respectability. Following the etiquette of public walking, O'Leary embodies restraint and does not draw attention to himself. In contrast, Weston appears more out of control and invites the attention of the audience. O'Leary represented the height of disciplined achievement on an international stage with Irish and British papers deriding Weston's "jerky" walk as "the reverse of graceful" while complimenting O'Leary as "statuesque."[122]

Irish-American newspapers also celebrated how O'Leary walked. The *Irish American Weekly* describes O'Leary as a sportsman and Weston as a flamboyant entertainer, who is not focused on the task at hand: "O'Leary walked in good, upright form, with his body thrown back, holding in each hand a piece of wood. Weston, on the contrary, walked with a riding whip in his hand, jesting with his friends and trying to keep time with the music."[123] During a subsequent race, the *Irish American Weekly* drew a direct connection between the performance of O'Leary's mobility and industrialization. Unlike the premodern, anti-Irish depiction, the paper describes his movement almost like a machine: "His feet work like clock-work—the true heel and toe motion—and every muscle in his body works with every step. His shoulders are carried well back and his arms bent at right angles at the elbow, the hands being held near the chest. In each hand he carries an ivory stick some eight inches long, weighted with lead and weighing about a quarter of a pound."[124] The papers attribute O'Leary's ability to beat his competitors to his superior discipline in his mobility.

Watched by thousands, including the many Irish who migrated to England, O'Leary took the lead from Weston during the 1877 match. When he reached his five-hundredth mile, the Irish in the crowd went wild, and some even joined O'Leary on the track for the lap. O'Leary continued to walk, finally completing 519 miles by the end of the six days and winning $14,000.[125] Newspapers complimented O'Leary, but they questioned the entertainment's ability to draw such a large crowd. The *Holloway Press* remarked, "[W]e only fail to understand how it is interesting enough to attract about eighty thousand to see it at its various stages."[126] Although the sport's popularity baffled some in London, through his walking, O'Leary attained wealth and for a short period of time was, arguably, "the most famous Irishman in all the world."[127]

Images of O'Leary's walking reinforced his status as a more respectable Irishman. The *Illustrated London News* published an engraving of O'Leary and Weston walking around Agricultural Hall during the 1877 match. O'Leary's clothes appear neat and orderly and his posture mimics the descriptions in training guides, including his erect and back-leaning posture and arms held at ninety degrees at his side. O'Leary remains focused on the track ahead, and his face is serious. In contrast, Weston

FIGURE 15. Daniel O'Leary walks with his shoulders back and focuses intently on his race against Edward Weston. "The Great Walking Feat at the Agricultural Hall." *Illustrated London News*, April 14, 1877. Mary Evans Picture Library.

looks at the viewer, as opposed to the track, and slightly smiles. His sleeves are rolled up. Leaning forward as he walks, he seems to carry a large handkerchief and a walking stick at his side, going against predominant pedestrian advice for posture and arm placement. Aside from the distinction made between the dress and posture of O'Leary and Weston, O'Leary also betrays no standard characteristics of stage or anti-Irish caricatures. He is portrayed as being equally, if not more, capable than Weston (see figure 15).

This widely perpetuated image of O'Leary did not escape the notice of the Irish in England, Ireland, and the United States. As Rohs notes, "At a time when physical culture was said to have the potential to unite different classes of society and male physical prowess," pedestrian victories were "viewed in sporting circles as evidence of American—or Irish—mastery of the English."[128] Before O'Leary started his victory tour around England and Ireland, he attended a celebratory dinner with Irish MPs. Proud of their countryman's victory over the English-backed pedestrian, they toasted "to a champion whose endurance,

fearlessness and courage were the same as those which had ever characterized the Irish race, and made its prodigies recognized as belonging
to the highest types of the human family."[129] Crediting O'Leary with
demonstrating Irish worthiness, they discussed how to extend the recognition of O'Leary's discipline and excellence to the nationalist cause.
One MP wondered how the successes of the Irish at home and abroad
might create an "opportunity of convincing the English people who
were open to conviction that the Irish members were prosecuting a just
cause, and support Irishmen in their endeavors to raise the country to
equality with England."[130] The *Irish American* championed O'Leary as
"a modest, retiring man; and the only consideration that has drawn
him into this contest is his conviction that the ubiquitous Celt should not
'take a back seat' for anyone, anywhere; and with this feeling on him he
tries to make good his convictions by deeds."[131] O'Leary's victory might
not have single-handedly delivered the Irish from anti-Irish prejudices
or English colonialism, but the MPs, workingmen's organizations, and
Irish-American newspapers viewed the success of Irish pedestrians as a
chance to transform negative perceptions of Irishness on national and
international stages.

Like its potential in American variety, pedestrianism spoke across
classes, and Irish workingmen in England echoed the MPs' views. At
one ceremony celebrating O'Leary's victory, the Irish Working Men of
Southwark London declared:

> As Irishmen, we are proud of your achievement, because of the name
> you bear, and the race from which you sprung—a race which has given
> as many distinguished men to the world, and made as important a page
> in history as any other on the surface of the globe. Early trained to manly
> exercises in your own land, and living a life of virtue, laid the foundation
> of the iron constitution that in manhood enabled you to win laurels in
> Europe and America, thus making your name known. . . . [Y]our suc-
> cess is the greater because it tends to promote those patriotic aspirations
> which give significance to the efforts of a people.[132]

The workingmen's statement went one step further than the MPs. They
tied O'Leary's success in sports to the physical training he received in
Ireland before he emigrated and to an essential Irish masculinity. Their

comments flip the anti-Irish script on the English and Americans who perpetuated the narrative that the unruly primitive Irish bodies that emigrated to their shores needed reform. The Irish workingmen repositioned Irish mobility, O'Leary's trained body, and his match victories not only as a way into a more respectable future, but also as acknowledgement of the labor and culture frequently ignored and erased by British colonialism.

O'Leary continued his successful pedestrian career, winning the Astley Belt, established by Sir John Astley, twice. In 1879, he lost the belt at a Gilmore's Garden match in New York to Englishman Charles Rowell. From the beginning of the race, observers noted O'Leary's flagging pace, but they complimented his form as compared to other walkers. He finally had to withdraw due to illness. Never able to entirely escape Irish stereotypes, O'Leary was accused of drunkenness, but his behavior on the track did not imply intoxication.[133] After his loss, O'Leary claimed Rowell's associates poisoned him; the accusation was never proven. As Algeo suggests, it is most likely that O'Leary's body gave out after the repeated strain of the endurance walks. After the 1879 loss, O'Leary retired, established the O'Leary Belt, and trained younger walkers.[134] The pedestrian craze began to wane by 1880. It remained a topic for mocking in the theatres, and pedestrians continued to appear in vaudeville into the twentieth century.[135]

The pedestrian craze provided an opportunity for the Irish to make a good living, gain respectability, and earn international fame. Performing disciplined mobility for mixed-class audiences became a vital component of their social rise, as their performances of mobility countered long-held Irish stereotypes. Although the Irish in America comprised a substantial part of the working classes and poor through the early twentieth century and anti-Irish prejudices remained, after the Civil War more Irish and Irish Americans began to move into the middle class. Newer immigrants, including southern and eastern Europeans and the Chinese, began to supplant the Irish's position as one of the most reviled immigrant groups. As the United States became more welcoming to the Irish, however slowly, these performances of disciplined mobility became crucial to transforming the image of the Irish as roving, lazy, violent intruders into one of patriotic, hardworking Americans.

THE FIVE MICROHISTORIES investigated in this book illustrate how dramaturgies of mobility helped create and circulate meanings around the Irish and their movement. Intertwined with race, gender, and class, mobility shaped Irish-American identity, anti-Irish and anti-Catholic prejudices, resistance to Anglo-Saxon narratives of Irish life, and access to social and economic advancement. This book's site of study, variety theatre, transitioned into vaudeville around the mid-1880s. The study ends here, but the dramaturgies and the meanings they helped propagate echoed throughout U.S. culture, transforming over time, as Irish and Irish Americans became increasingly socially mobile and new immigrants arrived on the country's shores. It would also be possible to trace the dramaturgies for these new immigrants as well as for the black Americans, Germans, and Chinese who frequently lived alongside the Irish during the 1860s and 1870s. The fragmented performances examined in this study raise many more questions than they answer. In this epilogue, I raise several more about the Irish and how dramaturgies of mobility create meaning across time and history.

These dramaturgies extended beyond the theatre and echoed for years. They transformed and gained new uses for the Irish, Irish Americans, and people in power. I center these final speculative thoughts on how dramaturgies surrounding return visits to Ireland and Irish migration journeys were disrupted and became repurposed for new ends. Drawing on Kotef's theorization of mobility and freedom, it is possible to understand how, as the Irish increasingly entered the middle class and acquired more of an "image of stability," at least compared to new migrants, their new status "served to facilitate their growing mobility."[1] As more Irish and Irish Americans acquired the financial ability to return home and advances in transportation made it more convenient and affordable, these travelers' experiences disrupted frequently repeated dramaturgies created through the imagined journey home. The "returned Yanks" reception in Ireland highlights the importance of audience in how meanings tied to movement are constructed and circulated. Finally, I point to the ways these dramaturgies are used in the United States' 2018 debates about migration.

In the last decades of the nineteenth century, social mobility still seemed out of reach for many Irish in the United States. Miller remarks that few post-Famine migrant letters encouraged relatives to migrate to America for economic opportunity. He notes that "most letters written during the period conveyed cautionary or negative information about the United States and the newcomers' likely prospects."[2] According to one migrant, "life in America was very trying on a person's nerves . . . there was always the fear that one might lose his position and become destitute."[3] Migrant Timothy Cashman reflected that "after forty years laboring in New England factories . . . [t]here never was good times for the ordinary *honest* worker."[4] Others lamented the similarities between Ireland and America for the working-class Irish: "[I]t was 'the same [in America] as in Ireland, . . . every year something new comes up to make the rich man richer and the poor man poorer.'[5] These experiences led some, like Irish migrant Frank Roney, to conclude that the "exalted idea of man's equality in the American republic was rather mythical."[6]

These conclusions do not appear surprising considering that in 1880 about half of Irish-American men still worked in unskilled jobs. At the turn of the century, in spite of increasing numbers of middle-class Irish Americans, significant numbers of Irish and Irish Americans remained in the working class, especially women. With unemployment and alcoholism continuing to plague daily life, "descriptions of lower-working-class Irish-American neighborhoods in the 1890s–1920s were often strikingly reminiscent of the destitution and demoralization observed at mid-century."[7] Learning about the harsh realities of U.S. life was a startling blow to some migrants. In 1883, one migrant told the New York immigration authorities that she left Ireland because "she was like many other fools in that country who were led to believe they would pick up money in the streets in America."[8]

By the late nineteenth and early twentieth century, however, a growing number of Irish Americans began to move into the middle class, defying the prevalent nineteenth-century image of Irish Americans as lazy and impoverished. Political and civil service positions helped Irish Americans gain respectability and exert power over their cities and towns.[9] It would be incorrect to suggest that mobility no longer played a role in Irish-American life, but with increasing numbers moving away from transient working-class life, the relationship shifted and more Irish-American families had the opportunity to establish a more rooted life. Despite the impression of the Irish community's "surface unity," this class shift reflected "a growing diversity and stratification" and an expansion of what constituted "Irishness" in the public imagination.[10] The term "lace curtain Irish" referred to the middle-class Irish population and "denot[ed] a certain level of financial achievement [as well as] . . . connot[ed] a self-conscious, anxious attempt to create and maintain a certain level and mode of gentility."[11] "Lace curtain" linked Irish social mobility with a decline in physical mobility and a more sedentary life. Becoming "lace curtain" Irish represented an ability to participate in consumer culture and live in a home with the trappings of middle-class respectability. The increase of the lace-curtain Irish created internal struggles in the Irish-American community, with "the desire to join the 'ins' conflict[ing] with the desire to lead the 'outs.' The wish to climb socially ran counter to the impulse to champion the rebellious, restless poor."[12] At the same time, constant migration caused the lower-class Irish communities in U.S. urban centers to grow.

For middle-class Irish and Irish Americans, their social mobility and less transient lives further enabled their physical movement in ways acceptable to middle-class culture. Their increased expendable income facilitated their participation in the consumer culture and the leisure economy, including the culture of international travel. Images of a return trip to Ireland were increasingly produced for middle-class Irish Americans in performances beyond the hibernicon. For example, travel lecturers started using the stereopticon by the mid-1870s through the turn of the century. Created in the 1850s, a stereopticon was a "projector of photographic slides."[13] Some lecturers also used their speeches to push their Irish nationalist politics. Similar to the hibernicon, the stereopticon performers also wanted to maintain their novelty. For example, in 1898, Father Sheehy took his audience through key battles in the Spanish-American War before starting his tour of Ireland.[14]

These stereopticon and lecture performances satisfied many of the same desires for nostalgic and romantic Irish images and spectacle that the hibernicon previously fulfilled. During these years, more affordable and efficient travel allowed more people than ever before to visit Ireland. More middle-class Irish Americans earned enough to afford a trip to Ireland. As a result, these performances frequently functioned as advertisements, as opposed to replacements, for the audiences' own Ireland experiences.

Irish Americans who visited and did not intend to resettle in Ireland became known as "returned Yanks." Although many visitors enjoyed their journeys, for others, their experience in Ireland disrupted their nostalgic memories, stories told by family members, and images of Ireland distributed in the United States. Many returned Yanks commented unfavorably on what they found in Ireland. After more than thirty years away, Irish migrant Timothy Cashman described his disappointment at seeing his hometown again. There was "mud and dirt all over everything," and he believed that "Irish poverty and emigration seemed as great . . . as when he had left his home."[15] Many Irish Americans were similarly disenchanted with their visits. Charles P. Daly, the son of Irish emigrants and a prominent judge in New York, ranted about his unhappy experience in his June 8, 1874, diary entry:

> I never travelled through a country that I was more willing to leave. . . .
> [T]he Irish in America were physically and intellectually far superior
> to the people we met with in Ireland. . . . I have seen a much greater
> number of fine [illegible] Irish people men and women of the humble
> and working classes in the [illegible] states than we saw in the whole of
> our journey through Ireland. . . . [T]he Irish appeared to us a dissatisfied
> people who were disposed to attribute their dissatisfaction to any cause
> but themselves. There are many causes for its historical [problems], but
> I apprehend the people themselves have much to do with it.[16]

Daly's low opinion of the Irish he met no doubt influenced their "un-favorable" opinions of the United States and Americans, which they apparently expressed quite openly to Daly.[17]

Arnold Schrier, who collected anecdotal evidence about returned Yanks around the turn of the century, describes the general type:

> He returned largely because of a sincere desire to see his family just once more, and also to glory in the admiration he was certain to receive in honor of the obvious evidence of his success in America: his grand clothes, his liberal supply of money, and just as important, the very fact that he was able to afford a return visit. He was duly accorded the admiration he sought, and with his vanity gratified and his funds exhausted, he once more took leave of Ireland, probably never to return again to the land of his birth.[18]

Generated in Ireland in response to Irish-American tourists, this type presented a counter to the romantic journey through Ireland presented in dramaturgies on the other side of the Atlantic. Irish anecdotes reflect the image of the wealthy, vain returned Irish visitor. For some, visual appearance made the distinction between the Irish and visitor instantly apparent. An Irish farmer commented, "People would make a great wonder of a Yankee having two or three suits, for the ordinary man at home would have one good suit for going to Mass in and it would have to do him for years and years."[19] A cook remembered the stir caused by a returned Yank who visited her family. Supposedly the local women tried to figure out which Mass she would attend so that they would not miss seeing her outfit.[20] They also remarked how the United States changed the characters of the former migrant or Irish American. Irish family and friends saw the visitors as more confident, hardworking, opinionated, and clean. According to an Irish teacher, "their shyness and gaucheries had left them."[21] The Irish also assumed that the returned Yanks were rich, and some visitors' looseness with money reinforced these expectations.[22] Although many Irish admired the visitors and their arrivals often warranted celebration, they also became targets for ridicule. The Catholic Church and pro-British authorities and residents also feared the ideas they might bring with them from the United States.[23]

Daly's visit highlights the sometimes-hostile response visitors received. As historian Marion Casey notes, "his or her visit was often unsettling because it highlighted how time had stood still in Ireland."[24] Reactions to visitors ranged from admiration to contempt. Although much of the evidence for Irish perceptions of returned Yanks is anecdotal, the impressions of returned Yanks as wealthy, well-dressed, vain visitors moved from anecdotes into literature, jokes, and the theatre. In 1908, the Gaelic writer Seamus O Dubhghaill described visiting Irish Americans in terms that could easily describe the stage stereotype: "There's another group, people who think a great deal of themselves, but whom I don't have much respect for—the Puncain—the Yankee. They come over here to us after spending a couple of years over there, they speak through their noses, and you would think with their hustle that they owned all of America and that the sun rose out of America's arse."[25] In Irish drama, Returned Yank characters are prosperous and bombastic. They illustrate all the reasons why the Irish should not migrate, and they reduce Irish Americans' usefulness to their large bank accounts.[26] According to scholar Philip O'Leary, "these comic treatments were rooted in a real concern about the influence American, and particularly Irish American, visitors to Ireland could have on Gaeltacht people."[27]

Social, economic, and political shifts within the Irish-American community also changed the meanings surrounding the physical and imagined journey to Ireland. Even though divisions and conflicts always existed among Irish and Irish Americans, rallying the Irish-American community around Irish causes became increasingly difficult in the first few decades of the twentieth century. Support for Irish-American nationalism weakened after 1890 with the failure of the Home Rule movement, but enthusiasm and political organization continued to exist. The Easter Rising of 1916 marked the beginning of the second mass Irish nationalist movement in America. Although the rebels' initial arrests did not inspire outrage, their execution and the postponement of Home Rule measures caused Irish Americans to rally around calls for Irish independence through any methods necessary. Between 1916 and 1922, Irish Americans sent $10 million across the Atlantic to support Irish independence efforts. The declaration of the Irish Free State in 1922 marked the end of Irish-American nationalism as a uniting force and major symbol of Irish-American identity. For many Irish Americans, the establishment of the Free State, even without the northern six counties, accomplished the movement's major goals.[28]

As the Irish-American connection with Ireland lessened, the hibernicon disappeared, and new visual mediums adopted and parodied the basic narrative. For example, the Edison company short film *European Rest Cure* (1904), directed by Edwin S. Porter, depicts tourists' first stop in Ireland on a European vacation. The Irish stereotypical characters convey none of the hibernicon's nuance, and no sentiment toward or loyalty to the country. The mishaps during the tourists' visit to the Blarney Stone are entirely for comic effect.[29] By the early twentieth century, for many Irish Americans, I suggest the imagined journey home no longer comprised part of their usable past. The narrative no longer mobilized Irish communities and nationalist sentiment like it did during the late nineteenth century. The dramaturgy from the 1870s reminded Irish and Irish Americans of Ireland's past glories and struggles, which seemed increasingly distant and irrelevant to their experiences in the United States. Many of the Irish Americans who viewed the film did not experience the trauma of their older relatives. Ireland may have occupied a mythic and beloved position for many Irish descendants, but the urgency and connection weakened. They did not envision themselves as part of a Celtic race on the move. They may have celebrated their ancestral past and enjoyed their vacation there, but they lived relatively settled lives in the United States, their home.

In addition to social and economic mobility, Irish and Irish Americans' position shifted in the United States as new migrants arrived. In 1882, the United States escalated its control of migrant movement by passing the first federal immigration law, the Chinese Exclusion Act. The act's preamble justified its regulations by explaining, "in the opinion of the Government of the United States the coming of Chinese laborers to this country endangers the good order of certain localities within the territory thereof."[30] The act banned Chinese laborers from migrating to the United States for ten years. Although it expanded the government's powers to regulate migration, the act also worked within the same rationale as previous state and local laws that targeted the

Irish and defined the U.S. nation by labeling a group as antithetical to American values. As Cresswell notes, "Both the Chinese immigrant and the tramp practiced mobility, but in doing so they were deemed to be practicing something other than citizenship. Both external and internal mobilities were presented as threats to the good order of particular kinds of spaces, which had been invested with moral (and legal) worth."[31] When the federal laws were passed, Anglo-American Protestants still may have despised them, but many saw the Irish as possible citizens and preferable to southern and eastern European or Chinese migrants.

The Irish and their dramaturgies continue to be touchstones in public conversations about migration in the United States. Proponents and opponents of the new migrant restrictions proposed by the Trump administration draw on the Irish's nineteenth-century migration journey to judge or defend migrants entering the country in the twenty-first century. As the president rails about refugees from what he refers to as "shithole countries" and imprisons Latinx immigrants while advocating for a border wall, Americans have looked to the Irish and the discrimination they faced as an answer. For some Republicans, referencing their Irish ancestors' journey has become a tactic for demonstrating their support for migration while backing the administration's antimigrant policies. For example, former press secretary Sean Spicer used his Irish heritage to express his support for migration while justifying his belief in Trump's border wall. In an interview in Ireland while promoting his book, Spicer explained, "As an Irish American, someone who understands the trials and tribulations that so many Irish folk felt coming to America, I'm very proud of America's history welcoming immigrants."[32] Whether intended or not, the juxtaposition between the celebrated Irish migration in his statements and the persecuted Latinx immigration at the border values Irish and Latinx bodies and mobilities differently in relation to the United States. The white Irish migrants become illustrative of "correct" immigration as compared to the Latinx migrants, even though they are similar in that they left their homes and came to the United States to seek a better life.

Even Republicans have used Irish migration to reject, however weakly, Trump's positions. When asked about Trump's comments about refugees from Haiti, Republican House Speaker Paul Ryan disagreed briefly, mostly speaking of his Irish heritage. He mentioned his family who "came from Ireland on what they called coffin ships then, came here and worked the railroads. The Irish were really looked down upon back in those days. I hear all these stories from my relatives about 'Irish Need Not Apply.'"[33] Discussing how his family worked its way into the middle class, he states that the migrant experience is the "beautiful story of America."[34] In this case, Ryan used his Irish ancestors' journey to offer an alternative narrative to the one presented by the president about migration and its relationship to the United States' past and future.

In addition to helping construct ideas surrounding contemporary migration debates, these dialogues reflect the changing role of mobility in the construction of Irish and Irish-American identity in the cultural imagination. Fear over undocumented migrants marching to the border and "invading" the country is personified in newspapers, on television, and on the internet as Latinx migrants. In part, this is unsurprising since they make up a large percentage of undocumented migrants. Undocumented migrants enter the United States in other ways, however, such as by overstaying visas, an approach that has received less public scrutiny and fewer attacks from the president. An estimated fifty thousand undocumented Irish currently live in the United States and remain at risk of deportation as a result of the Trump administration's more aggressive migrant enforcement policies. They are not depicted as dangerous invaders, if they are mentioned at all. When the Taoiseach of Ireland, Leo Varadkar, visited Washington, D.C., in March 2018, he portrayed the Irish as ideal American citizens and advocated for giving them a path to citizenship. Talking at a lunch with the speaker of the house, he stated, "I might simply highlight [the undocumented Irish's] situation — hardworking, law-abiding, tax-paying Irish men and women who share your hopes and your values, who are patriotic and loyal to America — and urge a sympathetic look at this issue."[35] After meeting with President Trump, the Taoiseach believed "enthusiasm" for a solution existed.[36]

Undocumented Irish still live in fear of deportation as the numbers of Irish deportations have increased over the past several years. Even though Irish migration did not stop after the nineteenth century, Irish mobility, even when technically in violation of U.S. law, no longer signifies a major threat to the United States. In some ways, Irish-American mobility remains trapped in nineteenth-century narratives, as illustrated by Spicer and Ryan's comments. The mobile Irish do not constitute an unpredictable, criminal specter that threatens to undermine American values. This image arguably results in part from the nativist and white supremacist language surrounding discussions of Latinx immigrants. I suggest that the image of the settled and assimilated Irish and Irish Americans acts in concert with their whiteness to limit the perceived threat of Irish migrant mobility in 2018. It is generally accepted that the Irish and their estimated thirty million descendants are here to stay.[37] Using repeated narratives about the negative impact of Latinx immigrants' mobility on the United States serves a dual purpose for white supremacist and nativist Americans. At the same time that they spread fear, they also hold out a nativist hope that Latinx migrants' mobility will prevent their settlement and enable them to return to their home countries. If the efforts to deport the Irish, Chinese, and others serve as any precedent, this hope also will inevitably be foiled.

NOTES

Introduction

1. Donald Trump, quoted in Erin Durkin and Nina Lakhani, "Trump Threatens to Close US-Mexico Border over Honduran Migrant Caravan," *Guardian*, October 18, 2018; accessed October 19, 2018, https://www.the guardian.com/us-news/2018/oct/18/trump-threatens-to-close-us-mexico -border-over-migrant-caravan.

2. Ibid.

3. Cesar Rios, quoted in Anna-Catherine Brigida, "A New Migrant Caravan from El Salvador Is Making Its Way North," *Washington Post*, October 28, 2018; accessed October 30, 2018, https://www.washingtonpost.com/world /the_americas/a-new-migrant-caravan-from-el-salvador-is-making-its-way -north/2018/10/28/201ecd86-dad0-11e8-8bacbfe01fcdc3a6_story.html? utm _term=.58cde8ce02eb.

4. Mauricio Landaverde, quoted in Brigida, "A New Migrant Caravan."

5. Salvador Sánchez Cerén, quoted in Brigida.

6. Jason Lemon, "MAGA Hat Wearing Border Vigilante Says U.S. Hasn't Taken in Immigrants Fleeing Hardships Before," *Newsweek*, November 21, 2018; accessed November 21, 2018, https://www.newsweek.com/maga-hat -wearing-border-vigilante-says-us-hasnt-taken-immigrants-fleeing-1226940.

7. Emma Larazus, "The New Colossus," quoted in Hunter, "The Story Behind the Poem."

8. Ken Lester, quoted in Lemon, "MAGA Hat."

9. "Literature," *New York Phoenix*, June 4, 1859, 6.

10. Ibid.

11. Bayor and Meagher, eds., *The New York Irish*; Barrett, *The Irish Way*; Casey and Lee, eds., *Making the Irish American*; Clark, *The Irish in Philadelphia*; Diner, *Erin's Daughters*; Dolan, *The Irish Americans*; Emmons, *The Butte Irish*; Kenny, *The American Irish*; Kenny, *Inventing Irish America*; Kerby Miller, *Emigrants and Exiles*; Scherzer, *Unbounded Community*; Shannon, *The American Irish*.

12. Kunowm, "American Studies as Mobility Studies," 215.

13. Ibid.

14. Brigham, *American Road Narratives*, 4.

15. Kunowm, 215–16. For example, see Dirlik, "American Studies in the

Time of Empire," 287–302; Graham and Raussert, eds., *Mobile and Entangled America(s)*; Greenblatt, "A Mobility Studies Manifesto," 250–53; Houseman, *The Rights of Mobility*; Pryor, *Colored Travelers*; Rabin, *Jews on the Frontier*; Turner, "The Significance of the Frontier in American History," 197–220; Tyrell, *Reforming the World*.

16. For example, see Davis, ed., *The Cambridge Companion to Performance Studies*; Desmond, *Meaning in Motion*; Foster, *Choreographing Empathy*; Taylor, *The Archive and the Repertoire*.

17. Urry, "Mobilities and Social Theory," 491.

18. Schweitzer, *Transatlantic Broadway*, 15; Augé, *Non-Places*; Clifford, *Routes*.

19. Cresswell, *On the Move*, 3.

20. Ibid.

21. Cresswell, "Towards a Politics of Mobility," 18.

22. Kotef, *Movement and the Ordering of Freedom*, 6.

23. Ibid., 11.

24. Ibid.

25. See Deluze and Guatari, *A Thousand Plateaus*; Certeau, *The Practice of Everyday Life*.

26. Arneil, "Disability, Self Image, and Modern Political Theory," 218–42; Kotef, 11, 14. For a discussion of disability studies' relationship to the new mobility paradigm, see Claes, De Schauwer, and Hove, "Disability Studies and Social Geography," 97–130.

27. Wolff, "On the Road Again," 253. See also Kaplan, *Questions of Travel*, 65–100; Massey, *For Space*, 45–47; Steggs, *Class, Self, Culture*, 45–52.

28. Kunowm, 216.

29. Wilkie, *Performance, Transport, and Mobility*, vi.

30. Haenni, *The Immigrant Scene*; Schweitzer.

31. Taylor, 2; see also Schechner, *Between Theater and Anthropology*, 36.

32. Profeta, *Dramaturgy in Motion*, 4.

33. Carleton, "The Rovin' Irish Boy," 27.

34. Ibid.

35. "How Paddy's Represented," 60.

36. Ibid.

37. Elliot, "Gender," 76.

38. Ibid.

39. Diner, 70–105, 178; McNamara, *The New York Concert Saloon*, 90.

40. See Kenny, "Diaspora and Comparison," 134–62.

41. Miller, "Introduction," in *Irish Immigrants in the Land of Canaan: 1675–1815*, 8.

42. Ibid.

43. Theodore Parker, quoted in Dolan, *The Irish Americans*, 62.

44. Miller, 8.

45. Miller, *Emigrants and Exiles*, 346–53, 503–6; Hirota, *Expelling the Poor*, 12, 139, 153.

46. Emmons, 67.

47. Scherzer, 40.

48. Emmons, 67. Historian Jules Tygiel explains how "[f]requent uprooting represented the normal pattern of the life course in the United States during the industrial era, and any study of the period must analyze this aspect of working-class existence, examining the ways in which people integrated transiency into their lives and how communities and institutions adapted to the realities of a mobile society" ("Tramping Artisans," 110).

49. McCaffrey, *The Irish Catholic Diaspora in America*, 7.

50. Hirota, 1–15, 129–55.

51. Dolan, *The Irish Americans*, 97–98.

52. Bernstein, *The New York City Draft Riots*, 113, 120, 157; Soennichsen, *The Chinese Exclusion Act of 1882*, 51–58; Tchen, 123–52.

53. Kattwinkel, "Negotiating a New Identity," 60.

54. Ibid., 61.

55. Hodges, "'Desirable Companions and Lovers,'" 107–24.

56. Moon, *Yellowface*, 57–85.

57. "John Chinaman," 43.

58. Ignatiev, *How the Irish Became White*; Roediger, *The Wages of Whiteness*; Jacobson, *Whiteness of a Different Color*; L. P. Curtis, *Apes and Angels*.

59. Arnesen, "Whiteness and the Historians' Imagination," 3–32; Barrett, "Whiteness Studies," 33–42; Foner, "Response to Eric Arnesen," 57–60; Goldstein, *The Price of Whiteness*; Guglielmo, *White on Arrival*; Hartman, "The Rise and Fall of Whiteness Studies," 22–38; Kenny, "Twenty Years of Irish American Historiography," 67–75; McMahon, *The Global Dimensions of Irish Identity*; Meagher, *The Columbia Guide to Irish American History*, 223.

60. Meagher, *The Columbia Guide*, 223.

61. Ibid.

62. Onkey, *Blackness and Transatlantic Irish Identity*, 7.

63. Guglielmo, 8–10; McMahon, 2.

64. McMahon, 13.

65. Ibid., 78.

66. Barrett, *The Irish Way*, 4.

67. In some ways, this conceptualization is similar to W. E. B. Du Bois's double consciousness. See Du Bois, *The Souls of Black Folk*.

68. McMahon, 78.

69. *Irish World*, January 28, 1871.

70. Ford, quoted in McMahon, 171.

71. Erdman, *Blue Vaudeville*; Kibler, *Rank Ladies*; Nasaw, *Going Out*; Snyder, *The Voice of the City*.

72. Mooney, *Irish Stereotypes in Vaudeville*. For foundational studies of variety theatre, see McNamara; Kattwinkel, "Introduction" and "Negotiating a New Identity"; Monod; Rodger, *Champagne Charlie* and *Just One of the Boys*.

73. Kattwinkel, "Negotiating a New Identity," 48.

74. Rohs, *Eccentric Nation*.

75. Butsch, *The Making of American Audiences*, 96–105; Monod; Kattwinkel, "Introduction" and "Negotiating a New Identity"; McNamara.

76. Rodger, *Champagne Charlie*, 6–8, 66–67, 73–80; Rodger, *Just One of the Boys*, 59.

77. Rodger, *Champagne Charlie*, 30–31. Monod argues that Josh Hart, manager of the Theatre Comique, started the improvements in variety first in New York in the 1870s. Monod, 180.

78. Rodger, *Champagne Charlie*, 72–84.

79. Rodger, *Just One of the Boys*, 47.

80. Rodger, *Champagne Charlie*, 25; Fields, 43.

81. Rodger, *Champagne Charlie*, 179; Kattwinkel, "Negotiating a New Identity," 47–48.

82. "The Hibernicon at Pike's," *New York Tribune*, September 23, 1868, 2.

83. Quoted in Murphy, "Irish-American Theatre," 222.

84. Mooney, 8–12; Murphy, "From Scapegoat to Grásta," 19–37.

85. Knobel, *Paddy and the Republic*, 62, 66–67, 68.

86. Williams, *'Twas Only an Irishman's Dream*, 171.

87. Ibid., 158, 171, 165.

88. Ibid., 118–33.

89. "Who is to Blame?," *Irish World*, June 5, 1875, 6.

90. Ibid.

91. "How Our Irish-Americans See Themselves Caricatured and Like It," *Irish-American*, February 24, 1883, 7.

92. See Dorman, "American Popular Culture and the New Immigration Ethnics," 179–93.

93. Miller, 106–7. Kattwinkel echoes this idea. Kattwinkel, "Negotiating a New Identity," 47.

94. Wilmeth, Review of *Champagne Charlie and Pretty Jemima*, 218.

95. Putnam, "To Study the Fragments/Whole," 615.

96. Kotef, 138.

Chapter One

1. Wertheim, *W. C. Fields from Burlesque and Vaudeville to Broadway*, 50–51; Gilbert, *American Vaudeville*, 269–78; Schulman, "Beaten, Battered, and Brawny," 102; DePastino, *Citizen Hobo*, 152–62; Cresswell, *The Tramp in America*, 130–70; Kusmer, *Down and Out*, 170–73.

2. This chapter does not claim to identify an originator of the comic tramp in variety. See also Henke, *Poverty and Charity*. The tramp would appear in the circus by the 1920s; Towsen, *Clowns*.

3. Brigham, *American Road Narratives*, 4.

4. For analysis of the Panic and depression, see Burrows and Wallace, *Gotham*, 1021–34.

5. Rorabaugh, *Craft Apprentice*, 198–210; D. T. Rodgers, *The Work Ethic in Industrial America*, 153–81; Carlebach, *Working Stiffs*, 19–54; Kasher, ed. *America and the Tintype*.

6. Monkkonen, *Police in Urban America*, 88–93; Kusmer, 35–56.

7. Ringenbach, *Tramps and Reformers*, 3–29; Cooper, "The 'Traveling Fraternity,'" 118–38; Letter to the Editor, *Printers' Circular* 5, no. 8 (October 1870): 330–31. Cresswell argues that tramps were "made up" in the 1870s; Cresswell, *The Tramp in America*, 13.

8. Ringenbach, 3–4, 16–25; Kusmer, 45–50; DePastino, 3–17.

9. Wayland, *Out-Door Relief and Tramps*, 10.

10. "The Tramp," *New York Times*, August 8, 1875, 9.

11. Stanley, "Beggars Can't Be Choosers," 1267. See also Stanley, *From Bondage to Contract*, 98–137; Fox, "Citizenship, Poverty, and Federalism," 565–69; Schmidt, *Free to Work*, 208–18.

12. "An Act Concerning Tramps," 45.

13. Millis, "The Law Affecting Tramps and Immigrants," 587–94.

14. Ocobock, "Introduction," 1.

15. Tiedemann, 145.

16. Harris, *The Man Who Tramps*, 18.

17. STAATS, *A Tight Squeeze or, The Adventures of a Gentleman*, 10.

18. Bellew, ed., *The Tramp*, 6.

19. Ibid., 21.

20. Ibid.

21. Ibid.

22. Ibid., 21–22.

23. A. P., *Mysteries and Miseries of the Great Metropolis*, 327–28.

24. Brewer, "What Shall We Do With Our Tramps?," 522.

25. "The Disease of Mendicancy," *Scribner's Monthly* 13, no. 3 (January 1877): 416–17, citing 416.

26. *Chicago Tribune*, July 12, 1877.

27. Brewer, 532.

28. Cresswell, *On the Move*, 160.

29. Sanborn, "The Tramp," 1.

30. Thanet, "The Indoor Pauper," 756.

31. O'Gorman, front cover clipping, Daybook of William O'Gorman, Overseer of the Poor Newtown, New York, Vol. II.

32. Hirota, 137.

33. *Boston Pilot*, May 12, 1883.

34. Hirota, 137.

35. Ibid., 137.

36. Ibid., 130.

37. Ibid., 139.

38. Quoted in Jacobson, 48.

39. "A Danger for Tramps," *New York Tribune*, March 19, 1882, 6.

40. Jacobson, 48.

41. Sanborn, 1.

42. Massachusetts, *Twelfth Annual Report of the Board of State Charities of Massachusetts*, 1876, Public Doc. 17, lxxxii, quoted in Hirota, 138; Brewer, 531.

43. DePastino, 15.

44. "City Summary," *New York Clipper*, January 31, 1874, 350.

45. "Dramatic," *Brooklyn Eagle*, February 16, 1874, 3. For more on the Panic and theatre in New York, see "Introductory Overture," *New York Clipper*, October 11, 1873, 222; "Introductory Overture," *New York Clipper*, November 15, 1873, 262; "Amusements in Hard Times," *New York Clipper*, November 22, 1873, 266; "Introductory Overture," *New York Clipper*, November 22, 1873, 270; "City Summary," *New York Clipper*, December 6, 1873, 286; "City Summary," *New York Clipper*, December 13, 1873, 294; *New York Clipper*, January 3, 1874, 314; "Introductory Overture," *New York Clipper*, January 10, 1874, 326; "City Summary," *New York Clipper*, January 31, 1874, 350; "Bankruptcy of Edwin Booth," *Brooklyn Daily Eagle*, February 9, 1874, 2; *New York Clipper*, February 21, 1874, 374; "Progress of the Operatic and Dramatic Season," *Brooklyn Daily Eagle*, November 6, 1874, 2; "New York," *Chicago Tribune*, April 25, 1874, 9D. See also Rodger, *Champagne Charlie*, 78–83; Alan Gevinson, "The Origins of Vaudeville," 149–315; and Butsch, 104.

46. *New York Clipper*, October 18, 1873, 230; *New York Clipper*, December 6, 1873, 288; *New York Clipper*, January 31, 1873, 347.

47. "Charity," *New York Clipper*, November 15, 873, 258; *New York Clipper*, November 22, 1873, 267; *New York Clipper*, November 29, 1873, 278; "City Summary," *New York Clipper*, December 13, 1873, 294.

48. McNamara; Rodger, *Champagne Charlie*; Kattwinkel, "Negotiating a New Identity" and "Tony Pastor's Vaudeville: Serving the New York Community," 50–75.

49. "City Summary," *New York Clipper*, March 21, 1874, 406. The *New York Clipper* documents the repeat performances through the end of May. See "City Summary," *New York Clipper*, October 10, 1874, 222; March 27, 1875, 414; May 16, 1874, 54; December 12, 1874, 294; October 14, 1876, 230; October 5, 1878, 222; October 19 and 26, 1878; April 3, 1875, 7; and May 1, 1875, 35. For other references, see Odell, *Annals of the New York Stage*, vol. 10, 266, and the *New*

York Herald, April 13, 1877, 11, and May 4, 1879, 17. For more on Harrigan, see Moody, *Ned Harrigan*.

50. Horton, *About Stage Folks*, 72.

51. "'Johnny' Wild is Dead," *New York Dramatic Mirror*, March 12, 1898, 23. Charles Edward Ellis repeats a similar sentiment in his *Authentic History of the Benevolent and Protective Order of Elks*, 275.

52. "Spirit of the Stage," *Spirit of the Times*, August 14, 1880, 44; "'Johnny' Wild is Dead," *New York Dramatic Mirror*, March 12, 1898, 23; "The Variety Stage," *Harper's Weekly*, April 12, 1902, 466.

53. "Spirit of the Stage," *Spirit of the Times*, September 29, 1883, 274.

54. "The Variety Stage," *Harper's Weekly*, April 12, 1902, 466; Ford, *Forty-Odd Years in the Literary Shop*, 99.

55. Gilbert, 37–85.

56. Cresswell, *The Tramp in America*, 14.

57. Kusmer, 106–7.

58. Cohen, *At Freedom's Edge*, 248.

59. Kolchin, *First Freedom*, 4–7, 11, 23. For more on black mobility after the Civil War, see Cohen, 248–98; Kusmer, 138–40; and Foner, *Reconstruction*, 200–201.

60. O'Gorman, clipping, Daybook of William O'Gorman, Vol. II, 155.

61. Kusmer, 138–39.

62. Garner, "The Simianization of the Irish," 216; Gough, *Kinship and Performance in the Black and Green Atlantic*, 1–83; Onkey, 1–32; L. P. Curtis; Lott, 95.

63. Cockrell, 199.

64. Kibler, *Censoring Racial Ridicule*, 22.

65. The advertisements in the *New York Clipper* during these years document the overlap in performers.

66. Lott, 95.

67. Ibid; Toll, 247, 249.

68. Harrigan, *Mulligan Guard Picnic*, one-act version, 27.

69. Ibid.

70. Ibid., 35.

71. Ibid.

72. Ibid. Jack seems to be performed white as demonstrated from his lack of dialect. Other characters also mix him up with other white characters when they switch clothing.

73. Courtright, *Private Boarding*, 3.

74. "Music and the Drama," *Spirit of the Times*, March 20, 1875, 134.

75. Wild, 4.

76. Ibid.

77. Harrigan, *Terrible Example*.

78. Ibid.

79. Harrigan, *Down Broadway*, 7–10. *Bummers* was a slang term for tramps used throughout the 1870s.

80. Ibid., 8–9.

81. Wild, arranged by Charles White, *One, Two, Three*, 6. *Business* refers to the actors' stage movements and actions, including scuffles and fighting.

82. Courtright, 4.

83. Harrigan, *Terrible Example*.

84. Courtright, 4.

85. Wild, 4–6.

86. Harrigan, *Terrible Example*.

87. Harrigan, *Down Broadway*, 10.

88. Courtright, 3.

89. Kasson, *Rudeness and Civility*, 130.

90. Stansell, *City of Women*, 90.

91. Kusmer, 57–72, 111–13; Cresswell, *The Tramp in America*, 89.

92. Harrigan, *Down Broadway*, 6.

93. *High Life and Low Life in New York*, 1869, 5.

94. *The Match Girl of New York*, 1873, 6.

95. Ibid., 6.

96. Ibid., 7.

97. Ibid., 15.

98. Kattwinkel, "Negotiating a New Identity," 59–61.

99. Williams, *'Twas Only an Irishman's Dream*, 161.

100. "The Army of Tramps," *National Labor Tribune* (Pittsburgh, Pa.), May 27, 1876.

101. Sanjek, *The Future of Us All*, 22–23.

102. O'Gorman, Daybook of William O'Gorman, vol. II, March 9, 1875.

103. Ibid., vol. II, April 23, 1875.

104. Ibid., vol. I, January 21, 1875.

105. Ibid., vol. I, December 21, 1874.

106. Letter to the Editor, Laurel Hill, January 14, 1876; clipping, O'Gorman, Daybook of William O'Gorman, vol. II.

107. Harrigan, *Terrible Example*.

108. Ibid.

109. Harrigan, "When the Soup House Comes Again," 8.

110. Ibid.

111. Harrigan, *Down Broadway*, 7.

112. Harrigan, "The Bummers," 7.

113. Ibid.; Harrigan, *Down Broadway*, 7.

114. Harrigan, "The Beggars," 5–6.

115. Ibid., 5.

116. Ibid., 6.

117. Harrigan, *Down Broadway*, 18–21.

118. Harrigan, *Mulligan Guard Picnic*, two-act version, act 1, 62.

119. Ibid., 64. The mention of the Bowery Theatre may have served as a metatheatrical reference to previous Wild performances there.

120. Ibid., 63.

121. Ibid., 67.

122. Wild, 4.

123. Harrigan, *Terrible Example*.

124. Ibid.

125. Harrigan, *Down Broadway*, 21.

126. Harrigan, *Terrible Example*.

127. "City Summary," *New York Clipper*, May 1, 1875, 38.

128. Harrigan, *Mulligan Guard Picnic*, two-act version, act 1, 67.

129. Ibid., act 2, 17. These pledges of loyalty occur throughout the play.

130. Ibid., act 2, 51.

131. Ibid., act 2, 51.

132. Ibid., 68.

133. Gilbert, 278.

Chapter Two

1. Thomas Meagher, quoted in McMahon, 118.

2. McMahon, 118.

3. Ibid., 112.

4. Ibid., 144.

5. Ibid., 121.

6. Meagher, quoted in McMahon, 119.

7. McMahon, 112.

8. Ibid., 2.

9. Pinkerton, *Strikers, Communists, Tramps, and Detectives*, 47.

10. Kusmer, 63–67.

11. Murphy, "From Scapegoat to Grásta," 19–37.

12. Joe English, "The Irish Volunteers," quoted in Moloney, *Far from the Shamrock Shore*, 23.

13. Ibid.

14. "Pat Murphy of Meagher's Brigade." For more Irish Civil War songs, see Williams, *'Twas Only an Irishman's Dream*, 113–17.

15. "What Irish Boys Can Do," broadside.

16. See Zellers, *Tony Pastor*.

17. Kattwinkel, "Negotiating a New Identity," 49.

18. Ibid., 51.

19. Ibid., 51.

20. Mooney, 67–88.

21. Ibid., 51.

22. Kattwinkel, "Negotiating a New Identity," 55; Mooney, 88–91.

23. McMahon, 167.

24. "The Eastern Question Revived," *New York Herald*, September 19, 1866, 6.

25. For example, see "Intervention," *Times-Picayune* (New Orleans, La.), December 31, 1871, 2.

26. "City Summary," *New York Clipper*, December 22, 1866, April 13, 1867, April 20, 1867, and March 12, 1870; *New York Herald*, March 7, 1870, 2, April 11, 1867, 7, and March 11, 1872.

27. Kotef, 139.

28. Ibid., 138.

29. Urry, *Sociology Beyond Societies*, 49.

30. Poole, *Irishman in Cuba*, 15.

31. Ibid.

32. Ibid., 16.

33. Poole, *Irishman in Greece*; *Americans in Turkey*.

34. Poole, *Irishman in Greece*, 8.

35. Poole, *Irishman in Cuba*, 3.

36. Ibid., 4.

37. *Americans in Turkey*, 23.

38. Ibid., 26, 24.

39. Rohs, 67.

40. Ibid., 70–71.

41. Poole, *Irishman in Cuba*, 4.

42. Ibid., 3.

43. Ibid., 15.

44. Ibid., 17.

45. Ibid., 18.

46. Ibid., 10.

47. *Americans in Turkey*, 28.

48. Poole, *Irishman in Greece*.

49. Ibid., 19.

50. Poole, *Irishman in Cuba*, 10.

51. Ibid., 33; Poole, *Irishman in Greece*, 26–29; *Americans in Turkey*, 34–35.

52. *Brooklyn Daily Eagle*, December 30, 1873, 3.

53. Ibid.

54. Ibid.

55. Ibid.

56. *Denver Tribune*, June 18, 1880, 1.

57. Walsh, "Michael Mooney and the Leadville Irish," 145.

58. Mike Mooney, "A Protest from the Irish," *Leadville (Colo.) Daily Herald,* November 16, 1881, 1.

59. Ibid.

60. Walsh, 8.

61. Mooney, 1; Walsh, 346.

62. Kenny, "The Molly Maguires in Popular Culture," 28.

63. Ibid., 27.

64. Bellesiles, *1877*, 110–60.

65. Pinkerton, 24. He also notes that not all tramps are violent and that some are hardworking men.

66. "The New York Central Road," *New York Evening Telegram,* July 24, 1877, 1.

67. "The Baltimore and Ohio Road," *New York Evening Telegram,* July 25, 1877, 1.

68. "The Great American Tramp," *New York Tribune,* December 20, 1885, 4.

69. Kusmer, 86.

70. Ibid.

71. Bellew, 20.

72. Ibid.

73. Harris, 21–22.

74. Ibid., 21.

75. Ibid., 272; see also Kusmer, 83–86, and Bellesiles, 262. Dime novels presented a complicated, multifaceted image of the tramp, some of which played into the tramp type linked to violence and labor. Denning, *Mechanic Accents,* 154–57.

76. For an account of the historical circumstances, see Kenny, *The Making of the Molly Maguires.* For an account of the executions, see Kenny, *The Making,* 245–46.

77. Ibid. For more on executions as forms of social control see Masur, *Rites of Execution,* 111; and Foucault, *Discipline and Punish,* 47–58.

78. Walsh, 128.

79. Denning, 118–48; Kenny, "The Molly Maguires in Popular Culture," 27–46.

80. Denning, 138–39.

81. Kenny, "The Molly Maguires in Popular Culture," 31–37; Denning, 120.

82. Denning, 118–48; Kenny, 27–46.

83. *Philadelphia Inquirer,* July 30, 1877, 5.

84. Denning, 140–43; *Philadelphia Inquirer,* August 2, 4, 6, and 8, 1877; *Leadville (Colo.) Daily Herald,* November 13 and 16, 1881.

85. *Philadelphia Inquirer,* August 6, 1877, 4.

86. Ibid.

87. *Baltimore Sun*, September 24, 1877, 1; *Trenton State Gazette*, December 11, 1877, 2.

88. Denning, 135–40; *New York Clipper*, March 25 and July 15, 1876; *Lowell (Mass.) Daily Courier*, October 5, 1876; *Roman Citizen* (Rome, N.Y.), January 4, 1878.

89. *New York Clipper*, July 15, 1876, 127; *Lowell (Mass.) Daily Courier*, October 5, 1876.

90. Cohan, *Poems and Sketches*, 114.

91. For more on Byers, see Blackstone, "Alexander Byers," 107–13.

92. Morton, *Black Diamond*. Newspaper articles were compared to the scripts, revealing that they are based on the same basic plot.

93. Ibid.

94. Denning, 135.

95. Morton, 3B.

96. Ibid., 3E.

97. Ibid., 5K.

98. Ibid., 4B.

99. Sofer, *Dark Matter*, 4.

100. Ibid., 5.

101. Morton, 3B.

102. Ibid., 4B.

103. Ibid., 1E.

104. Ibid., 4E.

105. Ibid.

106. Ibid.

107. Ibid., 7E.

108. Ibid.

109. Ibid., 6B.

110. Ibid., 5E.

111. Quoted in Odell, *Annals of the New York Stage*, vol. 11, 542–43.

112. Morton, 4E.

113. Ibid., 3E.

114. Ibid., 6E.

115. Ibid., 8E.

116. Ibid., 9E.

117. Ibid., 9E.

118. "Music and Drama," *Toronto Daily Mail*, March 15, 1881, 3; "Entertainments," *Lowell (Mass.) Daily Courier*, June 22, 24, and 25, 1885, 4.

119. It seems an afterpiece was sometimes performed during minstrel shows as well. For a selection of *Black Diamond* ads and reviews for various companies, see issues of the *New York Clipper* between 1876 and 1895.

120. "Rotten Eggs and Rocks," *Leadville (Colo.) Daily Herald*, December 13, 1883, 4.

Chapter Three

1. Vallillo, "George M. Cohan, Director," 6; Williams, "George M. Cohan," 192; Williams, *'Twas Only an Irishman's Dream*, 119; Snyder, 47–48.

2. Senelick, "Variety into Vaudeville," 1–15.

3. Brooks, *Bodies in Dissent*, 81.

4. For more on moving panoramas in the United States, see Oettermann, *The Panorama*, 342–43; Huhtamo, "Peristrephic Pleasures," 221, and *Illusions*, 177–78, 264; Hyde, *Panoramania*, 131–35; Bell, "The Sioux War Panorama," 279–99; Comment, *The Panorama*; Dahl, "Mark Twain and the Moving Panoramas," 20–32, and "Artemus Ward," 476–85; Hedgbeth, "Extant American Panoramas"; A. Miller, "Panorama, the Cinema, and the Emergence of the Spectacular," 34–69; Moody, *America Takes the Stage*, 234–38; and H. J. Powell, *Poole's Myriorama!*

5. Hanners, *"It Was Play or Starve,"* 35–53; Tenneriello, 51–89.

6. "Amusements," *New York Times*, February 24, 1859, 4.

7. Hoganson, *Consumers' Imperium*, 165.

8. Ibid., 165–66.

9. Ibid.

10. O'Kelly, *The Mambi-Land*; Bly, *Around the World in Seventy-Two Days*; Hoganson, 155–208.

11. Oettermann, 49.

12. Brooks, 96.

13. A. Miller, "Panorama," 46.

14. Tenneriello, 58–61; Altick, *The Shows of London*, 205–6.

15. A. Miller, "Panorama," 47.

16. Urry, *Mobilities*, 47.

17. Lengkeek, "Leisure Experience and Imagination," 173–85; Crouch, "Spacing, Performing, and Becoming," 1945–60; Salazar, "Tourism Imaginaries," 863–82.

18. Robinson, "Toys on the Move," 151.

19. Bense, Diary 1, October 17, 1885–August 15, 1886, 1.

20. Schivelbusch, *The Railway Journey*, 98.

21. Ibid.

22. For more on perception and panoramas, see A. Miller, "Panorama," 34–69.

23. *Daily Dramatic Chronicle*, January 30, 1866, 1; Hall and Hall, *Ireland*; Stirling, Willis, Bartlett, *The Scenery and Antiquities of Ireland*; Addey and Bartlett,

Picturesque Ireland, 78–79; El-Mudarrist and Salmon, *Romantic Travel through Bartlett's Engravings,* 17–18.

24. *Handbook for Travellers*; Ashworth, *The Saxon in Ireland*; Forbes, *Memorandums*; Otway, *A Tour*; Thackeray, *The Irish Sketchbook*. See also O'Connor, "Myths and Mirrors," 69–71; Cronin, "Fellow Travellers," 54–56; Meloy, "Touring Connemara," 45; Williams, *Tourism,* 30–31, 37, 41, 51–53, 127–28, 163; and Casey, "Ireland, New York and the Irish Image," 221–23.

25. Buzard, *The Beaten Track,* 4.

26. Kroeg, "Cockney Tourists," 213.

27. Macaulay, *Ireland in 1872,* v; for other instances, see Hall and Hall, 2–3, and Hooper, "The Isles/Ireland," 115.

28. Hall and Hall, 2–3.

29. Ibid.

30. Ashworth, 43; Macaulay, 4–5, 7–8, 11. See also Forbes; Martineau, *Letters from Ireland*; Meloy, 45; Hooper, 183; Williams, *Tourism,* 30–1, 37, 41, 51–53, 127–28, 153, 163; Casey, 221–22; Hall and Hall, *Hand-books for Ireland,* 87–88; and Optic, *Shamrock and Thistle,* 95, 215, 308.

31. Hall and Hall, *Hand-books,* 87–88.

32. Kroeg, 206, 211–14.

33. MacCannell, *The Tourist,* 101.

34. Jeffares, "Place, Space and Personality and the Irish Writer," 11.

35. Booth, "Irish Landscape in the Victorian Theatre," 160.

36. These representations also could be found in melodramas and variety afterpieces, including Dion Boucicault's Irish nationalist melodramas and variety afterpieces. Moody, *America Takes the Stage,* 205–38; Kattwinkel, "Negotiating a New Identity," 51; McFeeley, *Dion Boucicault,* 13–58, 77–106.

37. Booth, 163.

38. For example, see Ritchie, *Ireland,* iii–iv.

39. Salazar, "Tourism Imaginaries," 871.

40. O'Rourke, *Currier and Ives,* 11, 129, 131.

41. Williams, *Tourism,* 36.

42. McMahon, 25.

43. Casey, 229–28; Zuelow, *Making Ireland Irish,* xv–xxxiv; Bayne, *On an Irish Jaunting-Car*; Jones, *Shamrock-Land*; Mansfield and Mansfield, *Romantic Ireland.*

44. "Panorama of Ireland," *Irish-American,* January 25, 1851, 3. For a selection of references to panorama of Ireland shows during the 1850s, see *Philadelphia Inquirer,* January 2, 1851, 3; *Irish-American,* January 25, 1851, 3; *Weekly Herald* (Olympic, N.Y.), February 15, 1851, 1; *New York Daily Tribune,* February 19, 1851, 1; *New York Daily Tribune,* March 7, 1851, 4; *Irish-American,* March 15, 1851, 3; *Weekly Herald* (Olympic, N.Y.), May 3, 1851, 141; *New London (Conn.) Daily Chronicle,* August 7, 1851, 2; *Portsmouth (N.H.) Journal of Literature and Politics,* February 21, 1852, 2; *Brooklyn Daily Eagle,* April 20, 1852, 3; *New*

York Daily Tribune, April 23, 1852, 5; *Baltimore Sun,* November 24, 1852, 2; *Plain Dealer* (Cleveland), January 18, 1853, 2; *Cleveland Herald,* January 15, 1853; *Plain Dealer* (Cleveland), April 21, 1853, 3; *Milwaukee Daily Sentinel,* August 6 and 9, 1853; "Death of Chas. Ferguson, the Celebrated Irish Piper," *Irish-American,* May 1, 1869; "The Irish Union Pipes," *Irish-American,* May 1, 1852.

45. *Boston Herald,* January 7, 1863, 4.

46. *Charleston Courier,* June 20, 1853.

47. *Daily (Montgomery) Alabama Journal,* March 26, 1853, 2.

48. *Charleston Courier,* June 20, 1853, 3; *Daily (Montgomery) Alabama Journal,* March 15, 1853, 2, and March 23, 1853, 2; *Daily (St. Louis) Missouri Republican,* November 22, 1852, 2; *(Natchez) Mississippi Free Trader,* January 19, 1853, 1; *Daily American* (Auburn, N.Y.), June 26, 1856; "Continuation of the Examination of McEvoy Accused of the Murder of Thomas Applebee," *Chicago Times,* July 3, 1856, 3. For more on the infant phenomena during these years, see Vey, *Childhood and Nineteenth Century American Theatre.*

49. *Boston Herald,* January 7, 1863, 4.

50. *J. L. MacEvoy's New Hibernicon Songster,* 53–54.

51. "The Cyclorama of Ireland"; *MacEvoy's New Hibernicon,* broadside.

52. Rodger, *Champagne Charlie,* 98–99; see also Meade, "Kitty O'Neil and Her 'Champion Jig,'" 9–22; Williams, *'Twas Only,* 120–22.

53. For more on the hibernicon's Australian tours, see Granshaw, "Performing Cultural Memory," 76–101.

54. *Rody the Rover Songster,* 53–54.

55. *MacEvoy's New Hibernicon,* broadside.

56. Cohan Family Repertoire-Book, MS Thr 226 J. J. Cohan.

57. MacEvoy, "Barney Be Aisy," 34.

58. *McGill and Strong's Mirror of Ireland,* program, 3.

59. *Oswego (N.Y.) Daily Palladium,* February 12, 1864; *Oswego (N.Y.) Commercial Times,* June 12, 1864; *Daily Dramatic Chronicle* (San Francisco), January 30, 1866, 1; *Daily Morning Chronicle* (San Francisco), December 21, 1868, 1; Palmquist and Kailbourn, "J. H. Warwick," 578.

60. *New York Herald,* March 17, 18, and 24, 1863; *Irish-American,* March 14 and 28, 1863; April 4, 18, and 25, 1863; Harrison, *The Conventional Man,* 454; *West Australian* (Perth), October 27, 1882, 3; *Journal* (Graham's Town, South Africa), December 8, 1885, 2.

61. *Providence Evening Press,* September 28, 1871, 2.

62. Odell, *Annals of the New York Stage,* vol. 9, 195, 244, 373.

63. Tenneriello, 53. For a small selection of reports about these companies, see "A Tour of Ireland," *Syracuse (N.Y.) Daily Courier,* January 22, 1864, and May 17, 1876; *Daily (Columbus) Ohio Statesman,* April 17, 1865; *Daily Dramatic Chronicle* (San Francisco), January 30, 1866, 1; *San Francisco Chronicle,* September 10, 1870, and April 4, 1872; *Sacramento Bee,* November 2, 1870; *Hartford Daily*

Courant, November 22, 1870, 2; *Irish-American*, March 18, 1871, and December 28, 1878; *Daily Bulletin* (Auburn, N.Y.), April 15, 1871, 2; *New York Times*, April 14, 1872, May 7, 1872, July 26, 1874, and November 12, 1877; *Daily Citizen and News* (Lowell, Mass.), April 18, 1872, September 12 and 15, 1873; *Plain Dealer* (Cleveland), May 21, 1872, and May 23, 1874; *Daily Herald* (Hudson, New York), January 18, 1873; *Boston Daily Advertiser*, September 9, 1872, 1; *New York Evening Telegram*, April 10, 1873, 1; *St. Albans (Vt.) Daily Messenger*, May 20, 1873, 3; *Elkhart (Ind.) Daily Review*, March 24, 1874, 3; *Augusta (Ga.) Chronicle*, April 11, 1874, 2; *Bangor Daily Whig and Courier*, July 9, 1874; *New York Clipper*, August 21, 1875, 167; *St. Louis (Miss.) Globe-Democrat*, October 4, 1875, 5; *Brooklyn Daily Eagle*, December 31, 1875, 1; *Utica (N.Y.) Morning Herald*, May 8, 1876; and *Daily Commercial* (Vicksburg, Miss.), March 12, 1878.

64. Huhtamo, *Illusions*, 253; A. Miller, "Panorama," 46–47.

65. Huhtamo, *Illusions*, 247.

66. Sarah Davis to David Davis, Clover Lawn, January 21, 1872.

67. Davis to Davis, Clover Lawn "At Home Tuesday 10 p.m.," November 10, 1874.

68. *Irish-American*, March 14, 1863, 2.

69. "The 'Hibernicon,'" *Irish-American*, April 4, 1863, 2.

70. "Erin Go Braugh!" *Irish-American*, April 25, 1863, 1. See also "Ireland in America," *Irish-American*, April 13, 1872, 1.

71. *Times Picayune* (New Orleans, La.), March 21, 1874, 8.

72. "The Stage," *New York Evening Telegram*, April 8, 1872, 2.

73. "Announcements for the Week," *New York Evening Telegram*, April 22 and 29, 1872, 2.

74. *Cincinnati Daily Enquirer*, December 26, 1870, 1.

75. *McGill and Strong's Mirror of Ireland*, program, 3.

76. MacEvoy, "Invitation to 'Hibernicon,'" 1.

77. Ibid., 8.

78. Ibid.

79. *Irish-American*, June 5, 1852, 3.

80. Fenton, *The Young Ireland Rebellion and Limerick*, 167.

81. *Irish-American*, June 5, 1852, 3.

82. Ibid.

83. "Amusements," *New York Times*, September 9, 1868, 4.

84. "The Hibernicon," *Chicago Tribune*, September 21, 1869, 4.

85. Brown, *Irish-American Nationalism*, 8.

86. Thomas Davis, quoted in McMahon, 25.

87. McMahon, 25, 27. See also Brown, 8–10.

88. Graham, "Ireland and Irishness," 7.

89. "Constitution of the United Brotherhood, 1877," reprinted in *Special Commission Act, 1888*, 493. See Funchion, *Chicago's Irish Nationalists, 1881–1890*, 50.

90. Funchion, 53. See also K. Miller, *Emigrants and Exiles*, 538; Foner, *Politics and Ideology in the Age of the Civil War*, 154.

91. Foner, *Politics and Ideology*, 155; Brundage, "'In Time of Peace, Prepare for War,'" 321; Brown, 159–69; Miller, *Emigrants and Exiles*, 538–47.

92. Miller, 544–45.

93. Quoted in Miller, 548.

94. "Irish Funds," *Springfield (Ohio) Globe-Republic*, March 1, 1885.

95. "The Irish in America," *New York Times*, June 24, 1881, 4.

96. Miller, *Emigrants and Exiles*, 550.

97. Ibid., 551.

98. Quoted in Miller, 551.

99. Rohs, 210.

100. Williams, *'Twas Only*, 108, quoted at 109.

101. Brooks, 82.

102. Ibid.

103. Pollock, "Introduction: Making History Go," 4.

104. Ibid.

105. Ibid., 4.

106. *MacEvoy's New Hibernicon*, broadside.

107. Census and naturalization records as well as newspapers documented the migrant status of the MacEvoys, Gavin and Ryan, and McGill and Strong. MacEvoy, Naturalization Papers; United States Census Bureau, United States Census 1860, 615; *New York Evening Post*, March 25, 1863; *Rody the Rover Songster*, 4.

108. Rokem, *Performing History*, 25.

109. *New York Evening Post*, March 25, 1863.

110. "The Hibernicon at Pike's," *New York Tribune*, September 23, 1868, 2.

111. *Long-Islander*, September 26, 1879.

112. "Amusements," *New York Times*, September 9, 1868, 4.

113. *Rody the Rover Songster*, 3–4.

114. *MacEvoy's New Hibernicon*, broadside; *Rody the Rover Songster*, 56; *McGill and Strong's Mirror of Ireland*, program, 3.

115. *Daily Gazette* (Sterling, Ill.), March 3, 1882, 4.

116. *MacEvoy's New Hibernicon*, broadside.

117. Fanning, "Robert Emmet and Nineteenth Century Irish-America," 53.

118. Ibid., 55.

119. For more on Emmet and how his image proliferated through Irish-American culture, see Fanning, "Robert Emmet and Nineteenth Century Irish-America," 55–68.

120. E. S. Lloyd, "Lines," 16.

121. Dowling, "The Brigade at Fontenoy," 37.

122. Dowling, 36.

123. "I Hope That They Will Win," 39.

124. *Frank MacEvoy's New Hibernicon Songster*, 10. Frank MacEvoy does not seem to have been related, and it was common for imitation companies to use the MacEvoy name during the form's height.

125. Ibid., 11.

126. O'Mahony, "A Toast of the Sons of Ireland," 5.

127. MacEvoy, "Invitation to the 'Hibernicon,'" *MacEvoy's New Hibernicon*, broadside, 1.

128. "Terrible Times," 23.

129. Ibid.

130. "Paddy Burke," 50.

131. MS Thr 226 J. J. Cohan.

132. *MacEvoy's New Hibernicon*, broadside.

133. Ibid.

134. "Barney I Hardly Knew Ye," 14.

135. Subramanian, "Embodying the Space Between," 36.

136. MacPherson, *Women and the Irish Nation*.

137. *Lowell (Mass.) Daily Citizen*, November 22, 1876; "J. H. Ryan's Great Personation of the Irish Guide," "The Emerald Isle," broadside, 3; *San Francisco Chronicle*, April 4, 1872, 2; *Syracuse (N.Y.) Morning Standard*, March 19, 1881, 1; *Grand Forks Herald*, July 28, 1883, 1; *Daily Picayune* (New Orleans, La.), January 25, 1887; *Daily Inter Ocean* (Chicago), March 18, 1889, 4. See also Broadsides and Playbills, March and June 1871, in Program Book, 1871–1880, Tony Pastor Collection, *T-Mss 1995-028, Billy Rose Theatre Division, New York Public Library for the Performing Arts; *New York Dramatic Mirror*, June 20, 1908; and *Bangor Daily Whig and Courier*, August 30, 1872. It is harder to trace the hibernicon's female performers, especially since Barney remained the starring role. Nellie Cohan, Jerry Cohan's wife, and Dan Morris's wife both played Nora on and off for decades, but never reached the same level of acclaim as their husbands.

138. *St. Albans (Vt.) Daily Messenger*, October 8, 1890, 4.

139. Leavitt, *Fifty Years in Theatrical Management*, 296; McCabe, *George M. Cohan*, 6; Morehouse, *George M. Cohan*, 31.

140. Grau, *The Business Man in the Amusement World*, 66–67.

141. Tyler, *Whatever Goes Up*, 25.

Chapter Four

1. "Denounced by a Priest," *Kansas City Star*, March 5, 1884, 1; Orel, "Reporting the Stage Irishman," 66–77.

2. "Denounced by a Priest," 1.

3. Smith, "The Prospect for a Catholic Theatre," 1.

4. Balme, "The Bandmann Circuit," 31.

5. Rodger, *Champagne Charlie*, 70–74, 84, 85, 152–55, 166–67; Gevinson, 149–267.

6. Rodger, *Champagne Charlie*, 77.

7. Ibid.

8. For an example, see De Angelis and Harlow, *A Vagabond Trouper*, 33–56.

9. MacArthur, *The Man Who Was Rip Van Winkle*, 262. Balme characterizes agents as "the quintessential 'actor'" who "enabled other mediators [in the touring network] to function." Balme, "The Bandmann Circuit," 27; Rodger, *Champagne Charlie*, 75, 77.

10. Babbage, *"Phat Boys,"* 24–25.

11. Rodger, *Champagne Charlie*, 72–73, 77–82; Stover, *The Life and Decline of the American Railroad*, 47–96; Barnette, "Locomotive Leisure." For more on the tours, see selected newspapers: *San Francisco Chronicle*, September 10, 1870, 4; *Sacramento Bee*, November 2, 1870; *Hartford Daily Courant*, November 22, 1870, 2; *Irish-American*, March 18, 1871; December 28, 1878; *Daily Bulletin* (Auburn, N.Y.), April 15, 1871, 2; *San Francisco Chronicle*, April 4, 1872, 2; *New York Times*, April 14, 1872; May 7, 1872; July 26, 1874; November 12, 1877; *Lowell (Mass.) Daily Citizen and News*, April 18, 1872; September 12 and 15, 1873; *Plain Dealer* (Cleveland), May 21, 1872, 3; *Daily Herald* (Hudson, N.Y.), January 18, 1873; *Boston Daily Advertiser*, September 9, 1872, 1; *New York Evening Telegram*, April 10, 1873, 1; *St. Albans (Vt.) Daily Messenger*, May 20, 1873, 3; *Elkhart (Ind.) Daily Review*, March 24, 1874, 3; *Augusta (Ga.) Chronicle*, April 11, 1874, 2; *Plain Dealer* (Cleveland), May 23, 1874, 1; *Bangor Daily Whig and Courier*, July 9, 1874; *New York Clipper*, August 21, 1875, 167; *St. Louis (Miss.) Globe-Democrat*, October 4, 1875, 5; *Brooklyn Daily Eagle*, December 13, 1875, 1; *Utica (N.Y.) Morning Herald*, May 8, 1876; and *Syracuse (N.Y.) Daily Courier*, May 17, 1876.

12. Harrigan to Annie Harrigan, September 9, 1875, Scranton, Pa.; Harrigan, Harrigan Papers, Letters to Annie Harrigan, New York.

13. Ibid.

14. Harrigan to Annie Harrigan, May 14, 1876, Lawrence, Mass.; Harrigan, Harrigan Papers, Letters to Annie Harrigan, New York.

15. Harrigan to Annie Harrigan, May 9, 1876(?); Harrigan, Harrigan Papers, Letters to Annie Harrigan, New York.

16. Harrigan to Annie Harrigan, December 12, 1875, Columbus, Ohio; Harrigan, Harrigan Papers, Letters to Annie Harrigan, New York.

17. Harrigan to Annie Harrigan, n.d., 1875; Harrigan, Harrigan Papers, Letters to Annie Harrigan, New York.

18. Harrigan to Annie Harrigan, April 20, 1876, November 2, n.d., July 2, 1876; Harrigan, Harrigan Papers, Letters to Annie Harrigan, New York.

19. Farías, "Introduction." 2.

20. Cabranes-Grant, "From Scenarios to Networks," 510. Bruce Latour insists on investigating "connections leading from one local interaction to

the other places, times, and agencies through which a local site is made to do something." Without the constitutive relations, "you simply lose the grouping, which is not a building in need of restoration but a movement in need of continuation." Latour, *Reassembling the Social*, 173, 37.

21. Vium, "Fixating a Fluid Field," 82.

22. Gershon, "Bruce Latour," 166.

23. Dant, "Drivers and Passengers," 369.

24. Salazar, "Tourism Imaginaries," 869.

25. Ibid., 39; Balme, "The Bandmann Circuit," 30–31.

26. Balme, "The Bandmann Circuit," 26, 30.

27. Ibid., 30.

28. C. D. Johnson, *Church and Stage*; Wetmore, ed., *Catholic Theatre and Drama*; M. Powell, *God Off-Broadway*, 6–8. For more on the opposition of the Catholic clergy in Europe to nineteenth-century theatre, see Barish, *The Antitheatrical Prejudice*, 320–23.

29. O. Johnson, *Absence and Memory in Colonial American Theatre*, 171.

30. Panchok, "The Catholic Church and the Theatre in New York, 1890–1920," 7.

31. Panchok, 5, 9–11; Dubray, "Naturalism," 713–5.

32. Anbinder, *Nativism and Slavery*, 9–15; McCaffrey, "Irish and Irish America," 3; Higham, *Strangers in the Land*, 12–67. For more on anti-Catholicism, see Farrelly, *Anti-Catholicism in America*.

33. McMahon, 102.

34. Dolan, *The Immigrant Church*, 54; McMahon, 102.

35. J. Lloyd, "Who Would be a Nun?," 48–49.

36. Ibid., 49.

37. Synod 1866, quoted in Panchok, 27–28n10. I am relying on Panchok's translations of the Latin decrees for my analysis. Panchok includes full translations of the decrees pertaining to theatre in her footnotes.

38. Ibid., 27–28n10.

39. Fourth Synod, quoted in Panchok, 29n13.

40. Ibid.

41. Fourth Provincial Council, quoted in Panchok, 30n15.

42. Plenary of Bishops 1885, quoted in Panchok, 30n16.

43. Fifth Synod 1886, quoted in Panchok, 33n23. Panchok discusses how, after 1886, even though the Catholic leadership felt the need to reissue the theatre ban, they didn't spend much time, if any, discussing the matter in council.

44. It is not clear whether Burtsell's theatre hobby was truly unusual or not. In many other ways, Burtsell was an atypical priest. Along with his clergy friends, he started a group that discussed and debated church policies, such as priests' celibacy and the church's treatment of women.

45. Burtsell, Diary, November 27, 1865.

46. Ibid., May 1, 1865.

47. Burtsell, *The Diary of Richard L. Burtsell*, 304.

48. As Burtsell set up his new parish, he stopped keeping his diary for about four years between 1868 and 1872. A diary for 1879 also is missing.

49. Burtsell, Diary, February 24, 1867, Box 2.

50. Ibid., March 20, 1867.

51. Smith, "An Inside View of the Stage," 141; Smith, *The Parish Theatre*, 7.

52. Smith, "An Inside View of the Stage," 141.

53. Ibid.

54. Ibid.

55. Gilley, "The Roman Catholic Church and the Nineteenth-Century Irish Diaspora," 199–200. See also McKenna, 1–8.

56. K. Miller, *Emigrants and Exiles*, 527.

57. Ibid., 527.

58. Gilley, 197. See also McCaffrey, *The Irish Catholic Diaspora in America*, 82–84.

59. Diner, 127.

60. Ibid., 137.

61. Colligan, *Canvas Documentaries*, 8; Comment, 117–18.

62. Colligan, ix–xii, 6, 9–11, 16–18; Huhtamo, *Illusions in Motion*, 1–20, 175–82.

63. Smith, *The Parish Theatre*, 11.

64. Dolan, *Immigrant Church*, 99.

65. Diner, 137. "Catholic Church Fairs," *Boston Daily Globe*, November 13, 1877, 2; McDannell, "Going to the Ladies' Fair," 236.

66. See McDannell, 236; Lynch-Brennan, *The Irish Bridget*, 140; Diner, 137.

67. "Church Fairs," *Chicago Daily Tribune*, January 22, 1882, 4; Gordon, *Bazaar and Fair Ladies*, 105.

68. McDannell, 240–41. According to McDannell, German, French, Italian, Polish, and Canadian national parishes held bazaars instead of fairs for fundraisers.

69. Ibid., 244.

70. "Three Catholic Church Fairs," *New York Times*, December 14, 1883, 3; "Jottings by the Way," *Boston Daily Globe*, November 3, 1877, 2; McDannell, 242–43; Diner, 137.

71. Burtsell, *The Diary of Richard L. Burtsell*, 257.

72. *New York Times*, April 26, 1879, 4.

73. "Church Fairs," *New York Times*, December 18, 1868, 8.

74. Quoted in Diner, 138.

75. See issues of the *Catholic Herald* from 1878–1879. See also McDannell, 240.

76. McDannell, 239.

77. For more information, see McDannell, 240–41, 250.

78. *Review* (Decatur, Ill.), October 17, 1882, 3; "The Hibernicon at Pike's,"

New York Tribune, September 23, 1868; *Rocky Mountain News* (Denver, Colo.), March 2 and 5, 1884; "The Mirror of Ireland," *Hartford Daily Courant*, November 22, 1870, and September 14, 1871; *Sacramento Bee*, November 2, 1870; *Long Island City Star*, October 22, 1886, 2; *Baltimore Sun*, 23 November 23, 1865, May 24, 1870; November 24, 1874; *Courier and Union* (Syracuse, N.Y.), March 1, 1864; *Courier and Republican* (Buffalo, N.Y.), April 14, 1871; Odell, *Annals of the New York Stage*, vol. 9, 764, 773. New York's Church of the Epiphany illustrates the lasting impact of buildings supported by the hibernicon. It served the parish until 1963, when a fire destroyed it.

79. "Resolutions," *Utica (N.Y.) Daily Observer*, January 23, 1864.

80. Ibid.

81. *Courier and Union* (Syracuse, N.Y.), March 1, 1864.

82. *Utica (N.Y.) Daily Observer*, January 28, 1864.

83. Ibid.

84. Ibid.

85. "MacEvoy's New Hibernicon—A Card," *Cincinnati Daily Enquirer*, December 8, 1872, 5.

86. *Philadelphia Press*, May 5, 1870, 3.

87. *Public Ledger* (Philadelphia), December 27, 1872, 1.

88. See Burtsell's diary entries for 1865–67; Dolan, *Immigrant Church*, 65.

89. "The Parish of the Epiphany," *New York Times*, January 11, 1869, 8.

90. Burtsell, End of the Year Financial Report for 1869.

91. Burtsell, Diary, April 1, 3, 5, and 6, 1872; September 20, 23, and 24, 1875; December 26, 27, and 28, 1876, Box 1 and 2.

92. Burtsell, *The Diary of Richard L. Burtsell*, 227.

93. "The Hibernicon at Pike's."

94. Ibid.

95. Ibid.

96. Burtsell, Diary, April 3, 1872, Box 2.

97. Ibid., April 5, 1872.

98. Ibid.

99. McCarthy, *Respectability and Reform*, 21.

100. Burtsell, Diary, April 10, 1872, Box 2.

101. McCaffrey, *The Irish Catholic Diaspora in America*, 91–115.

102. Gilley, 189.

103. A true ANT approach to theatrical touring would not place such emphasis on representation. However, it is the intersection of approaches that makes it possible to understand what made the partnerships possible.

104. For examples, see Smith and White, "That Little Church Around the Corner," 33; "When These Old Clothes Are New," 11; Ryan, "Rollicking Rody"; MacEvoy, "Barney Be Aisy," 4; MacEvoy, "Widow Mavrone," 1–4; "Paddy's Wedding," 1.

105. For more on the church in Irish-American life, see K. Miller, *Emigrants and Exiles*, 527.

106. "Birth of Saint Patrick," 51.

107. Ryan, "St. Patrick's Day," 37. See also "The Dear Little Shamrock," 31.

108. Ibid.

109. "Father Tom O'Neil," 46.

110. Ibid.

111. Ibid., 46–47.

112. Ibid., 47.

113. Burtsell, Diary, March 27, 1865, Box 1.

114. Gilley, 191–92.

115. K. Miller, *Ireland and Irish America*, 265.

116. *MacEvoy's New Hibernicon*, broadside; *Gavin and Ryan's Emerald Isle*, program, 51, 53.

117. *Irish Citizen*, September 26, 1868, 5.

118. *Gavin and Ryan's Emerald Isle*, program, 52–53.

119. Ibid.

120. Ibid., 57.

121. Ibid., 53.

122. Ibid.

123. See also *McGill and Strong's Mirror of Ireland*, program; "The Emerald Isle," broadside.

124. Schweitzer, 6.

125. Ibid.

126. "The Hibernicon Then and Now," *New York Clipper*, November 1, 1884, 519.

127. Ibid.

128. Burtsell, Diary, December 26, 27, and 28, 1876.

129. Ibid.

130. Harry Miner, *Harry Miner's American Dramatic Directory*.

131. *The Statute Law of the State of New York*, 403; Havemeyer Papers; Wickham Papers.

132. *The Statute Law of the State of New York*, 404; *The Charter of the City of New York*, 143; Wallace and Patton, *Springfield City Code*, 258.

133. *Corrector* (Sag Harbor, N.Y.), October 11, 1879.

134. Ibid.

135. *Brooklyn Daily Eagle*, April 16, 1910, 5. The company was Dan Morris Sullivan's Hibernicon. If it was indeed the same Dan Morris Sullivan, he performed with hibernicon companies on and off from the 1870s.

136. "A Notable Benefit," *New York Times*, November 21, 1886, 2; *New York Times*, February 13, 1887, 11; "In and About the City," *New York Times*, January 15, 1888, 3; *New York Times*, November 15, 1891, 7; Smith, "Augustine Daly," 142.

137. Smith, *The Parish Theatre*, 12.

138. For more on the Catholic Actors Guild, see Panchok, "The Catholic Church and the Theatre in New York, 1890–1920," 497–535.

139. See Kane, "'Staging a Lie,'" 111–45; Kibler, *Censoring Racial Ridicule*, 51–81.

140. Panchok, 15.

Chapter Five

1. "The Walking Mania," *Philadelphia Inquirer*, April 2, 1879; "Pedestrian Fever," *New York Clipper*, March 8, 1879.

2. "Pedestrian Fever."

3. "Pedestrianism Gone Mad," *New York Times*, February 14, 1879, 5.

4. Ibid.

5. Rohs, 166.

6. Ibid.

7. Ibid., 167.

8. Cresswell, *On the Move*, 142.

9. Kasson, 62.

10. Ibid.

11. Butsch, 66; Kasson, 34–63.

12. Butsch, 72.

13. Kasson, 57.

14. Diner, 67.

15. Ibid., 68.

16. Butsch, 66–78.

17. Jefferson, quoted in Butsch, 80.

18. Butsch, 77–78.

19. For example, see Butsch, 66–78.

20. Amato, *On Foot*, 7, 10–11; Ingold, "Culture on the Ground," 321–22; Jarvis, *Romantic Writing and Pedestrian Travel*, 1–14, 22–4; Urry, *Sociology*, 51–59; Wallace, *Walking, Literature, and English Culture*, 11.

21. Jarvis, 2–6, 29–33; Wallace, 10–14; Benesch, "Modern(s) Walking," viii.

22. Amato, 103.

23. Jarvis, 29. For more on walking as a practice and trope, see Wallace, quote at 9, 14; Jarvis, 29–33; Solnit, 79–132.

24. It was not until the 1850s that sidewalks became a regular feature of city life in U.S. cities. Monkkonen, *America Becomes Urban*, 161; Hart, "Transport and the City," 109; Blomley, 57–58; Amato 162–63; Schultz, *Constructing Urban Culture*, 175–76.

25. Loukaitou-Sideris and Ehrenfeucht, *Sidewalks*, 5; Stansell, "Women, Children, and the Uses of the Streets," 310; Amato, 162–63; McShane, 279–85.

26. Scobey, "Anatomy of the Promenade," 204.

27. Ibid., 217–18.

28. Stansell, *City of Women*, 90–95.

29. Ibid., 90.

30. McAllister, *White People Do Not Know How to Behave*, 25.

31. A. A. to William Havemeyer, January 17, 1873, Office of the Mayor, Early Mayor Records, 1826–1897, Municipal Archives, City of New York, microfilm, roll 24.

32. Ibid.

33. Ibid.

34. John Kelly to William Havemeyer, March 13, 1873, Office of the Mayor, Early Mayor Records, 1826–1897, Municipal Archives, City of New York, microfilm, roll 27.

35. Jacob Drinker to Hon. John T. Hoffman, August 8, 1867, in *New York City Museum of Complaint*.

36. M. C. Boyer, *Dreaming the Rational City*, 8.

37. "Through Broadway," *Atlantic Monthly* XVIII (December 1866): 727; quoted in Scobey, "Anatomy of the Promenade," 212.

38. Stansell, "Women, Children, and the Uses of the Streets," 323.

39. Loukaitou-Sideris and Ehrenfeucht, "Constructing the Sidewalks," 108; M. C. Boyer, 14–15. See Paul Boyer, *Urban Masses and Moral Order in America*, 233–83.

40. Boyer, *Dreaming the Rational City*, 14; Scobey, *Empire City*, 178.

41. Blomley, 3–4, 58–64; Scobey, *Empire City*, 219–20; Amato, 64; Bluestone, "'The Pushcart Evil,'" 70–81; Schultz and McShane, "To Engineer the Metropolis," 393. See also "The Law of the Sidewalk," *New York Times*, August 28, 1879, 4.

42. Quoted in Novak, *The People's Welfare*, 124–25.

43. "The Law of the Sidewalk," 4.

44. Blomley, 70.

45. See Darwin, *The Descent of Man*, 137–39; Jefferis and Nichols, *Searchlights on Health*, 34.

46. For more on the connections between emerging sciences and Irish representation in England, as well as the difference between simianism and prognathism, see Curtis, 109–47.

47. Simms, *Nature's Revelations of Character*, 367–68. See also Stanton, *Physiognomy*.

48. Cresswell, *One the Move*, 142.

49. Simms, 373.

50. Ibid., 374–75.

51. "How to Walk Well," *Health Reformer* (September 1871): 85. For more on history of posture, see Gilman, "'Stand Up Straight,'" 57–83.

52. Amato, 181–83, 217–18; Blomley, 57–58.

53. Amato, 181.

54. Ingold, 326.

55. Riess, *Sport in Industrial America, 1850–1920,* loc. 128, 141, 188; Cumming, *Runners and Walkers,* 38–39, 42, 44–45, 47.

56. Riess, loc. 188.

57. Algeo, *Pedestrianism,* 17–25; Cumming, 70.

58. "Pedestrianism Gone Mad," *New York Times,* February 14, 1879, 5.

59. Shaulis, "Pedestriennes," 29–50; Algeo, 105–18.

60. Goulding, *The Amateur's Guide,* 5. See also James, *Practical Training,* 21; Harding, *The American Athlete,* 21.

61. "Pedestrianism," *Chicago Daily Tribune,* April 2, 1876, 5; Shaulis, 32–35; Algeo, 110.

62. Algeo, 105–15.

63. Shaulis, 32–39. For more on Anderson, see also Algeo, 105–15.

64. "Pedestrian Exercise for Women," *Brooklyn Daily Eagle,* December 29, 1878.

65. *Spirit of the Times,* January 18, 1879, 633.

66. Shaulis, 43.

67. "In the Depths," *Chicago Daily Tribune,* April 20, 1879, 3. For some of these venues, it is unclear whether they are simply saloons or are part-time variety houses. Since newspapers seem to have classified these venues similarly and with the same disdain, this section considers the dialogue that surrounded both types of places for pedestrianism.

68. "Legs and Beer," *Chicago Daily Tribune,* April 15, 1879, 5; "The Walking Mania," *Philadelphia Inquirer,* April 2, 1879, 2.

69. "The Walking Mania," 2.

70. "Legs and Beer," 5. For more on the donkey and women in the saloon, see "Pedestrianism: The Business Squelched," *Chicago Daily Tribune,* April 22, 1879, 8.

71. "Legs and Beer," 5. See also "Variety Halls," *New York Clipper,* May 3, 1879, 47; "Stopping Sunday Walks," *New York Times,* March 24, 1879, 8.

72. These concerns were possibly tied in to anxiety over women "walking the plank" in 1850s saloons. Shaulis, 32; Cumming, 38, 48–49.

73. Kasson, 130.

74. Ibid.

75. "The Female Pedestrians," *New York Times,* March 27, 1879, 5.

76. "Mme. Anderson," *Chicago Daily Tribune,* March 14, 1879, 3.

77. "Public Brutality," *Chicago Daily Tribune,* March 11, 1879, 9.

78. "Legs and Beer," 5.

79. Shaulis, 30.

80. "Broken-Down Female Pedestrians," *New York Clipper*, April 4, 1879, 4. See also "Our Amusements," *Milwaukee Daily Sentinel*, November 20, 1868.

81. Martin, *Dance Marathons*, xxi.

82. "Haps and Mishaps of Pedestrians," *New York Times*, February 2, 1879, 7.

83. Ibid.

84. "Mme. Anderson," 3.

85. "Stopping Sunday Walks," *New York Times*, March 24, 1879, 8; *Philadelphia Inquirer*, December 24, 1879, 4; "Objecting to Female Pedestrians," *New York Times*, March 29, 1879, 5; "Legs and Beer," 5. See also Shaulis, 40.

86. "The Board of Aldermen," *New York Times*, December 24, 1879, 3.

87. The relationship between female pedestrians and variety extended beyond the craze's conclusion. No longer able to support herself through pedestrianism, Madame Anderson started singing in variety theatres. "Sporting and Dramatic," *National Police Gazette*, March 6, 1880, 35, 128.

88. Algeo, 27–28, 42.

89. "O'Leary, The Pedestrian: The Weston Contest," *Irish American Weekly*, April 14, 1877, 5.

90. Ibid.

91. Stephen Rohs, *Eccentric Nation*, 165–66, quote at 166.

92. "Pedestrianism and How to Train Therefor," *New York Clipper*, January 13, 1866, 316. See also Chadwick, ed., *Beadle's Dime Hand-book of Pedestrianism*.

93. Goulding, 7.

94. Wilcox, "Irish American in Sports," 443–46; Redmond, *Irish and the Making of American Sport*, 42–44, 325.

95. Laurie Jr., *Vaudeville*, 132; Kattwinkel, *Tony Pastor Presents*, 82n15.

96. "Dramatic," *New York Clipper*, October 24, 1874, 238; "City Summary," *New York Clipper*, August 7, 1869, 142; "To Correspondents," *New York Clipper*, November 6, 1875, 250. For other instances throughout the country, see "Variety Halls," *New York Clipper*, August 5, 1876, September 9, 1876, February 2, 1878, October 5, 1878, March 30, 1878, May 3, 1879, and May 10, 1879; and "The Boylston Museum," *Boston Daily Globe*, March 27, 1879, 2.

97. "Pedestrianism," *New York Clipper*, October 10, 1874, 219. For another similar instance, see "Variety Halls," *New York Clipper*, January 13, 1877, 335.

98. "Variety Halls," *New York Clipper*, January 9, 1875, 327.

99. *New York Clipper*, April 9, 1870, 2; "The Ring," *New York Clipper*, March 14, 1874, 394; "The Ring," *New York Clipper*, June 10, 1876, 82; "City Summary," *New York Clipper*, March 29, 1879, 6; "Variety Halls," *New York Clipper*, May 3, 1879, 47.

100. *New York Clipper*, November 7, 1874, 255; Laurie, 132.

101. "A Herculean Task," *Boston Daily Globe*, April 4, 1878, 1; "Trying to Beat O'Leary Time," *New York Times*, April 22, 1878, 5; "Pedestrian Match," *Wheeling (W.Va.) Register*, October 1, 1878, 1; "Muscular Manifestations," *Boston Daily Globe*, January 11, 1879, 1. See also McNamara, 109–20.

102. *The Fawn*, in *Tony Pastor Presents*, 79.

103. *New York Clipper*, March 29, 1879, April 5, 1879, and October 18, 1879; Moody, *Ned Harrigan*, 91; Rohs, 177, 181.

104. *Daily Evening Bulletin* (San Francisco), March 24, 1876; "City Summary," *New York Clipper*, July 28, 1877, 142.

105. H. M. L., "Walk, Walk, Walk," sheet music (Cleveland: S. Brainard's Sons, 1867), 5.

106. *Age* (Melbourne), May 18, 1865, 8.

107. Horton, *About Stage Folks*, 7.

108. "Pedestrianism," *Daily Alta California*, April 9, 1868, 1.

109. *New York Clipper*, March 21, 1868, 398; *New York Herald*, March 13, 1868, 12; "Pedestrianism," *Daily Alta California*, April 9, 1868.

110. *New York Clipper*, March 21, 1868, 398.

111. Ibid. See also *New York Herald*, March 13, 1868, 12.

112. "The Long Walk," *Boston Investigator*, May 20, 1868, 22.

113. "Pedestrianism," *Daily National Intelligencer* (Washington, D.C.), April 27, 1868; "The Thousand Mile Walk," *Daily Alta California*, May 15, 1868, 1.

114. "Pedestrianism," *Daily National Intelligencer* (Washington, D.C.), April 27, 1868.

115. "The Great Walking Match," *Daily National Intelligencer* (Washington, D.C.), May 25, 1868.

116. Quoted in Algeo, 27–28.

117. "Athletic," *New York Clipper*, April 19, 1879.

118. "Twenty-Mile Run," *New York Clipper*, April 12, 1878, 21.

119. Algeo, 80–83; Rohs, 175.

120. "O'Leary, the Pedestrian," *Irish American Weekly*, April 15, 1876, 8.

121. "O'Leary, the Pedestrian," *Irish American Weekly*, March 3, 1877, 6.

122. Quoted in Algeo, 73.

123. "O'Leary, the Pedestrian," *Irish American Weekly*, April 14, 1877, 5.

124. "Daniel O'Leary: Another Feat of Endurance," *Irish American Weekly*, July 14, 1877.

125. Algeo, 79–82.

126. Quoted in Algeo, 80.

127. Ibid., 82.

128. Rohs, 168.

129. "O'Leary the Pedestrian: The Dinner to the Champion," *Irish American Weekly*, May 19, 1877, 3.

130. Ibid.

131. "The Pedestrian Match," *Irish American Weekly*, November 27, 1875, 4.

132. "O'Leary, the Pedestrian: Presentation to the Champion," *Irish American Weekly*, May 26, 1877, 8.

133. "The Pedestrian Match," *Irish American*, March 22, 1879, 1.

134. Algeo, 134.

135. Hoyt, *Rag Baby*, 132. Thanks to Travis Stern for pointing out *Rag Baby*'s connection to pedestrianism.

Epilogue

1. Kotef, 11.

2. Miller, *Emigrants and Exiles*, 502.

3. Quoted in Miller, 502.

4. Ibid.

5. Ibid.

6. Roney, *Irish Rebel*, 179–81.

7. Miller, *Emigrants and Exiles*, 506.

8. Quoted in Miller, 518.

9. Ibid., 496.

10. Shannon, 142.

11. Ibid.

12. Ibid., 145.

13. Musser, *The Emergence of Cinema*, 30.

14. Ibid.

15. Timothy Cashman, quoted in Casey, 253.

16. Daly, Diary of Trip to Ireland, June 8, 1874.

17. Ibid.

18. Schrier, *Ireland and the American Emigration*, 132–33.

19. Quoted in Schrier, 133.

20. Ibid., 133.

21. Quoted in Schrier, 134–35.

22. Ibid., 135–37.

23. Ibid., 140; Wyman, *Round-Trip to America*, 162. See also Lynch-Brennan, 57–59; Diner, 50–51.

24. Casey, 254–55.

25. Seamus O Dubhghaill quoted in O'Leary, "Yank Outsiders," 253.

26. Ibid., 253–54.

27. O'Leary, 259. See also Smith, *The Art of Disappearing*; Birmingham, "In Honor of General Regan," 618–25; Fanning, *The Irish Voice in America*, 189–97.

28. Brundage, 321–334; Miller, *Emigrants and Exiles*, 541–44; Kenny, "American-Irish Nationalism," 293–97; McNickle, "When New York Was Irish and After," 350–51.

29. Porter, *European Rest Cure.*

30. Chinese Exclusion Act of 1882, 58. Sess. I, Chap. 126; 22 Stat. 58. 47th Cong.; approved May 6.

31. Cresswell, *On the Move,* 160.

32. "'Every day at the White House felt like an eternity' says Sean Spicer," *RTE,* January 13, 2018; accessed September 15, 2018, https://www.rte.ie /entertainment/2018/0112/932993-every-day-was-an-eternity-says-sean-spicer/.

33. Ryan, "My Family Came from Ireland on Coffin Ships," *Irish Times,* January 18, 2018, video; accessed August 15, 2018, https://www.irishtimes .com/news/world/us/paul-ryan-my-family-came-from-ireland-on-coffin -ships-1.3353582.

34. Ibid.

35. Suzanne Lynch, "Trump Signals Support for Deal on Undocumented Irish in U.S.," *Irish Times,* March 15, 2018; accessed September 18, 2018, https://www.irishtimes.com/news/politics/trump-signals-support-for-deal -on-undocumented-irish-in-us-1.3428885.

36. Ibid.

37. Donie O'Sullivan, "White, Irish, and Undocumented in America," *CNN,* March 16, 2017; accessed September 18, 2018, https://www.cnn.com /2017/03/16/us/white-irish-undocumented-trnd/index.html.

BIBLIOGRAPHY

A. P. *The Mysteries and Miseries of the Great Metropolis.* New York: D. Appleton, 1875.

"An Act Concerning Tramps." *Laws of the State Affecting the Interests in the City and County of New York Passed by the Legislature of 1880.* New York: Martin B. Brown, 1880.

Addey, Markenfield, and William H. Bartlett. *Picturesque Ireland: Historical and Descriptive,* Vol. 1. New York: Worthington, 1890.

Algeo, Matthew. *Pedestrianism: When Watching People Walk Was America's Favorite Spectator Sport.* Chicago: Chicago Review Press, 2014.

Altick, Richard D. *The Shows of London: A Panorama History of Exhibitions, 1600–1862.* Cambridge, Mass.: Belknap Press, 1978.

Amato, Joseph. *On Foot: A History of Walking.* New York: New York University Press, 2004.

Americans in Turkey. Tony Pastor Collection, 1861–1908. Harry Ransom Center, University of Texas at Austin.

Anbinder, Tyler. *Nativism and Slavery: The Northern Know-Nothings and the Politics of the 1850s.* New York: Oxford University Press, 1992.

Arneil, Barbara. "Disability, Self-Image, and Modern Political Theory." *Political Theory* 37, no. 2 (2009): 218–42.

Arnesen, Eric. "Whiteness and the Historians' Imagination." *International Labor and Working-Class History,* no. 60 (Fall 2001): 3–32.

Ashworth, John Harvey. *The Saxon in Ireland, or The Rambles of an Englishman in Search of a Settlement in the West of Ireland.* London: John Murray, 1851.

Augé, Marc. *Non-Places: Introduction to an Anthropology of Supermodernity.* Translated by John Howe. New York: Verso, 1995.

Babbage, E. F. *"Phat Boys": Eighteen Years on the St. Lawrence.* Rochester, N.Y.: Democrat and Chronicle Print, 1891.

Balme, Christopher B. "The Bandmann Circuit: Theatrical Networks in the First Age of Globalization." *Theatre Research International* 40, no. 1 (2015): 19–36.

Barish, Jonas A. *The Antitheatrical Prejudice.* Berkeley: University of California Press, 1981.

Barnette, Jane Stewart. "Locomotive Leisure: The Effects of Railroads on Chicago Area Theatre, 1870–1920." PhD diss., University of Texas at Austin, 2003.

"Barney I Hardly Knew Ye." *Barney and Nora Songster of Charles MacEvoy's Original Hibernicon.* New York: Robert M. DeWitt, 1872. Borowitz Collection. Kent State Special Collections.

Barrett, James R. *The Irish Way: Becoming American in the Multiethnic City.* New York: Penguin Press, 2012.

———. "Whiteness Studies: Anything Here for Historians of the Working Class?" *International Labor and Working-Class History* 60 (Fall 2001): 33–42.

Bayne, S.G. *On an Irish Jaunting-Car Through Donegal and Connemara.* New York: Harper and Brothers, 1902.

Bayor, Ronald H., and Timothy J. Meagher, eds. *The New York Irish.* Baltimore: Johns Hopkins University Press, 1997.

Bell, John. "The Sioux War Panorama and American Mythic History." *Theatre Journal* 48, no. 3 (1996): 279–99.

Bellesiles, Michael. *1877: America's Year of Living Violently.* New York: New Press, 2010.

Bellew, Frank, ed. *The Tramp.* New York: Dick and Fitzgerald, 1878.

Benesch, Klaus. "Modern(s) Walking: An Introduction." In *Walking and the Aesthetics of Modernity: Pedestrian Mobility in Literature and the Arts,* edited by Klaus Benesch and Francois Specq, v–xi. New York: Palgrave Macmillan, 2016.

Bense, Evangeline Isabelle. Diary 1, October 17, 1885–August 15, 1886. Manuscript and Archives, New York Public Library.

Bernstein, Iver. *The New York City Draft Riots.* New York: Oxford University Press, 1990.

Berry, John M., and Frances Panchok. "Church and Theatre." *U.S. Catholic Historian* 6, no. 2/3 (Spring/Summer 1987): 151–79.

Birmingham, George A. "In Honor of General Regan." *Harper's Monthly Magazine* 118 (March 1909): 618–25.

"Birth of Saint Patrick." *J. L. MacEvoy's New Hibernicon Songster.* New York: DeWitt, 1881. Harris Collection of Poetry and Plays. Brown University.

Blackstone, Sarah J. "Alexander Byers: Play Pirate Extraordinaire." *Theatre History Studies* 14 (1994): 107–13.

Blomley, Nicholas. *Rights of Passage: Sidewalks and the Regulation of Public Flow.* New York: Routledge, 2011. E-book.

Bluestone, Daniel M. "'The Pushcart Evil': Peddlers, Merchants, and NYC's Streets, 1890–1940." *Journal of Urban History* 18, no. 1 (November 1991): 70–81.

Bly, Nellie. *Around the World in Seventy-Two Days.* New York: Pictorial Weeklies, 1890.

Booth, Michael R. "Irish Landscape in the Victorian Theatre." In *Places, Personality and the Irish Writer,* edited by Andrew Carpenter, 159–72. Gerrards Cross: Colin Smythe, 1977.

Boyer, M. Christine. *Dreaming the Rational City: The Myth of American City Planning*. Cambridge, Mass.: MIT Press, 1983.

Boyer, Paul. *Urban Masses and Moral Order in America, 1820–1920*. Cambridge, Mass.: Harvard University Press, 1978.

Brewer, William H. "What Shall We Do With Our Tramps?" *New Englander* 37 (July 1876): 521–32.

Brigham, Ann. *American Road Narratives: Reimagining Mobility in Literature and Film*. Charlottesville: University of Virginia Press, 2015.

Brooks, Daphne A. *Bodies in Dissent: Spectacular Performances of Race and Freedom, 1850–1910*. Durham, N.C.: Duke University Press, 2006.

Brown, Thomas N. *Irish-American Nationalism*. Philadelphia: J. B. Lippincott, 1966.

Brundage, David. "'In Time of Peace, Prepare for War': Key Themes in the Social Thought of New York's Irish Nationalists, 1890–1916." In *The New York Irish*, edited by Ronald H. Bayor and Timothy J. Meagher, 321–34. Baltimore: Johns Hopkins University Press, 1997.

Burrows, Edwin G., and Mike Wallace. *Gotham: A History of New York City to 1898*. New York: Oxford University Press, 1999.

Burtsell, Richard. Diary. Richard Burtsell Papers, Collection Number 022.001. Archives of the Archdiocese of New York. St. Joseph's Seminary, Dunwoodie.

———. *The Diary of Richard L. Burtsell, Priest of New York: The Early Years, 1865–1868*, edited by Nelson J. Callahan. New York: Arno Press, 1978.

———. End of the Year Financial Report for 1869, Church of the Epiphany. Richard Burtsell Papers, Collection Number 022.001. Archives of the Archdiocese of New York. St. Joseph's Seminary, Dunwoodie.

Butsch, Richard. *The Making of American Audiences*. New York: Cambridge University Press, 2000.

Buzard, James. *The Beaten Track: European Tourism, Literature, and the Ways to Culture, 1800–1918*. New York: Oxford University Press, 1993.

Cabranes-Grant, Leo. "From Scenarios to Networks: Performing the Intercultural in Colonial Mexico." *Theatre Journal* 63, no. 4 (December 2011): 499–520.

Carlebach, Michael. *Working Stiffs: Occupational Portraits in the Age of Tintypes*. Washington, D.C.: Smithsonian Institution, 2002.

Carleton, William. "The Rovin' Irish Boy." *Sheridan, Mack, and Day's 'Grand Combination' Songster*. New York: DeWitt, 1874. Music Division of the Library for the Performing Arts, New York Public Library.

Casey, Marion R. "Ireland, New York and the Irish Image in American Popular Culture, 1890–1960." PhD diss., New York University, 1998.

Casey, Marion, and J. J. Lee, eds. *Making the Irish American: History and Heritage of the Irish in the United States*. New York: New York University Press, 2006.

Chadwick, Henry, ed. *Beadle's Dime Hand-book of Pedestrianism*. New York: Beadle, 1867.

The Charter of the City of New York: Chapter 378 of the Laws of 1897. Brooklyn: N.p., 1899.

Claes, Lien, Elisabeth De Schauwer, and Geert Van Hove. "Disability Studies and Social Geography Make a Good Marriage: Research on Life Trajectories of People with Intellectual Disabilities and Additional Mental Health Problems." In *Emerging Perspectives on Disability Studies*, edited by Matthew Wappett and Katrina Arndt, 97–130. New York: Palgrave, 2013.

Clark, Dennis. *The Irish in Philadelphia: Ten Generations of Urban Experience*. Philadelphia: Temple University Press, 1973.

Clifford, James. *Routes: Travel and Translation in the Late Twentieth Century*. Cambridge: Harvard University Press, 1997.

Cockrell, Dale. *Demons of Disorder: Early Blackface Minstrels and Their World*. New York: Cambridge University Press, 1997.

Cohan, Jerry. *Poems and Sketches*. Ossining-on-Hudson: Physioc, 1911.

Cohan Family Repertoire-Book. MS Thr 226 J. J. Cohan. Harvard Theatre Collection, Harvard University.

Cohen, William. *At Freedom's Edge: Black Mobility and the Southern White Quest for Racial Control, 1861–1915*. Baton Rouge: Louisiana State University Press, 1991.

Colligan, Mimi. *Canvas Documentaries: Panoramic Entertainments in Australia and New Zealand*. Victoria: Melbourne University Press, 2002.

Comment, Bernard. *The Panorama*. London: Reaktion Books, 1999.

Cooper, Patricia A. "The 'Traveling Fraternity': Union Cigar Makers and Geographic Mobility, 1900–1919." In *Walking to Work: Tramps in American, 1790–1935*, edited by Eric H. Monkkonen, 118–38. Lincoln: University of Nebraska Press, 1984).

Courtright, William. *Private Boarding*. New York: Clinton T. DeWitt, 1877.

Coyne, J. Stirling, N. P. Willis, and W. H. Bartlett. *The Scenery and Antiquities of Ireland*. London: George Virtue, 1841–1842.

Cresswell, Tim. *On the Move: Mobility in the Modern Western World*. New York: Routledge, 2006.

———. "Towards a Politics of Mobility." *Environment and Planning D: Society and Space* 28, no.1 (2010): 17–31.

———. *The Tramp in America*. London: Reaktion Books, 2001.

Cronin, Michael. "Fellow Travellers: Contemporary Travel Writing and Ireland." In *Tourism in Ireland: A Critical Analysis*, edited by Barbara O'Connor and Michael Cronin, 51–67. Cork: Cork University Press, 1993.

Crouch, D. "Spacing, Performing, and Becoming: Tangles in Mundane." *Environment and Planning A* 35, no. 11 (2003): 1945–60.

Cumming, John. *Runners and Walkers: A Nineteenth Century Sports Chronicle.* Chicago: Regnery Gateway, 1981.

Curtis, Jr., L. Perry. *Apes and Angels: The Irishman in Victorian Caricature.* London: David and Charles, 1971.

Dahl, Curtis. "Artemus Ward: Comic Panoramist." *New England Quarterly* 32, no. 4 (December 1959): 476–85.

———. "Mark Twain and the Moving Panoramas." *American Quarterly* 13, no. 1 (Spring 1961): 20–32.

Daly, Charles P. Diary of Trip to Ireland. Manuscript and Archives Room, New York Public Library.

Dant, Tim. "Drivers and Passengers." *Routledge Handbook of Mobilities*, edited by Peter Adey, David Bissell, Kevin Hannam, Peter Merriman, and Mimi Sheller, 367–75. New York: Routledge, 2014.

Darwin, Charles. *The Descent of Man, and Selection in Relation to Sex.* New York: D. Appleton, 1872.

Davis, Sarah. Letter to David Davis. Clover Lawn. January 21, 1872. David Davis Papers. Box 8, Folder B23. Abraham Lincoln Presidential Library.

———. Letter to David Davis. Clover Lawn "At Home Tuesday 10 p.m." November 10, 1874. David Davis Papers. Box 9, Folder B27. Abraham Lincoln Presidential Library.

Davis, Tracy C., ed. *The Cambridge Companion to Performance Studies.* New York: Cambridge University Press, 2008.

De Angelis, Jefferson, and A. F. Harlow. *A Vagabond Trouper.* New York: Harcourt, Brace, 1931.

"The Dear Little Shamrock," *W. F. Lawlor's Original Barney the Guide Songster.* New York: Robert M. DeWitt, 1871. Harris Collection of Poetry and Plays. Brown University.

de Certeau, Michel. *The Practice of Everyday Life.* Translated by Steven Rendell. Berkeley: University of California Press, 1988.

Deluze, Gilles, and Félix Guatari. *A Thousand Plateaus.* Translated by Brian Massumi. New York: Continuum, 1987.

Denning, Michael. *Mechanic Accents: Dime Novels and Working-Class Culture in America.* New York: Verso, 1987.

DePastino, Todd. *Citizen Hobo: How a Century of Homelessness Shaped America.* Chicago: University of Chicago Press, 2003.

Desmond, Jane C. *Meaning in Motion.* Durham: Duke University Press, 1997.

Diner, Hasia R. *Erin's Daughters in America: Irish Immigrant Women in the Nineteenth Century.* Baltimore: Johns Hopkins University Press, 1983.

Dirlik, Arif. "American Studies in the Time of Empire." *Comparative American Studies* 2, no. 3 (2004): 287–302.

Dolan, Jay P. *The Immigrant Church: New York's Irish and German Catholics, 1815–1865*. Notre Dame: University of Notre Dame Press, 1983.

———. *The Irish Americans: A History*. London: Bloomsbury Press, 2008.

Dorman, James H. "American Popular Culture and the New Immigration Ethnics: The Vaudeville Stage and the Process of Ethnic Ascription." *American Studies* 36, no. 2 (1991): 179–93.

Dowling, Bartholomew. "The Brigade at Fontenoy." *W. F. Lawlor's Original Barney the Guide Songster*. New York: Robert M. De Witt, 1871. Harris Collection of Poetry and Plays, Songsters. Brown University.

Drinker, Jacob. In *New York City Museum of Complaint: Municipal Collection, 1751–1969*, edited by Matthew Bakkom. Göttingen: Steidl, 2009.

Du Bois, W. E. B. *The Souls of Black Folk*. New York: Dover, 1903.

Dubray, C.A. "Naturalism." *The Catholic Encyclopedia*, Vol. 10, edited by Charles G. Herbermann, Edward A. Pace, Condé B. Pallen, Thomas J. Shahan, and John J. Wynne, 713–15. New York: Encyclopedia Press, 1913.

Elliot, Alice. "Gender." *Keywords of Mobility: Critical Engagements*, edited by Noel B. Salazar and Kiran Jayaram, 73–92. New York: Berghahn Books, 2016.

Ellis, Charles Edward. *An Authentic History of the Benevolent and Protective Order of Elks*. Chicago: Published by the Author, 1910.

El-Mudarrist, Hussein I., and Olivier Salmon. *Romantic Travel through Bartlett's Engravings from Europe to the Middle East*. Aleppo, Syria: Ray Publishing and Science, 2007.

"The Emerald Isle." Broadside. Boston: F. A. Searle, 1873. American Broadsides and Ephemera, Series 1, 24041.

Emmons, David M. *The Butte Irish: Class and Ethnicity in an American Mining Town, 1875–1925*. Urbana: University of Illinois Press, 1990.

Erdman, Andrew L. *Blue Vaudeville: Sex, Morals, and the Mass Marketing of Amusement, 1895–1915*. Jefferson: McFarland, 2007.

Fanning, Charles. *The Irish Voice in America: 250 Years of Irish-American Fiction*. 2nd ed. Lexington: University Press of Kentucky, 2000.

———. "Robert Emmet and Nineteenth Century Irish-America." *New Hibernia Review* 8, no. 4 (Winter 2004): 53–83.

Farías, Ignacio. "Introduction: Decentering the Object of Urban Studies." In *Urban Assemblages: How Actor-Network Theory Changes Urban Studies*, edited by Ignacio Farías and Thomas Bender, 1–24. New York: Routledge, 2010.

Farrelly, Maura Jane. *Anti-Catholicism in America, 1620–1860*. New York: Cambridge University Press, 2017.

"Father Tom O'Neil." *W. F. Lawlor's Original Barney the Guide Songster*. New York: Robert M. De Witt, 1871. Harris Collection of Poetry and Plays, Songsters. Brown University.

The Fawn. In *Tony Pastor Presents: Afterpieces from the Vaudeville Stage*, edited by Susan Kattwinkel, 63–82. Westport, CT: Greenwood Press, 1998.

Fenton, Laurence. *The Young Ireland Rebellion and Limerick*. Cork: Mercier, 2010.

Fields, Armond. *Tony Pastor, Father of Vaudeville*. Jefferson, N.C.: McFarland, 2007.

Foner, Eric. *Politics and Ideology in the Age of the Civil War*. New York: Oxford University Press, 1980.

———. *Reconstruction: America's Unfinished Revolution*. New York: Harper and Row, 1988.

———. "Response to Eric Arnesen." *International Labor and Working-Class History*, no. 60 (Fall 2001): 57–60.

Forbes, Sir John. *Memorandums Made in Ireland in the Autumn of 1852*. 2 vols. London: Smith, Elder, 1853.

Ford, James L. *Forty-Odd Years in the Literary Shop*. New York: E.P. Dutton, 1921.

Foster, Susan Leigh. *Choreographing Empathy: Kinesthesia in Performance*. New York: Routledge, 2011.

Foucault, Michel. *Discipline and Punish: The Birth of the Prison*. Translated by Alan Sheridan. New York: Vintage Books, 1979.

Fox Jr., James W. "Citizenship, Poverty, and Federalism: 1787–1882." *University of Pittsburgh Law Review* 60, no. 2 (Winter 1999): 421–578.

Frank MacEvoy's New Hibernicon Songster. Philadelphia: Merrihew and Son, 1874. American Antiquarian Society.

Funchion, Michael F. *Chicago's Irish Nationalists, 1881–1890*. New York: Arno, 1976.

Garner, Steve. "The Simianization of the Irish: Racial Ape-ing and Its Contexts." In *Simianization: Apes, Gender, Class, and Race*, edited by Wulf D. Hund, Charles W. Mills, and Silvia Sebastiani, 197–221. Münster: LIT Verlag, 2015.

Gershon, Ilana. "Bruce Latour." In *From Agamben to Žižek: Contemporary Critical Theorists*, edited by Jon Simons, 161–76. Edinburgh: Edinburgh University Press, 2010.

Gevinson, Alan. "The Origins of Vaudeville: Aesthetic Power, Disquietude, and Cosmopolitanism in the Quest for an American Music Hall." PhD diss., Johns Hopkins University, 2007.

Gilbert, Douglas. *American Vaudeville: Its Life and Times*. New York: Whittlesey House, 1940. Reprint, New York: Dover, 1963.

Gilley, Sheridan. "The Roman Catholic Church and the Nineteenth-Century Irish Diaspora." *The Journal of Ecclesiastical History* 35, no. 2 (April 1984): 188–207.

Gilman, Sander L. "'Stand Up Straight': Notes Towards a History of Posture." *Journal of Medical Humanities* 35 (2014): 57–83.

Goldstein, Eric L. *The Price of Whiteness: Jews, Race, and American Identity.* Princeton: Princeton University Press, 2008.

Gordon, Beverly. *Bazaar and Fair Ladies: The History of the American Fundraising Fair.* Knoxville: University of Tennessee Press, 1998.

Gough, Kathleen M. *Kinship and Performance in the Black and Green Atlantic: Haptic Allegories.* New York: Routledge, 2014.

Goulding, John. *The Amateur's Guide: Or, Training Made Easy, For Modern Outdoor Amusements.* New York: Peck and Snyder, 1879.

Graham, Brian. "Ireland and Irishness: Place, Culture and Identity." In *In Search of Ireland: A Cultural Geography*, edited by Brian J. Graham, 1–16. New York: Routledge, 1997.

Graham, Maryemma, and Wilifred Raussert, eds. *Mobile and Entangled America(s).* New York: Routledge, 2016.

Granshaw, Michelle. "Performing Cultural Memory: The Traveling Hibernicon and the Transnational Irish Community in the United States and Australia." *Nineteenth Century Theatre and Film* 41, no. 2 (Winter 2014): 76–101.

Grau, Robert. *The Business Man in the Amusement World.* New York: Broadway Publishing Company, 1910.

Greenblatt, Stephen. "A Mobility Studies Manifesto." In *Cultural Mobility: A Manifesto*, edited by Stephen Greenblatt, Ines G. Zupanov, Reinhard Meyer-Kalkus, Heike Pául, Påul Nyíri, and Friederike Pannewick, 250–53. Cambridge: Cambridge University Press, 2010.

Guglielmo, Thomas. *White on Arrival: Italians, Race, Color, and Power in Chicago, 1890–1945.* New York: Oxford University Press, 2004.

Haenni, Sabine. *The Immigrant Scene: Ethnic Amusements in New York, 1880–1920.* Minneapolis: University of Minnesota Press, 2008.

Hall, Samuel Carter, and Anna Maria Hall. *Hand-books for Ireland.* London: Virtue, Hall, and Virtue, 1853.

———. *Ireland: Its Scenery, Character, etc. In Three Volumes.* London: How and Parsons, 1841–43.

Handbook for Travellers in Ireland. London: John Murray, 1866.

Hanners, John. *"It Was Play or Starve": Acting in the Nineteenth-Century American Popular Theatre.* Bowling Green, Ohio: Bowling Green State University Popular Press, 1993.

Harding, William E. *The American Athlete: A Treatise on the Rules and Principles of Training for Athletic Contests, and the Regimen of Physical Culture.* New York: Richard K. Fox, 1881.

Harrigan, Edward. "The Beggars," *Down Broadway Gallant 69th Songster.* New York: A. J. Fisher, 1875. American Antiquarian Society.

———. "The Bummers." *Down Broadway Gallant 69th Songster.* New York: A. J. Fisher, 1875. American Antiquarian Society.

———. *Down Broadway* [1875]. Edward Harrigan Papers. Manuscripts and Archives Division. The New York Public Library. Astor, Lenox and Tilden Foundations.

———. Letters to Annie Harrigan, New York. Edward Harrigan Papers. *T-Mss. 1941–003. Billy Rose Theatre Division, The New York Public Library for the Performing Arts.

———. *Mulligan Guard Picnic* [one-act version; 1878]. Edward Harrigan Papers. Manuscripts and Archives Division. The New York Public Library. Astor, Lenox and Tilden Foundations.

———. *Mulligan Guard Picnic* [two-act version; likely 1880]. Edward Harrigan Papers. Manuscripts and Archives Division. The New York Public Library. Astor, Lenox and Tilden Foundations.

———. *Terrible Example* [1874]. Edward Harrigan Papers. Manuscripts and Archives Division. The New York Public Library. Astor, Lenox and Tilden Foundations.

———. "When the Soup House Comes Again." *Harrigan and Hart's When the Soup House Comes Again Songster.* New York: A. J. Fisher, 1874. Harris Collection of American Plays and Poetry. John Hay Library, Brown University.

Harris, Lee O. *The Man Who Tramps: A Story of Today.* Indianapolis: Douglass and Carlton, 1878.

Harrison, Robert A. *The Conventional Man: The Diaries of Ontario Chief Justice Robert A. Harrison, 1856–1878.* Toronto: University of Toronto, 2003.

Hart, Tom. "Transport and the City." In *Handbook of Urban Studies,* edited Ronan Paddison, 102–23. London: Sage, 2001.

Hartman, Andrew. "The Rise and Fall of Whiteness Studies." *Race and Class* 46, no. 2 (2004): 22–38.

Havemeyer Papers. Police, Dept. of Licensing of Theaters, Concert Halls, etc., 1874. Office of the Mayor, Early Mayor Records, 1826–1897. Municipal Archives, City of New York.

Head, Sir Francis B. *A Fortnight in Ireland.* London: John Murray, 1852.

Hedgbeth, Llewellyn. "Extant American Panoramas: Moving Entertainments of the Nineteenth Century." PhD diss., New York University, 1977.

Henke, Robert. *Poverty and Charity in Early Modern Theater and Performance.* Iowa City: University of Iowa Press, 2015.

Higham, John. *Strangers in the Land: Patterns of American Nativism, 1860–1925.* New Brunswick: Rutgers University Press, 1955.

High Life and Low Life in New York [1869]. Tony Pastor Collection 1861–1908. Harry Ransom Center. University of Texas at Austin.

Hirota, Hidetaka. *Expelling the Poor: Atlantic Seaboard States and the Nineteenth-Century Origins of American Immigration Policy.* New York: Oxford University Press, 2017.

Hodges, Graham. "'Desirable Companions and Lovers': Irish and African Americans in the Sixth Ward, 1830–1870." In *The New York Irish*, edited by Ronald H. Bayor and Timothy J. Meagher, 107–24. Baltimore: Johns Hopkins University Press, 1997.

Hoganson, Kristin L. *Consumers' Imperium: The Global Production of American Domesticity, 1865–1920*. Chapel Hill: University of North Carolina Press, 2007.

Hooper, Glenn. "The Isles/Ireland: The Wilder Shore." In *The Cambridge Companion to Travel Writing*, edited by Peter Hulme and Tim Youngs, 174–90. New York: Cambridge University Press, 2002.

Horton, William Ellis. *About Stage Folks*. Detroit: Free Press Printing Company, 1902.

Houseman, Gerald L. *The Rights of Mobility*. Port Washington: Kennikat, 1979.

"How Paddy's Represented." *Billy Ashcroft's Irish Character Songster*. New York: DeWitt, 1874. Music Division of the Library for the Performing Arts, New York Public Library.

Hoyt, Charles. *Rag Baby* [1884]. English and American Drama of the Nineteenth Century Series, Microopaque.

Huhtamo, Erkki. *Illusions in Motion: Media Archaeology of the Moving Panorama and Related Spectacles*. Cambridge: MIT Press, 2013.

———. "Peristrephic Pleasures: On the Origins of the Moving Panorama." In *Allegories of Communication: Intermedial Concerns from Cinema to the Digital*, edited by John Fullerton and Jan Olsson, 215–48. Rome, Italy: J. Libbey Publishing, 2004.

Hunter, Walt. "The Story Behind the Poem on the Statue of Liberty." *The Atlantic*, January 16, 2018. Accessed October 1, 2018. https://www.the atlantic.com/entertainment/archive/2018/01/the-story-behind-the-poem -on-the-statue-of-liberty/550553/.

Hyde, Ralph. *Panoramania*. London: Trefoil Publications, 1988.

Ignatiev, Noel. *How the Irish Became White*. New York: Routledge, 1995.

"I Hope That They Will Win." *Sheehan and Coyne's McManus' Trip Abroad Songster*. New York: New York Popular Publishing Co., 1882. Harris Collection of Poetry and Plays, Songsters. Brown University.

Ingold, Tim. "Culture on the Ground: The World Perceived Through the Feet." *Journal of Material Culture* 9, no. 3: 315–40.

"J. H. Ryan's Great Personation of the Irish Guide." *J. H. Ryan's Dublin Bard Songster*. New York: DeWitt, 1877. Special Collections. Princeton University.

J. L. MacEvoy's New Hibernicon Songster. New York: DeWitt, 1881. Harris Collection. Brown University.

Jacobson, Matthew Frye. *Whiteness of a Different Color: European Immigrants and the Alchemy of Race*. Cambridge, Mass.: Harvard University Press, 1998.

James, Ed. *Practical Training, for Running, Walking, Rowing, Wrestling, Boxing Jumping, and All Kinds of Athletic Feats*. New York: Ed James, 1877.

Jarvis, Robin. *Romantic Writing and Pedestrian Travel*. New York: St. Martin's, 1997.

Jeffares, A. Norman. "Place, Space and Personality and the Irish Writer." In *Place, Personality and the Irish Writer*, edited by Andrew Carpenter, 11–40. New York: Harper and Row, 1977.

Jefferis, B. G., and J. L. Nichols. *Searchlights on Health: Light on Dark Corners A Complete Sexual Science and a Guide to Purity and Physical Manhood, Advice to Maiden, Wife, and Mother, Love, Courtship, and Marriage*. Toronto: J. L. Nichols, 1894.

"John Chinaman." *"First She Would Then She Wouldn't" Songster*. New York: Robert M. DeWitt, 1873. Music Division of the Library for the Performing Arts, New York Public Library.

Johnson, Claudia Durst. *Church and Stage*. Jefferson: McFarland and Company, 2008.

Johnson, Odai. *Absence and Memory in Colonial American Theatre*. New York: Palgrave, 2006.

Jones, Plummer F. *Shamrock-Land: A Ramble Through Ireland*. New York: Moffat, Yard, 1908.

Kane, Paula M. "'Staging a Lie': Boston Catholics and the New Irish Drama." In *The Irish World Wide: History, Heritage, Identity: Religion and Identity*. Vol. 5, edited by Patrick O'Sullivan, 111–45. New York: Leicester University Press, 1996.

Kaplan, Karen. *Questions of Travel: Postmodern Discourses of Displacement*. Durham: Duke University Press, 1996.

Kasher, Stephen, ed. *America and the Tintype*. Göttingen, Germany: Steidl, 2008.

Kasson, John F. *Rudeness and Civility: Manners in Nineteenth-Century Urban America*. New York: Hill and Wang, 1990.

Kattwinkel, Susan. "Introduction." In *Tony Pastor Presents: Afterpieces from the Vaudeville Stage*, edited by Susan Kattwinkel, 1–8. Westport, CT: Greenwood Press, 1998.

———. "Negotiating a New Identity: Irish Americans and the Variety Theatre in the 1860s." In *Interrogating America through Theatre and Performance*, edited by William W. Demastes and Iris Smith Fischer, 47–64. New York: Palgrave, 2007.

———. "Tony Pastor's Vaudeville: Serving the New York Community." *The Library Chronicle of the University of Texas at Austin* 25, no. 3 (1995): 50–75.

Kenny, Kevin. *The American Irish: A History*. New York: Routledge, 2000.

———. "American-Irish Nationalism." In *Making the Irish American*, edited by

Marion Casey and J. J. Lee, 293–97. New York: New York University Press, 2006.

———. "Diaspora and Comparison: The Global Irish as a Case Study." *The Journal of American History* 90, no. 1 (June 2003): 134–62.

———. *The Making of the Molly Maguires.* New York: Oxford University Press, 1998.

———. "The Molly Maguires in Popular Culture." *Journal of American Ethnic History* 14, no. 4 (Summer 1995): 27–46.

———. "Twenty Years of Irish American Historiography." *Journal of American Ethnic History* 28, no. 4 (Summer 2009): 67–75.

Kibler, M. Alison. *Censoring Racial Ridicule: Irish, Jewish, and African American Struggles over Race and Representation, 1890–1930.* Chapel Hill: University of North Carolina Press, 2015.

———. *Rank Ladies: Gender and Cultural Hierarchy: Gender and Cultural Hierarchy in American Vaudeville.* Chapel Hill: University of North Carolina Press, 1999.

Knobel, Dale T. *Paddy and the Republic: Ethnicity and Nationality in Antebellum America.* Middletown, Conn.: Wesleyan University Press, 1986.

Kolchin, Peter. *First Freedom: The Responses of Alabama's Blacks to Emancipation and Reconstruction.* Tuscaloosa: University of Alabama Press, 2008.

Kotef, Hagar. *Movement and the Ordering of Freedom: On Liberal Governances of Mobility.* Durham: Duke University Press, 2015.

Kroeg, Susan. "Cockney Tourists, Irish Guides, and the Invention of the Emerald Isle." *Eire-Ireland* 44, nos. 3 and 4 (Fall/Winter 2009): 200–228.

Kunowm, Rüdiger. "American Studies as Mobility Studies: Some Terms and Constellations." In *Re-Framing the Transnational Turn in American Studies*, edited by Winfried Fluck, Donald E. Pease, and John Carlos Rowe, 214–30. Hanover, N.H.: Dartmouth College Press, 2011. ProQuest E-book Central.

Kusmer, Kenneth L. *Down and Out, On the Road: The Homeless in American History.* New York: Oxford University Press, 2002.

Latour, Bruno. *Reassembling the Social: An Introduction to Actor-Network-Theory.* New York: Oxford University Press, 2005.

Laurie Jr., Joe. *Vaudeville: From the Honky-Tonks to the Palace.* New York: Henry Holt, 1953.

Leavitt, Michael Bennett. *Fifty Years in Theatrical Management.* New York: Broadway Publishing, 1912.

Lengkeek, J. "Leisure Experience and Imagination—Rethinking Cohen's Modes of Tourist Experience." *International Sociology* 16, no. 2 (2001): 173–85.

Lhamon Jr., W.T. *Raising Cain: Blackface Performance from Jim Crow to Hip Hop.* Cambridge, Mass.: Harvard University Press, 1998.

Lloyd, Edward Stewart. "Lines." *John M. Burke's "Dublin Carman's" Songster.* New York: De Robert M. De Witt, 1871. Harris Collection of Poetry and Plays, Songsters. Brown University.

Lloyd, J. "Who Would be a Nun?" *The Moet and Shandon Songster.* New York: Robert M. DeWitt, 1870. Music Division at the Library of the Performing Arts, New York Public Library.

Lott, Eric. *Love and Theft: Blackface Minstrelsy and the American Working Class.* New York: Oxford University Press, 1993.

Loukaitou-Sideris, Anastasia, and Renia Ehrenfeucht. "Constructing the Sidewalks: Municipal Government and the Production of Public Space in Los Angeles, CA, 1880–1920." *Journal of Historical Geography* 33 (2007): 104–24.

———. *Sidewalks: Conflict and Negotiation over Public Space.* Cambridge: MIT Press, 2009.

Lynch-Brennan, Margaret. *The Irish Bridget: Irish Immigrant Women in Domestic Service in America, 1840–1930.* Syracuse: Syracuse University Press, 2009.

MacArthur, Benjamin. *The Man Who Was Rip Van Winkle: Joseph Jefferson and Nineteenth-Century American Theatre.* New Haven: Yale University Press, 2007.

Macaulay, James. *Ireland in 1872: A Tour of Observation.* London: Henry S. King, 1873.

MacCannell, Dean. *The Tourist: A New Theory of the Leisure Class.* Berlin: Schocken Books, 1976.

MacEvoy, Charles. "Barney Be Aisy," *W. F. Lawlor's Original Barney the Guide Songster.* New York: Robert M. DeWitt, 1871. Harris Collection of Poetry and Plays, Songsters. Brown University.

———. "Invitation to 'Hibernicon.' " *Barney and Nora Songster of Charles MacEvoy's Original Hibernicon.* New York: Robert M. DeWitt, 1872. Borowitz Collection, Kent State Special Collections.

———. Naturalization Papers. New York Superior Court, Bundle 254, Record 7. National Archives, New York City.

MacEvoy, John. "Widow Mavrone." New York: C.H. Ditson and Co, 1872. American Memory, Library of Congress.

MacEvoy's New Hibernicon. Broadside. Boston: F. A. Searle, n.d. American Broadsides and Ephemera Series I, 10F455D54A460CF8.

MacPherson, D. A. J. *Women and the Irish Nation: Gender, Culture, and Irish Identity, 1890–1914.* New York: Palgrave, 2012.

Mahar, William J. *Behind the Burnt Cork Mask: Early Blackface Minstrelsy and Antebellum American Popular Culture.* Urbana: University of Illinois Press, 1999.

Mansfield, M. F., and B. McM. Mansfield. *Romantic Ireland.* Boston: L.C. Page, 1905.

Martin, Carol. *Dance Marathons: Performing American Culture of the 1920s and 1930s.* Jackson: University Press of Mississippi, 1994.

Martineau, Harriet Ashworth. *Letters from Ireland.* London: John Chapman, 1852.

Massey, Doreen. *For Space.* Thousand Oaks: SAGE, 2005.

Masur, Louis P. *Rites of Execution: Capital Punishment and the Transformation of American Culture 1776–1865.* New York: Oxford University Press, 1989.

The Match Girl of New York [1873]. Tony Pastor Collection 1861–1908. Harry Ransom Center. University of Texas at Austin.

McAllister, Marvin. *White People Do Not Know How to Behave at Entertainments Designed for Ladies and Gentlemen of Colour: William Brown's African and American Theater.* Chapel Hill: University of North Carolina Press, 2003.

McCabe, John. *George M. Cohan: The Man Who Owned Broadway.* Cambridge: Da Capo, 1980.

McCaffrey, Lawrence. "Irish and Irish America: Connections and Disconnections." *U.S. Catholic Historian* 22, no. 3 (Summer 2004): 1–18.

———. *The Irish Catholic Diaspora in America.* Washington, D.C.: Catholic University Press, 1997.

McCarthy, Tara M. *Respectability and Reform: Irish American Women's Activism, 1880–1920.* Syracuse: Syracuse University Press, 2018.

McDannell, Colleen. "Going to the Ladies' Fair: Irish Catholics in New York City, 1870–1900." In *The New York Irish*, edited by Ronald H. Bayor and Timothy J. Meagher, 234–51. Baltimore: Johns Hopkins University Press, 1997.

McFeeley, Deirdre. *Dion Boucicault: Irish Identity on Stage.* New York: Cambridge University Press, 2012.

McGill and Strong's Mirror of Ireland. Program. Worcester, MA: 1872. American Broadsides and Ephemera Series I: 1760–1900.

McKenna, Kevin. *The Battle for Rights in the United States Catholic Church.* New York: Paulist Press, 1989.

McMahon, Cian T. *The Global Dimensions of Irish Identity: Race, Nation, and the Popular Press.* Chapel Hill: University of North Carolina Press, 2015.

McNamara, Brooks. *The New York Concert Saloon.* New York: Cambridge University Press, 2002.

McNickle, Chris. "When New York Was Irish and After." In *The New York Irish*, edited by Ronald H. Bayor and Timothy J. Meagher, 337–56. Baltimore: Johns Hopkins University Press, 1997.

McShane, Clay. "Transforming the Use of Urban Space: A Look at the Revolution in Street Pavements, 1880–1924." *Journal of Urban History* 5, no. 3 (May 1979): 279–307.

Meade, Don. "Kitty O'Neil and Her 'Champion Jig': An Irish Dancer on the New York Stage." *New Hibernia Review* 6, no. 3 (Autumn 2002): 9–22.

Meagher, Timothy J. *The Columbia Guide to Irish American History.* New York: Columbia University Press, 2005.

———. *Inventing Irish America: Generation, Class, and Ethnic Identity in a New England City, 1880–1928.* Notre Dame: University of Notre Dame Press, 2001.

Meloy, Elizabeth. "Touring Connemara: Learning to Read a Landscape of Ruins, 1850–1860." *New Hibernia Review* 13, no. 3 (Autumn 2009): 21–46.

Miller, Angela. "Panorama, the Cinema, and the Emergence of the Spectacular." *Wide Angle* 18, no. 2 (April 1996): 34–69.

Miller, Kerby. *Emigrants and Exiles: Ireland and the Irish Exodus to North America.* New York: Oxford University Press, 1985.

———. "Introduction." In *Irish Immigrants in the Land of Canaan 1675–1815*, edited by Kerby A. Miller, Arnold Schrier, Bruce D. Boling, and David N. Doyle, 3–10. Oxford: Oxford University Press, 2003.

———. *Ireland and Irish America: Culture, Class, and Transatlantic Migration.* Dublin: Field Day Publications, 2008.

Millis, Harry A. "The Law Affecting Tramps and Immigrants." *Charities Review* 7 (September 1897): 587–94.

Miner, Harry, ed. *Harry Miner's American Dramatic Directory for the Season of 1884–5.* New York: Wolf and Palmer Dramatic Publishing, 1884.

Moloney, Mick. *Far from the Shamrock Shore.* New York: Crown Publishers, 2002.

Monkkonen, Eric H. *America Becomes Urban: The Development of U.S. Cities and Towns, 1780–1810.* Berkeley: University of California Press, 1988.

———. *Police in Urban America, 1860–1920.* New York: Cambridge University Press, 1981.

Monod, David. *The Soul and Pleasure: Sentiment and Sensation in Nineteenth-Century American Mass Entertainment.* Ithaca, N.Y.: Cornell University Press, 2016.

Moody, Richard. *America Takes the Stage: Romanticism for American Drama and Theatre, 1750–1900.* Bloomington: Indiana University Press, 1955.

———. *Ned Harrigan: From Corlear's Hook to Herald Square.* Chicago: Nelson-Hall, 1980.

Moon, Krystyn R. *Yellowface: Creating the Chinese in American Popular Music and Performance, 1850s–1920s.* New Brunswick: Rutgers University Press, 2005.

Mooney, Jennifer. *Irish Stereotypes in Vaudeville, 1865–1905.* New York: Palgrave, 2015.

Morehouse, Ward. *George M. Cohan: Prince of American Theatre.* Westport: Greenwood Press, 1972.

Morton, Charles. *Black Diamond, 1914.* Sherman Theatre collection, Special Collections Research Center, Southern Illinois University Carbondale.

Murphy, Maureen. "From Scapegoat to Grásta: Popular Attitudes and Stereotypes in Irish American Drama." In *Irish Theater in America: Essays on Irish Theatrical Diaspora*, edited by John P. Harrington, 19–37. Syracuse, N.Y.: Syracuse University Press, 2009.

———. "Irish-American Theatre." In *Ethnic Theatre in the United States*, edited by Maxine Seller, 221–35. Westport, CT: Greenwood Press, 1983.

Musser, Charles. *The Emergence of Cinema: The American Screen to 1907.* Vol. 1

of *History of the American Cinema*. Berkeley: University of California Press, 1994.

Nasaw, David. *Going Out: The Rise and Fall of Public Amusement*. New York: Basic Books, 1993.

Novak, William J. *The People's Welfare: Law and Regulation in Nineteenth Century America*. Chapel Hill: University of North Carolina Press, 1996.

Ocobock, Paul. "Introduction: Vagrancy and Homelessness in Global and Historical Perspective." In *Cast Out: Vagrancy and Homelessness in Global and Historical Perspective*, edited by A. L. Beier and Paul Ocobock, 9–30. Athens, OH: Ohio University Press, 2009. ProQuest E-book Central.

O'Connor, Barbara. "Myths and Mirrors: Tourist Images and National Identity." In *Tourism in Ireland: A Critical Analysis*, edited by Barbara O'Connor and Michael Cronin, 68–85. Cork: Cork University Press, 1993.

Odell, George C. D. *Annals of the New York Stage*. Vol. 9: *1870–1875*. New York: Columbia University Press, 1937.

———. *Annals of the New York Stage*. Vol. 10: *1875–1879*. New York: Columbia University Press, 1938.

———. *Annals of the New York Stage*. Vol. 11: *1879–1882*. New York: Columbia University Press, 1939.

Oettermann, Stephan. *The Panorama: History of a Mass Medium*. New York: Zone Books, 1997.

O'Gorman, William. Daybook of William O'Gorman, Overseer of the Poor Newtown, New York, Vols. I and II. New York Historical Society.

O'Kelly, James J. *The Mambi-Land, or Adventures of a Herald Correspondent in Cuba*. Philadelphia: J. B. Lippincott, 1874.

O'Leary, Philip. "Yank Outsiders: Irish Americans in Gaelic Fiction and Drama of the Irish Free State, 1922–1939." In *New Perspectives on the Irish Diaspora*, edited by Charles Fanning, 253–65. Carbondale: Southern Illinois University Press, 2000.

O'Mahony, N. J. "A Toast of the Sons of Ireland." *Rody the Rover Songster and Emerald Isle Lecture Book*. New York: De Witt Publishers, 1873. Mick Moloney Irish-American Music and Popular Culture Collection. Part IV, Box 48, Folder 29. Archives of Irish America. Tamiment Library/Robert F. Wagner Labor Archives.

Onkey, Lauren. *Blackness and Transatlantic Irish Identity: Celtic Soul Brothers*. New York: Routledge, 2010.

Optic, Oliver. *Shamrock and Thistle, or Young America in Ireland and Scotland: A Story of Travel and Adventure*. Boston: Lee and Shepard, 1868.

Orel, Gwen. "Reporting the Stage Irishman: Dion Boucicault in the Irish Press." In *Irish Theater in America*, edited by John P. Harrington, 66–77. Syracuse, N.Y.: Syracuse University Press, 2009.

O'Rourke, Kevin. *Currier and Ives: The Irish and America*. New York: Harry N. Abrams, Inc., 1995.

Otway, Rev. Caesar. *A Tour in Connaught*. Dublin: William Curry, 1839.

"Paddy Burke." *John M. Burke's Dublin Carman's Songster*. New York: DeWitt, 1871.

"Paddy's Wedding." *Howarth's Grand Hibernica Songster*. Trenton: Wm. S. Sharp, [1885?]. Harris Collection of Poetry and Plays, Songsters. Brown University.

Palmquist, Peter E., and Thomas R. Kailbourn. *Pioneer Photographers of the Far West: A Biographical Dictionary, 1840–1865*. Stanford: Stanford University Press, 2000.

Panchok, Frances. "The Catholic Church and the Theatre in New York, 1890–1920." PhD diss., Catholic University of America, 1976.

"Pat Murphy of Meagher's Brigade." American Song Sheets, David M. Rubenstein Rare Book & Manuscript Library, Duke University.

Pinkerton, Allan. *Strikers, Communists, Tramps, and Detectives*. New York: G. W. Carleton, 1878.

Pollock, Della. "Introduction: Making History Go." In *Exceptional Spaces: Essays in Performance and History*, edited by Della Pollock, 1–48. Greensboro: University of North Carolina Press, 1998.

Poole, J. F. *Irishman in Cuba*. Tony Pastor Collection, 1861–1908. Harry Ransom Center, University of Texas at Austin.

———. *Irishman in Greece*. Tony Pastor Collection, 1861–1908. Harry Ransom Center, University of Texas at Austin.

Porter, Edwin S., dir. *European Rest Cure*. Thomas A. Edison, and Paper Print Collection. United States: Edison Manufacturing Co, 1904. Video. American Memory Collection. Library of Congress. https://www.loc.gov /item/00694197/.

Powell, Hudson John. *Poole's Myriorama!: A Story of Travelling Panorama Showmen*. Bradford on Avon: ELSP, 2002.

Powell, Matthew. *God Off-Broadway: The Blackfriars Theatre of New York*. Lanham: The Scarecrow Press, 1998.

Profeta, Katherine. *Dramaturgy in Motion: At Work on Dance and Movement in Performance*. Madison: University of Wisconsin Press, 2015.

Program Book, 1871–1880. Tony Pastor Collection. *T-Mss. 1995-028. Billy Rose Theatre Division, New York Public Library for the Performing Arts.

Pryor, Elizabeth Stordeur. *Colored Travelers: Mobility and the Fight for Citizenship before the Civil War*. Chapel Hill: University of North Carolina Press, 2016.

Putnam, Laura. "To Study the Fragments/Whole: Microhistory and the Atlantic World." *Journal of Social History* 39, no. 3 (Spring 2006): 615–30.

Rabin, Shari. *Jews on the Frontier: Religion and Mobility in Nineteenth Century America*. New York: New York University, 2017.

Redmond, Patrick R. *Irish and the Making of American Sport, 1835–1920*. Jefferson: McFarland, 2014.

Riess, Steven A. *Sport in Industrial America, 1850–1920*. Wheeling, IL: Harlan Davidson, 1995. Reprinted, Chichester, UK: John Wiley, 2013. Kindle edition.

Ringenbach, Paul T. *Tramps and Reformers, 1873–1916*. Westport, CT: Greenwood, 1973.

Ritchie, Leitch. *Ireland: Picturesque and Romantic*. London: Longman, Orme, Brown, Green, and Longmans, 1838.

Robinson, Shanna. "Toys on the Move: Vicarious Travel, Imagination, and the Case of Traveling Toy Mascots." In *Travel and Imagination*, edited by Garth Lean and Russell Staiff, 149–64. New York: Routledge, 2016. E-book.

Rodger, Gillian M. *Champagne Charlie and Pretty Jemima: Variety Theater in the Nineteenth Century*. Urbana: University of Illinois Press, 2010.

———. *Just One of the Boys: Female-to-Male Cross-Dressing on the American Variety Stage*. Urbana: University of Illinois Press, 2018.

Rodgers, Daniel T. *The Work Ethic in Industrial America*. Chicago: University of Chicago Press, 1978.

Rody the Rover Songster and Emerald Isle Lecture Book. New York: De Witt, 1873. Mick Moloney Irish-American Music and Popular Culture Collection. Part IV, Box 48, Folder 29. Archives of Irish America, Tamiment Library/ Robert F. Wagner Labor Archives.

Roediger, David R. *The Wages of Whiteness: Race and the Making of the American Working Class*. New York: Verso, 1991.

Rohs, Stephen. *Eccentric Nation: Irish Performance in Nineteenth-Century New York City*. Madison, N.J.: Fairleigh Dickinson University Press, 2009.

Rokem, Freddie. *Performing History: Theatrical Representations of the Past in Contemporary Theatre*. Iowa City: University of Iowa Press, 2000.

Roney, Frank. *Irish Rebel and California Labor Leader: An Autobiography*. Edited by Ira B. Cross. Berkeley: University of California Press, 1931.

Rorabaugh, W. J. *Craft Apprentice: From Franklin to the Machine Age in America*. New York: Oxford University Press, 1988.

Ryan, J. H. "Rollicking Rody." *Rody the Rover Songster and Emerald Isle Lecture Book*. New York: De Witt Publishers, 1873. Mick Moloney Irish-American Music and Popular Culture Collection. Part IV, Box 48, Folder 29. Archives of Irish America, Tamiment Library/Robert F. Wagner Labor Archives.

———. "St. Patrick's Day." *Rody the Rover Songster and Emerald Isle Lecture Book*. New York: De Witt Publishers, 1873. Mick Moloney Irish-American Music and Popular Culture Collection. Part IV. Box 48, Folder 29. Archives of Irish America. Tamiment Library/Robert F. Wagner Labor Archives.

Salazar, Noel B. "Tourism Imaginaries: A Conceptual Approach." *Annals of Tourism Research* 39, no. 2 (2011): 863–82.

Sanborn, Franklin B. "The Tramp—His Cause and Cure." *The Independent* 30 (1878): 1.

Sanjek, Roger. *The Future of Us All: Race and Neighborhood Politics in New York City*. Ithaca, N.Y.: Cornell University Press, 1998.

Schechner, Richard. *Between Theater and Anthropology*. Philadelphia: University of Pennsylvania Press, 1985.

Scherzer, Kenneth A. *Unbounded Community: Neighborhood Life and Social Structure in New York, 1830–1875*. Durham: Duke University Press, 1992.

Schivelbusch, Wolfgang. *The Railway Journey: The Industrialization and Perception of Time and Space*. Berkeley: University of California Press, 1987.

Schmidt, James D. *Free to Work: Labor, Law, Emancipation, and Reconstruction, 1815–1880*. Athens, GA: University of Georgia Press, 1998.

Schrier, Arnold. *Ireland and the American Emigration, 1850–1900*. Minneapolis: University of Minnesota Press, 1958.

Schulman, Max. "Beaten, Battered, and Brawny: American Variety Entertainers and the Working-Class Body." In *Working in the Wings: New Perspectives on Theatre History and Labor*, edited by Elizabeth A. Osborne and Christine Woodworth, 95–108. Carbondale: Southern Illinois University Press, 2015.

Schultz, Stanley K. *Constructing Urban Culture: American Cities and City Planning, 1800–1920*. Philadelphia: Temple University Press, 1989.

Schultz, Stanley K., and Clay McShane. "To Engineer the Metropolis: Sewers, Sanitation, and City Planning in Late-Nineteenth-Century America." *Journal of American History* 65, no. 2 (September 1978): 389–411.

Schweitzer, Marlis. *Transatlantic Broadway: The Infrastructural Politics of Global Performance*. New York: Palgrave Macmillan, 2015.

Scobey, David. "Anatomy of the Promenade: The Politics of Bourgeois Sociability in Nineteenth-Century," *Social History* 17, no. 2 (May 1992): 203–27.

———. *Empire City: The Making and Meaning of the New York City Landscape*. Philadelphia: Temple University Press, 2002.

Senelick, Laurence. "Variety into Vaudeville: The Process Observed in Two Manuscript Gagbooks." *Theatre Survey* 19, no. 1 (May 1978): 1–15.

Shannon, William V. *The American Irish*. Amherst: University of Massachusetts Press, 1989.

Shaulis, Dahn. "Pedestriennes: Newsworthy but Controversial Women in Sporting Entertainment." *Journal of Sport History* 26, no.1 (Spring 1999): 29–50.

Simms, Joseph. *Nature's Revelations of Character*. N.p.: Author, 1873.

Smith, Dexter, and C.A. White. "That Little Church Around the Corner." *W. F. Lawlor's Original Barney the Guide Songster*. New York: Robert M. DeWitt, 1871. Harris Collection of Poetry and Plays, Songsters. Brown University.

Smith, John Talbot. "An Inside View of the Stage," *Donahoe's Magazine* 56, no. 2 (1906): 141.

———. *The Art of Disappearing*. New York: William H. Young and Company, 1902.

———. "Augustine Daly." In *Memories of Daly's Theatres*, 135–43. New York: Augustine Daly, 1896.

———. *The Parish Theatre*. New York: Longmans, Green, 1917. Reprint, n.p.: General Books, 2009.

———. "The Prospect for a Catholic Theatre." *Rosary Magazine* (September 1920): 1.

Snyder, Robert W. *The Voice of the City: Vaudeville and Popular Culture in New York*. New York: Oxford University Press, 1989.

Soennichsen, John. *The Chinese Exclusion Act of 1882*. Santa Barbara: Greenwood, 2011.

Sofer, Andrew. *Dark Matter: Invisibility in Drama, Theater, and Performance*. Ann Arbor: University of Michigan Press, 2013.

Solnit, Rebecca. *Wanderlust: A History of Walking*. New York: Penguin, 2000.

Special Commission Act, 1888: Reprint of the Shorthand Notes of the Speeches, Proceedings and Evidence Taken Before the Commissioners. Vol. IV. London: H.M.S.O., 1890.

STAATS. *A Tight Squeeze or, The Adventures of a Gentleman*. Boston: Lee and Shepard, 1879.

Stanley, Amy Dru. "Beggars Can't Be Choosers: Compulsion and Contract in Postbellum America." *Journal of American History* 78, no. 4 (March 1992): 1265–93.

———. *From Bondage to Contract: Wage Labor, Marriage, and the Market in the Age of Slave Emancipation*. Cambridge: Cambridge University Press, 1998.

Stansell, Christine. *City of Women: Sex and Class in New York, 1789–1860*. Urbana: University of Illinois Press, 1986.

———. "Women, Children, and the Uses of the Streets: Class and Gender Conflict in New York City, 1850–1860." *Feminist Studies* 8, no. 2 (Summer 1982): 309–35.

Stanton, Mary Olmstead. *Physiognomy: A Practical and Scientific Treatise*. San Francisco: San Francisco News Company, 1881.

The Statute Law of the State of New York, vol. III. New York: George S. Diossy, 1881.

Steggs, Beverley. *Class, Self, Culture*. New York: Routledge, 2004.

Stover, John F. *The Life and Decline of the American Railroad*. New York: Oxford University, 1971.

Subramanian, Sheela. "Embodying the Space Between: Unmapping Writing about Racialised and Gendered Mobilities." In *Gendered Mobilities*, edited by Tanu Priya Uteng and Tim Cresswell, 35–46. Burlington, Vt.: Ashgate, 2008.

Taylor, Diana. *The Archive and the Repertoire: Performing Cultural Memory in the Americas*. Durham: Duke University Press, 2003.

Tchen, John Kuo Wei. "Quimbo Appo's Fear of Fenians: Chinese-Irish-Anglo Relations in New York City." In *The New York Irish*, edited by Ronald H. Bayor and Timothy J. Meagher, 123–52. Baltimore: Johns Hopkins University Press, 1997.

Tenneriello, Susan. *Spectacle Culture and American Identity, 1815–1940*. New York: Palgrave Macmillan, 2013.

"Terrible Times." *Miles Morris Irish Gems*. New York: A.J. Fisher, 1873.

Thackeray, William Makepiece. *The Irish Sketchbook*. London: Smith, Elder, 1887.

Thanet, Octave. "The Indoor Pauper: A Study." *Atlantic Monthly* 47, no. 284 (June 1881): 749–61.

Tiedemann, Christopher. *A Treatise on the Limitations of Police Power in the United States*. St. Louis: F. H. Thomas Law Book, 1886.

Toll, Robert C. *Blacking Up: The Minstrel Show in Nineteenth-Century America*. New York: Oxford University Press, 1974.

Towsen, John H. *Clowns*. New York: Hawthorn Books, 1976.

Turner, Frederick Jackson. "The Significance of the Frontier in American History" (1894). In *In Search of the American Dream*, edited by Jane L. Scheiber and Robert C. Elliott, 197–220. New York: New American Library, 1974.

Tygiel, Jules. "Tramping Artisans: Carpenters in Industrial America, 1880–90." In *Walking to Work: Tramps in America, 1790–1935*, edited by Eric H. Monkkonen, 87–117. Lincoln: University of Nebraska Press, 1984.

Tyler, George C. *Whatever Goes Up: The Hazardous Fortunes of a Natural Born Gambler*. Indianapolis: Bobbs-Merrill, 1934.

Tyrell, Ian. *Reforming the World: The Creation of America's Moral Empire*. Princeton: Princeton University Press, 2010.

United States Census Bureau. United States Census 1860. Chicago Ward 3. Cook County, Illinois. p. 615. Family number 593, dwelling 441, lines 12–18. June 4, 1860. Family History Library film M653_165. Image 65. Ancestry. com (803165).

Urry, John. *Mobilities*. Malden, Mass.: Polity Press, 2007.

———. "Mobilities and Social Theory." In *The New Blackwell Companion to Social Theory*, edited by Bryan S. Turner, 477–95. Hoboken: Wiley-Blackwell, 2009.

———. *Sociology Beyond Societies: Mobilities for the Twenty-First Century*. New York: Routledge, 2000.

Vallillo, Stephen M. "George M. Cohan, Director." PhD diss., New York University, 1987.

Vey, Shauna. *Childhood and Nineteenth Century American Theatre*. Carbondale: Southern Illinois University Press, 2015.

Vium, Christian. "Fixating a Fluid Field: Photography as Anthropology in Migration Research." In *Methodologies of Mobility: Ethnography and Engagement*, edited by Alice Elliot, Roger Norum, and Noel B. Salazar, 172–94. New York: Berghahn Books, 2017.

Wallace, Anne D. *Walking, Literature, and English Culture: The Origins and Uses of Peripatetic in the Nineteenth Century*. New York: Oxford University Press, 1993.

Wallace, Joseph, and James W. Patton. *Springfield City Code*. Springfield: H.W. Rokker, 1884.

Walsh, James Patrick. "Michael Mooney and the Leadville Irish: Respectability and Resistance at 10,200 Feet, 1875–1900." PhD diss., University of Colorado, 2010.

Wayland, Francis. *Out-Door Relief and Tramps: Papers Read at the Saratoga Meeting of the American Social Science Association, before the Conference of State, September 5 and 6, 1877*. New Haven: Hoggson and Robinson, 1877.

Wertheim, Arthur Frank. *W. C. Fields from Burlesque and Vaudeville to Broadway*. New York: Palgrave, 2014.

Wetmore, Jr., Kevin J., ed. *Catholic Theatre and Drama: Critical Essays*. Jefferson: McFarland, 2010.

"What Irish Boys Can Do." New York: J. Wrigley, n.d. Broadsides, British Library.

"When These Old Clothes Are New." *W. F. Lawlor's Original Barney the Guide Songster*. New York: Robert M. DeWitt, 1871. Harris Collection of Poetry and Plays, Songsters. Brown University.

Wickham Papers. Police Dept., Licensing of Theaters [Concerning], 1875–1876. Office of the Mayor. Early Mayor Records, 1826–1897. Municipal Archives, City of New York.

Wilcox, Ralph. "Irish American in Sports: The Nineteenth Century." In *Making the Irish American*, edited by John Joseph Lee and Marion R. Casey, 443–56. New York: New York University Press, 2006.

Wild, John. *One, Two, Three*. Arranged by Charles White. New York: Robert M. DeWitt Publisher, 1875.

Wilkie, Fiona. *Performance, Transport, and Mobility: Making Passage*. New York: Palgrave, 2015.

Williams, William H. A. "George M. Cohan." In *Ireland and the Americas: Culture, Politics, and History*, Vol. 2, edited by James Patrick Byrne, Phillip Coleman, and Jason King, 192–93. Santa Barbara, CA: ABC-CLIO, 2008.

———. *Tourism, Landscape, and the Irish Character*. Madison: University of Wisconsin Press, 2008.

———. *'Twas Only an Irishman's Dream: The Image of Ireland and the Irish in American Popular Song Lyrics, 1800–1920*. Chicago: University of Illinois Press, 1996.

Wilmeth, Don. Review of *Champagne Charlie and Pretty Jemima: Variety Theater in the Nineteenth Century*, by Gillian M. Rodger. *Journal of American History* 98, no. 1 (June 2011): 217–18.

Wolff, Janet. "On the Road Again: Metaphors of Travel in Cultural Criticism." *Cultural Studies* 6 (1992): 224–39.

Wyman, Mark. *Round-Trip to America: The Immigrants Return to Europe, 1880–1930*. Ithaca, N.Y.: Cornell University Press, 1993.

Zellers, Parker. *Tony Pastor: Dean of the Vaudeville Stage*. Ypsilanti: Eastern Michigan University Press, 1971.

Zuelow, Eric G. E. *Making Ireland Irish: Tourism and National Identity since the Irish Civil War*. Syracuse, N.Y.: Syracuse University Press, 2009.

INDEX

STUDIES IN THEATRE HISTORY AND CULTURE

Representing the Past: Essays in Performance Historiography
Edited by Charlotte M. Canning and Thomas Postlewait

The Roots of Theatre: Rethinking Ritual and Other Theories of Origin
By Eli Rozik

Sex for Sale: Six Progressive-Era Brothel Dramas
By Katie N. Johnson

Shakespeare and Chekhov in Production: Theatrical Events and Their Audiences
By John Tulloch

Shakespeare on the American Yiddish Stage
By Joel Berkowitz

The Show and the Gaze of Theatre: A European Perspective
By Erika Fischer-Lichte

Stagestruck Filmmaker: D. W. Griffith and the American Theatre
By David Mayer

Strange Duets: Impresarios and Actresses in the American Theatre, 1865–1914
By Kim Marra

Susan Glaspell's Poetics and Politics of Rebellion
By Emeline Jouve

Textual and Theatrical Shakespeare: Questions of Evidence
Edited by Edward Pechter

Theatre and Identity in Imperial Russia
By Catherine A. Schuler

Theatre, Community, and Civic Engagement in Jacobean London
By Mark Bayer

Theatre Is More Beautiful Than War: German Stage Directing in the Late Twentieth Century
By Marvin Carlson

Theatres of Independence: Drama, Theory, and Urban Performance in India since 1947
By Aparna Bhargava Dharwadker

The Theatrical Event: Dynamics of Performance and Perception
By Willmar Sauter

Traveler, There Is No Road: Theatre, the Spanish Civil War, and the Decolonial Imagination in the Americas
By Lisa Jackson-Schebetta

The Trick of Singularity: "Twelfth Night" and the Performance Editions
By Laurie E. Osborne

The Victorian Marionette Theatre
By John McCormick

Wandering Stars: Russian Emigré Theatre, 1905–1940
Edited by Laurence Senelick

Women Adapting: Bringing Three Serials of the Roaring Twenties to Stage and Screen
By Bethany Wood

Writing and Rewriting National Theatre Histories
Edited by S. E. Wilmer